THE SHERPA GUIDE:
PROCESS-DRIVEN
EXECUTIVE
COACHING

Brenda Corbett
Judith Colemon

Australia · Brazil · Canada · Mexico · Singapore · Spain · United Kingdom · United States

The Sherpa Guide: Process-Driven Executive Coaching
Brenda Corbett and Judith Colemon

Printed in the United States of America by RRD—Crawfordsville

2 3 4 5 08 07 06

This book is printed on acid-free paper.

ISBN 0-324-40707-6

Library of Congress Cataloging in Publication Number is available. See page 351 for details.

For more information about our products, contact us at:

Thomson Learning Academic Resource Center
1-800-423-0563

Thomson Higher Education
5191 Natorp Boulevard
Mason, Ohio 45040
USA

Dedication

We are in awe of how God orchestrates things. We are clear that He places people in our lives just at the appointed time to fulfill His purpose.

We embrace Karl Corbett, our editor. Karl, we cannot fully express our gratitude for masterfully editing our words and bringing order to this book. Thank you for exhibiting endless patience in navigating the bantering in stereo, and most importantly, for your unselfish demeanor and willingness to supply great energy, support, and enthusiasm to both of us.

To our clients who have trusted us to be their Sherpa and to get them to the Summit, certainly this book would not exist without you, especially JPF. Thank you.

—BRENDA CORBETT AND JUDITH COLEMON

To my family and friends, my circle of love and support. Thank you for seeing in me what I often cannot see in myself.

To Brenda, my friend and co-writer, Thank you for encouraging me, challenging me, and absolutely knowing that I could do this. I am really proud of us and appreciate more than you can imagine your commitment to this partnership.

—JUDITH

To our children, Dan, Dani, and Nora: we have lived this together. Now you must each live it on your own. God Bless you.

And Mamie, thank you for undying support and encouragement.

To Judith, my friend and partner, Thank you for your unending enthusiasm and contribution to not only this book, but also to my life. You are an inspiration and a mentor to me.

To Karl, The finest man I have ever known.

—BRENDA

Contents

 *Preface*

THE LARGEST GENERATION in the U.S. and abroad is ready to retire, many from management and executive positions. The void at the top is a huge vacuum, drawing in what talent is left behind. The number of companies citing "leadership development" as their number-one training priority increases dramatically year after year. To help prepare these emerging leaders, money flows like a rising tide. Someone will have to get these upcoming executives ready to express themselves as leaders.

Like the snake oil salesmen of America's Wild West, an odd variety of self-proclaimed gurus has emerged to answer the call. Corporate America is betting its money on "the coach" as a cure-all. At hourly rates rivaled only by a life of crime, a well-regarded coach can make a fortune. They're the rock stars of human resources.

Aesthetics coaches, life coaches, business coaches, and executive coaches flock to where the money is. Some are brilliant, most are mediocre, and, like the patent medicines of the Wild West, some are quite dangerous. With no meaningful training or certification process, it's hard to tell which end of the spectrum a given coach falls on.

Finally, with this book and the Sherpa process, there's a gold standard that defines what executive coaching is and what it is not. Like Bill Gates' idea called Windows, the authors of *The Sherpa Guide* have developed the "operating system" for executive coaching. The Sherpa process has produced the first "Executive Coaching Certification" from a major university. It's becoming the recognized standard that every credible coach will follow.

Whether you would like to be an effective coach, develop a coaching program, or simply become a better developer of human capital, *The*

Sherpa Guide has answers:

What does it take to be a coach?

How good can I be?

How would I coach an executive, step by step?

How long does it take?

Can I turn this into a business?

In *The Sherpa Guide,* you'll uncover the secrets of becoming a world-class executive coach, and come away with hundreds of pages of process-specific resources.

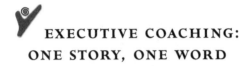

EXECUTIVE COACHING:
ONE STORY, ONE WORD

Coaching one person can make a difference in the lives of countless others. Teaching an executive to change just one word in a single sentence can improve an entire organization's morale, teamwork, and productivity.

Those truths hit home for us recently. An executive we were coaching received a transfer and a promotion. John's direct staff was a warm, familial group. They looked up to him with the utmost respect. Losing John would be devastating to them. We grappled with the decision on how to break the news to them. What would be the best way to handle this situation? How would the staff respond?

The executive's take: "Tell them I'm still part of the company. I'll come by and see them once in a while. In one sentence, I am not going to abandon the ship."

John's approach is perfect for a task-based, business relationship. But when delivered to a tight-knit group that feels like family, this response is clearly flawed. John's group doesn't want to be thought of as a "ship" from which their captain can jump at any time. We changed one word of the message, modifying the last sentence to say: "I am not going to abandon YOU." John found that hard to say. It was only one word, but it brought him closer to those people than he ever could have imagined. John delivered his farewell and said: "I am not going to abandon YOU." That's exactly what they needed to hear.

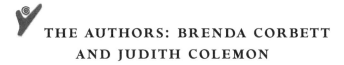

THE AUTHORS: BRENDA CORBETT AND JUDITH COLEMON

When we met, we were in a pressure cooker, recruiting and retaining staff during an employees' market. We were senior managers for very different organizations, but we became partners, looking out for each other in a time of crisis.

We recognized our philosophies were similar. We had a certain chemistry that made collaboration fun and productive. Even early on, our relationship contained elements of the Sherpa coaching process. We shared our professional strengths and weaknesses. We put our skill sets and personal experience on the table. We knew we could trust each other for support, because we constantly shared our expectations. We set goals, made a commitment, and threw ourselves into a relationship that resulted in *The Sherpa Guide*.

We would like to think there's something special about us that gives us the intuitive ability to guide others to success. Maybe our experience in leadership, always being front and center, has helped us become coaches. Is coaching a skill you can develop? Of course. Our ability to coach, and to share this with you, is the result of our partnership, which has forced us to clearly define the parameters of successful coaching.

Why do we do coach? Senior management can be a lonely place. Executives need support because their mistakes are more costly, and their good decisions are more valuable than anyone else's. A process-driven coach can be their best ally.

Brenda's Story

As a kid, I volunteered in hospitals in my native Quebec. Being there, I became a confidante. I heard stories my patients had never shared before. Now, as a coach, I give my clients something no one else gives them:

complete dedication. I learn more about clients' professional lives than their spouse, their family, their friends will ever know.

I often say to my clients: "When you and I meet, yours is the only opinion I care about. I will use your opinion, your world-view, as our foundation." This helps my client understand my orientation and motivation. Coaching also means a commitment to finding the truth. Regardless of what I hear, I refuse to develop preconceived notions about anyone in my client's life—boss, co-workers, partners, or subordinates. Because I never take sides, I can help my clients grow, change, and develop, even in difficult circumstances.

 ## STORIES FROM THE SUMMIT

Sixty years old. After 30 years, Jason knew everything there was to know about water purification, but he didn't know enough about life. Jason had issues. No one at his office understood him. His wife wasn't concerned. His friends had no idea how to help him.

Did Jason's problems stem from childhood? I don't know. I don't care. Coaching is not therapy. We don't address the past. We develop solutions TODAY.

All Jason needed was a way to control his anger at work. After six weeks, he had three likely solutions. One he discarded; the other two he used. He applied his two techniques every day, and we talked about them each week when we met. Jason began to control his anger, instead of being controlled by it.

He used his techniques for weeks, and then months. One day, Jason told me: "I have conquered anger. I have beaten my biggest obstacle, because you cared about me. You were so dedicated to helping me find the solution. Thanks, Sherpa."

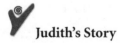
Judith's Story

I was taught early in life to think big and take on the consequences. Now, as a coach, everything I was taught and all the things I love have come together in one avocation.

I never enjoyed committees. My early careers had me going one-on-one with people who could make or break my career. Whether I was running a boutique or managing entertainers, I always made my own calls. As a CEO attracted to new ventures, I've learned how to communicate a vision that helps people discover why their professional life matters.

The Sherpa model is profound, because it takes into account a crucial fact: no matter how much a client trusts you, you can't make their decisions for them. In coaching, I challenge clients to solve problems for themselves. I serve as a guide. I listen more than I talk. I am comfortable with silence. With the Sherpa process, my clients decide the path their life takes.

 ## Stories from the Summit

> *Martha's son owns a catering business. It's a small company, but he's up to 20 employees and making a small fortune.*
>
> *In a few months, Martha plans to leave her full-time job so she can help her son build capacity and depth in his business. After 20 years, she's ready to step away from the familiar, ready to start a career in catering. Something's wrong, though. Martha is more nervous than excited. She's doing the research, saving her money, getting ready to live out the dream. It's not making her happy.*
>
> *Martha engages a Sherpa coach. Martha learns why she's nervous, and exactly how miserable she'll be if she makes this move. With the Sherpa process, she can measure, quantify, and prove that her staying put is best for everyone. Life goes on at the catering company without her, and Martha's happy, doing what she's always done.*

Introduction

WHEN HOLLYWOOD'S ELITE started hiring personal trainers, they created a fitness industry that's still booming. Today, executive coaching is the hottest consulting concept on the planet. Executive coaches work on the professional fitness of business leaders. Those who do it well are richly rewarded, whether they're staff consultants or work independently.

It's quite fashionable for executives to have a coach, so people have rushed to fill the demand. Becoming a coach requires no test, no training, and no licensing. So there are a lot of dubious coaches, concepts, and certifications floating around.

What you are about to read is the very first coaching process that's been defined in significant detail. In fact, it's the only real process available. Backed by the executive education program of a major university, the Sherpa process has held up to close scrutiny by seasoned veterans of adult education and received their unequivocal endorsement. Since there's no significant competition, the Sherpa process is the only credible standard for executive coaching.

Years ago, software companies that jumped on board the Windows platform aligned their future with Bill Gates. Their competitors, relying on proprietary standards, faded into obscurity. Today, executive coaches who adopt the Sherpa process will be mainstream, instead of being shut out of this lucrative career.

We'd like to see you succeed. When it's done right, coaching can be rewarding, both financially and personally. Harvard Business School says: "Executive coaching is a major growth industry. 10,000 coaches work for businesses today and that's expected to exceed 50,000 in five years. Executive coaching is also highly profitable, with fees ranging from $1,500 to $15,000 a day." You are about to uncover the secrets of becoming a world-class executive coach. Follow *The Sherpa Guide* and you'll be far more effective than your peers in this new and exciting field.

HOW THIS BOOK WILL GUIDE YOU

The problem with most business books? They'll talk all day about what to do and never tell you exactly and clearly how to do it. We've written this book to be different, and to be truly helpful to you. *The Sherpa Guide* offers:

- A clear, predictable process for business coaching.
- A timeline for every coaching engagement.
- A way to avoid the pitfalls of a very complex and delicate business.

We are detailed and specific about every last thing that may happen as you coach. This book is written as your guide through a coaching engagement, a guide that never leaves you in doubt about what to do and how to do it. The Sherpa process will guide your client, too. Every client will get a companion piece to this book, a client journal with quizzes, assessments, and exercises that identify and solve problems in business behavior.

To start with, read the book all the way through at least once. The first few chapters explain our philosophy on coaching: what it is and what it is not. You'll find assessments to see how good you'll be as a coach and ways to hone your skills. Then we will take you step-by-step through ten routes to create positive change for your client.

Have a highlighter or bookmarks available to help you remember what you really like. When you begin working with clients, pick this book up and use it as a guide, rehearsing and taking notes before each meeting. Know the client's journal by heart, too: every exercise a client might use.

You're learning a trade that's being defined clearly for the first time. It takes work to be really good. Do the work; you'll be richly rewarded.

CHAPTER 1

Base Camp

L IFE COACHES, CONSULTANTS AND MENTORS use the name "coach," as do presentation trainers and coaches who 'create beautiful spaces.' There's no real consensus about how the word "coach" should be used. *The Sherpa Guide* brings order to this confusion by telling you exactly what executive coaching is and how it works, step-by-step.

What You'll Find in This Chapter:

- **Executive Coaching**
- **The Sherpa**
- **Your Role as a Sherpa Coach**
- **What Makes a Good Coach?**

EXECUTIVE COACHING

In our world, executive coaching is a personal and frequent one-on-one meeting designed to produce specific, positive changes in business behavior within a fixed time frame.

We strongly advocate face-to-face coaching. Face-to-face meetings force honesty, impose concentration, and guarantee a personal commitment to success. That's what we mean when we talk about coaching. Personal, live coaching has the advantage of rapport and immediacy. That's the path we follow in *The Sherpa Guide*. Develop your coaching skills in person, and you can apply the Sherpa process in other venues, if the need arises.

Some coaches offer services by phone or email. We've seen coaches try to sell this concept by saying it "removes visual distractions," but a long-distance relationship cannot produce world-class results. Most communication is visual, nonverbal.

Phone and email are convenient and allow a coach to have greater reach, but we discourage those media. Over the phone, visual stimuli are removed. Email takes away even more, stripping inflection and tone of voice from a relationship. If your clients want leadership advice in text format, send them to the library for a self-help book.

Have you ever multitasked, tried to do something else while talking on the phone? Coaching clients will, too. Use the phone sparingly, only when you know your clients well enough to know they'll avoid distractions and focus completely on your conversation. Use email only for client support in-between meetings and never in place of a meeting.

Technology has added another option for coaching, that of a point-to-point video. This technology allows you, the coach, sitting at your desk, to communicate directly with your client, anywhere in the world, sitting at theirs. Using a webcam, along with a headset and microphone, a coach can "meet virtually" with their client. To offer videoconference coaching to your clients, you and they will both need to have a high-quality camera and headset. You, as a coach, will need to sign up for a conferencing service. This allows you to initiate conferences and invite your clients to them. As of this writing, free conferencing services produce low-quality video, with delays so significant they'll take away from the coaching experience. High-end videoconferencing is fairly smooth and trouble-free. Over time, the quality of sound and images will only improve, making coaching over the Web more and more like a live meeting.

STORIES FROM THE SUMMIT

> *Allen is a dynamic sales manager. He manages a dozen salespeople across the U.S. and Canada. He loves to make deals, but Allen has trouble communicating. He talks a good talk, but is not much of a listener.*
>
> *One week, when Allen was out of town, I agreed to spend an hour on the phone with him, not because it's the best way to coach, but because Allen manages his workforce over the phone. We talked about what it really meant to "listen" on the phone.*
>
> *Allen learned about asking leading questions to keep people engaged in a phone conversation, and how to make better connections with what was really going on in the field.*

Live coaching demands focus. It ensures that everyone gets something out of their investment. The client gets undivided attention. The coach gets results, a great reputation, and great references that help produce future business.

THE SHERPA

In the Himalayas, the native guides that assist climbers to the top of Everest are called Sherpas. Sherpas have a global reputation because:

- They are accustomed to the altitude, just as an experienced executive coach understands what life is like for a manager or an executive.
- They can predict bad weather that makes a climb dangerous or impossible. A Sherpa coach knows the dangers of professional life, and what might make a leader's journey unsuccessful.
- They design routes for the climb since they know the terrain. The Sherpa process is designed with a clear choice of paths executives can take to reach their own summit.
- They offer suggestions, ideas, and improvements on the "tools of the trade": skills and resources needed for the climb. As coaches, Sherpas have an inventory of tools designed to aid in any executive's climb to the top.

- They are unobtrusive unless they have a specific thought to share. Just like the mountain escorts, a Sherpa coach guides his client to figure things out for himself, unless intervention is demanded by circumstance.

In our executive coaching, we take on the role of the Sherpa, enabling, advising, and assisting in difficult environments with limited options. Our clients, like climbers on Everest, endure the hardships, put forth the effort, and are subject to the risks involved in reaching their goals. Ultimately, they must reach the summit through their own skill and determination.

During the arduous climb, a Sherpa does not make decisions. The Sherpa makes recommendations and gives tips, tricks, and techniques to make the climb easier. A good Sherpa never does the climbing for the client. Once the Sherpa has offered all the alternatives, the client has to make their own choices. With this relationship in mind, we call ourselves Sherpas, and have named our detailed process for coaching the Sherpa Process™. We are guides. We are supporters, and we walk side by side with our clients up to the summit.

In Chapter 2, we'll review the logistics of a coaching engagement: the meetings, arrangements, and communication needed to properly manage a coaching engagement.

Once coaching begins, the Sherpa process has a philosophy and detailed content that leads a client through six phases:

- Taking Stock
- Global View
- Destination
- Charting the Course
- Agenda
- The Summit

Beginning in Chapter 3, you'll find this process rolled out in great detail. Leading up to that point, we'll define what executive coaching is. We'll reveal who's most likely to be good at it. You'll learn why having a

SHERPA EXECUTIVE COACHING

Graphic design by Daniel Region, Blue Mesa Productions, Hudson, New York
(© Sasha Corporation)

well-defined process makes executive coaching a predictable and legitimate course of action for almost any organization.

One disastrous day on Everest, two of the world's most famous climbing guides and their clients diced with death and lost. *Into Thin Air: Death on Everest* is a fascinating movie about that day. This tragic story makes for gripping drama. Provide your client with a copy at your first meeting. Tell them: "Whether or not you enjoy this movie, you'll learn from it. What I would like you to do is this: watch the movie and notice the relationships and the roles of the Sherpa guides. Come back next meeting and tell me what a Sherpa does, and you'll understand my role as a coach."

The movie also holds an important lesson for coaches: know the rules and follow them. To make great things happen, a Sherpa coach respects and follows the Sherpa process. No shortcuts and no detours. Every situation is unique. Without following proven routines, there's no way a coach can locate the path that leads to the client's goals.

YOUR ROLE AS A SHERPA COACH

Keep in mind your role as a coach. You are working with and for the client, but you are not on the field of play. In fact, the Sherpa coach *must* remain on the sidelines.

Years ago, an overzealous college football coach crossed that line, with disastrous results. Ohio State's Woody Hayes, during the 1978 Gator Bowl, actually interfered with an opposing team's player, Charlie Bauman, during a game with Clemson. As Bauman stepped out of bounds on the Ohio State sideline after an interception that had sealed Clemson's victory, Hayes stepped up and punched the opposing player. He crossed the line. The result: Hayes' career ended on a note that many would remember far more clearly than his superb coaching record, one of the best in NCAA history. Keep this example in mind as you enter the world of coaching.

The only time a coach consults with his players is during a time-out. Even then, the players leave the field to talk with him. Your weekly meeting is the equivalent of that sideline consultation: off the field, during a "time-out" period. That's why we hold off-site meetings: to help you resist the temptation to pick up the ball and run with it, or otherwise interfere with the flow of the game.

Your client must be trained to observe their situation and environment clearly and with detachment. Their view must be based on reality rather than emotion. The "big picture" is crucial to long-term goals, and a client must be able to describe it accurately to be able to choose the right path.

Coaching must be focused on performance and results, nothing else. Sherpa coaching is focused solely on the performance of the individual in a work environment. This is why coaches are hired: to produce tangible results. Executives want to feel better about their working environment, but this is only part of the picture. Good coaching should create positive results that can be seen throughout the workplace.

Business coaching must be controlled, efficient, and productive or it will be a waste of everyone's time. The Sherpa's personal agenda and life story are not part of the coaching experience. You must keep your experience, your life, separate from the client's. It is sometimes valuable to share personal anecdotes that illustrate how techniques are applied, but be careful to do this sparingly. Any story you tell should be brief, three sentences or less. You don't learn unless you are listening.

Steven Berglas, a professor at UCLA's Anderson School of Management, writes in *The Harvard Business Review:* "Coaches can make bad situations worse, because they don't have the background to deal with psychological problems." He's right. Sherpa coaching is not therapy. We do not discuss personal matters with the client. We do not discuss family issues with the client. There are times when work/life balance is discussed from the client's perspective. This happens so we understand who in the client's life truly supports them. We can't solve marriage, family, or personal issues. We can help clients balance their work more effectively, so they have time to work on other issues. Sherpas make this distinction clear in the first client meeting.

If the client brings up family, children, or personal matters, a good coach will redirect the conversation:

CLIENT: "My spouse is always angry with me."

SHERPA: "Does anything like that happen at work? Do you provoke anyone's anger at work? What do you do when someone is angry with you?"

When your client shares a situation at home, it will often reveal a problem at work. A Sherpa listens carefully, to "connect the dots," and focuses on professional behavior. You may spend a lot of time redirecting in your early meetings. Once your client understands that you don't, under any circumstances, get into personal matters, he will abide by your standards and respect them.

Even though the Sherpa and client don't discuss personal matters, the coaching client will get better at solving personal issues. When the Sherpa respects and adheres to the process, the client will begin to handle every aspect of life differently. You will hear stories about personal victories, in areas you did not even cover during your coaching sessions.

STORIES FROM THE SUMMIT

> *Joanna is the CEO of a community health center. She is an efficient, task-driven manager. Joanna misses the mark when it comes to connecting with her staff. She can delegate, problem solve, and reprimand, but she can't connect. Her Sherpa taught her "People don't care how much you know . . . until they know how much you care."*
>
> *Joanna applied that truth to her relationship with every key staff member. She changed fundamentally. About three months after coaching ended, Joanna called, and told her coach that she'd renewed her relationship with her stepdaughter, based on what she'd learned in coaching. For her, it worked in both her public and private lives.*

The essential task for the Sherpa is to understand individual clients' needs. This means identifying a client's communication style and communication needs: How does this person express and interpret things? What's the best way to reach them? The Sherpa will, in turn, teach clients to understand the communication needs of everyone around them. This is the key to the Sherpa/client relationship.

There's an ideal way to communicate with each and every person. When you understand someone's communication needs, you can master a relationship with them. When a Sherpa identifies a client's communication needs and style, they can help the client understand himself and those with different styles. The Sherpa develops clients who become open to new ways of listening and expressing their thoughts. Every Sherpa and every client must work with this concept, all the time.

Your clients will need different things. Some people need to feel validated. Others need constant encouragement. Some need to be in control. And some are overwhelmed by fear, and need to be reassured. Ask yourself: "What does this client need me to say? What is important to him right now?

Why is he using those particular words? What is he looking for when he says that?" When you do that, you are delving deep into the nature of communication, the most important area of coaching. Ultimately, by meeting your client's needs, you'll teach them to meet the needs of others.

STORIES FROM THE SUMMIT

Larry is the president of a regional utilities company in the Midwest. Larry is a direct and short-tempered man. When Larry visits Marcy with a question, Marcy knows Larry's communication needs. He wants a concise answer and he wants it now. If Marcy opts to add detail to a story, Larry gets agitated and shuts down. When detail is necessary, she'll prepare Larry for a more lengthy conversation, and he'll be ready to listen a little longer.

Identifying a person's communication need is key. Don't be afraid to push. It is your role to be assertive enough to push your client to explain more carefully, in greater detail, and more honestly.

Sherpa coaches are not therapists. Sherpas are not always trainers, either. Trainers typically have complete control of their process, and they deliver all the answers. In coaching, the Sherpa doesn't completely control the pace, and the client has to come up with his own realizations and solutions.

Unlike therapy or training, a Sherpa coach is paid to confront and to challenge clients' answers. Clients must be involved! They must have revelations, or you are not doing your job well.

WHAT MAKES A GOOD COACH?

If you are considering a role as a coach, you'd like to know if you've got what it takes. You're curious about where you can make improvements and channel your energy to get better.

Here are the top ten qualities of a good Sherpa coach:

1. **Good listener**
2. **Inquisitive**

3. Objective observer

4. Centered, in control of a dialogue

5. Direct, honest, even blunt

6. Flexible

7. Intuitive

8. Remembers

9. Believable

10. And most of all, trustworthy.

You *must* have, or develop, these skills to be an effective coach. To be happy and successful as a coach, you must be able to admit your own weaknesses and develop new strengths and qualities. Here is more detail on how these characteristics come into play in the coaching field:

1. *GOOD LISTENER.* All coaches benefit from good listening skills. If you're a big talker, love to tell stories, and be the center of attention, curb those tendencies when you coach. If you get easily bored listening to people's stories, you'll have to work extra hard to be a coach. Coaches are great listeners. That means more than hearing and understanding. In the dictionary, listening is defined as "the conscious effort to hear." Great coaches can listen to a story and then form a picture of the personality types and relationships underlying the action.

This quality, being a good listener, is at the top of our list for good reason. To evaluate your listening skills, turn to Appendix and run through assessment SC 1-1.

STORIES FROM THE SUMMIT

Lori wanted to be a coach; she'd been an enthusiastic, high-level manager for 20 years. Lori took on the challenge of coaching and failed. The clients she encountered did not like her.

They were ready to spill the details of their lives, and they were paying quite well for the privilege. Lori could not keep her life out of the client/coach relationship. She would constantly say: "That reminds me of a situation I experienced . . ." The client would always lose direction. The "story of Lori" overwhelmed conversation. She needed to stop talking—to really listen—but Lori never mastered the skill. She dropped out of coaching in short order.

2. INQUISITIVE.   Asking questions allows your client to work on their area of focus and solve their own problems. Sherpas use questions such as: *"What do you mean? Can you explain that in more detail? Can you rephrase that for me? How could you have handled that differently? Why is that hard for me to believe? Why do you think he did that?"* That inquisitive nature, really wanting to know more, creates a learning environment for your clients. They notice that, and it makes a big difference to your relationship.

 ## STORIES FROM THE SUMMIT

In our meetings, Dana kept telling me it was impossible to complete all the work her boss assigned. I asked, "Does your boss expect you to do all this work by yourself?" "No," Dana said, "but everyone else is overloaded, too."

"Let's look at the options." I said. "Turn to a blank page in your journal and draw for me what it looks like to have too much work to do." Dana's picture showed her bent over with an oversize box on her back. I asked, "What will happen if you don't get rid of some of that weight? Draw that for me." Her next picture showed her collapsed with the box on top of her. "Can this go on?" I continued, "What are you going to do about it? Is everyone else really so overloaded?"

It took time to figure out why Dana was overloaded. It took time to find workable answers to the problem. Once she'd admitted things couldn't continue as they were, once she'd acknowledged she needed to do something about it, we were on our way.

Sherpas work with clients until the clients can reach a satisfactory answer on their own. Often, a coach does not have to say much more than "Why is that?" and wait for a response. If your client is avoiding a difficult truth, or coming up with answers that won't solve the problem, challenge that client, again and again, until he gets it right. This can be frustrating for your client. Be sensitive enough to challenge them in a way that's encouraging at the same time. Be honest in a caring way. That's what you're paid to do.

3. OBJECTIVE OBSERVER. Experts believe that less than 30 percent of relational communication comes through the words you say. As a perceptive coach, you must notice body language, voice inflection, and mannerisms. You must analyze the way your client chooses words, such as using "feel" versus "think." Pay close attention to the messages a client's actions send you. Clients often can't understand the ramifications and dynamics of a situation they describe to you. Upon hearing it back from you, they'll see things, and draw conclusions they couldn't arrive at on their own.

Our clients keep a personal record called a journal, which includes their notes, homework assignments, and assessments. Notice the way they complete their journals. How do they react to your questions and remarks? How do they approach their homework? What do they miss? What do they want to talk about, and what do they need to talk about? Are they a willing participant? A Sherpa's silence is a powerful tool that helps the Sherpa learn secrets about what is really going on with clients.

STORIES FROM THE SUMMIT

> *I noticed that Jeff was beginning to tap his foot rapidly, and use his hand to cover his mouth. I asked him why. Jeff told me that when he did this, it meant that I was getting close to the core of the problem. He hated that there was "nowhere to hide." He was getting a little nervous. Noticing those signals allowed me to extract honesty from my client.*

4. CENTERED, IN CONTROL OF A DIALOGUE. Make sure you understand the Sherpa coaching process. Then let the process do its job. The Sherpa process is based on 12 one-hour meetings. It is easy to get involved in a client's dramatic week and make little progress in a given meeting. It is easy to fall into the "therapy trap," asking about the past ("Why did your father act that way?"). Don't let your client steer any meeting in that direction. While flexibility is important, you can't lose control of the structure of the meeting. The process is important. Use it and believe in it. If the conversation gets off on a tangent, try comments like this to bring it back to the agenda:

> "Mary, it seems like this was an emotional experience for you. How do you relate this to our discussion about your values?"

> "What does this really mean, when you think about the expectation process we just covered?"

> "Why are you spending so much energy with that situation? If we get back to discussing accountability, we might find some answers for you."

The Sherpa directs what is said. The Sherpa also controls the client's environment. That includes carefully selecting when and where you meet off-site.

Stories from the Summit

> *Alexis was a 38-year-old executive moving up in her company. She knew she needed coaching, but was not committed to doing her homework. Alexis called on the third meeting and asked to meet one hour later than usual, so she could finish her homework. She literally wanted to "cram." Her coach had to be in control, and said: "We meet as scheduled. We can complete the homework together as part of the process." To make a coaching relationship work, set limits, communicate guidelines, and show leadership.*

5. DIRECT, HONEST, EVEN BLUNT. Stop or redirect a conversation if it is going in the wrong direction. Your job is to stay focused on the end game and your client's next step to success. Be caring while you "tell it like it is."

As a coach, you are in a position of control and authority. Occasionally, a client will become very emotional about things that seem trivial. These feelings are very real, but they are nonproductive. You can shut down a line of conversation without conflict and without being judgmental. "Our goal today is to . . .".

STORIES FROM THE SUMMIT

A client company was planning how to allocate some new space. Their goal was to place people to make communication between team members more efficient. Mark was upset with the space planner. He seemed to think the planner would scale down his office and move it to the far side of the building, to a spot with no windows. Mark argued with the planner, ranting and raving, "You are always being unreasonable about something!"

When he told me the story, I stopped him mid-sentence and said: "Mark . . . you are whining." He looked at me, surprised, and began to laugh. Then we took apart his story about the chain of command and who would ultimately make the decision about his office location. It wasn't even the planner's decision. So I asked, "Why did you bother to get upset over this? What are you so angry about, really?" By being direct, a good coach turns negative behavior into self-discovery.

Directness is not always forceful or negative. Often, a client will share a story with you, seemingly endless, with lots of tangents. Stop the conversation and summarize the story for them. Then ask: "What does this mean?" As described, this tactic may seem abrupt, but your client will see the results and appreciate your actions.

Don't be afraid to use words like:

"Stop for a second."
"Don't go there."
"Did you just hear yourself?"
"What's our goal today? How does this relate?"

Believe it or not, clients not only depend on your directness, they crave it. At work, everyone is so busy avoiding confrontation that it's hard to get a straight story. A client will hold you, their coach, in the highest regard, because you make it easy for them and because you are honest.

6. FLEXIBLE. Flexibility is the most important skill a Sherpa coach can develop. Understand your client's needs and desires, take their lead, but follow the Sherpa process as closely as you can. You might have to step out of your comfort zone, abandon your agenda, and go with the client's, at times. You might have a topic chosen for a given meeting. Instead, the events of the client's week might end up as the focus of your meeting.

As a Sherpa, you will sometimes run across a client whose needs exceed the boundaries of your weekly dialogue. If there are things going on in a client's office that you must see, to be able to believe your client's perspective, what should you do? Go to their workplace and observe. It is important that a client knows you are interested in improving their work environment and serious about doing whatever it takes.

 ## STORIES FROM THE SUMMIT

Marsha is in sales and marketing for her organization. She is at the top of her game, yet her co-workers can barely stand to be in her presence. Marsha is very high-energy, direct, and rallies her team in a manner that she thinks is great. So why the problems? Marsha is oblivious to the needs of her teammates.

To understand, Marsha's coach went to see this for herself. She followed Marsha for a few hours of her workday. When people saw Marsha coming, they would avoid eye contact, pick up their walking pace, anything to avoid a conversation. The problem was real, and the coach knew from direct experience how Marsha's forcefulness was being received.

A coach must be flexible enough to find a way to get to the bottom of things, to see things from a different angle. It is the job of the coach to be flexible, so the client gets results beyond their expectations.

7. INTUITIVE. A good coach can anticipate a client's reaction to almost any situation. The intuitive coach trusts herself to ask the right question and provoke the right response. With intuition, a coach knows when to push a client out of their comfort zone and when to avoid that. Intuition can be learned, developed, and improved. Make sure you work on yours.

8. REMEMBERS. Memory and timing are also consistent instincts of a good coach. A Sherpa remembers all the issues that confront each client and never loses focus. As a sounding board, you must be able to reiterate the situations your client shares with you, acting as an objective observer. Some people can keep reams of information organized in their heads. Most people can't. As a Sherpa, you must offer the appearance to each client that he is the center of your universe, at least for that hour every week. The more people you coach, the more their stories and situations will run together. Your best bet is to write down what your clients say in these meetings. Keep an "organizational chart" for each client, listing the key people in their working life.

Refer to a client's checklist before you start each session. Write down the homework you assigned last time, print out any emails sent during the week, and bring those to each meeting, too. Create a folder bearing your client's initials or first name, and make sure that it is in your "portable office" each time you meet.

Create a good memory for your client, too. Record keeping is part of the Sherpa journey. Review the client's journal each meeting to see what has (and has not) been accomplished between meetings. The journal can be extremely valuable to your client. You must help them acquire ownership of their journal. The only way to do this is to use it at every opportunity. You'll see a sample of the client's journal pages in Appendix, along with an order form, so you can provide a Sherpa journal for each client.

STORIES FROM THE SUMMIT

> *Valerie is a well-qualified professional in a male-dominated field. She has excellent job skills, yet she feels inferior to her peers. When she first met her Sherpa coach, Valerie complained about her daily routine of retrieving*

> *morning coffee for her peers. It was apparent that Valerie had a weakness in the area of self-confidence.*
>
> *Three to four weeks later, Valerie said, "I feel like my officemates are using me." Her coach responded, "I remember our talk three weeks ago. You put yourself in this position by getting everyone's coffee every morning. This is not about them.*
>
> *What are you going to do about this situation? How are you going to change things?" That's the prod Valerie needed to start changing an unpleasant situation she had created. Her coach's memory of a comment the previous month was critical.*

A Sherpa with a good memory can hold clients accountable for what they say they want to do, and to be. This tells clients you listen and care about what they say. A good memory creates good will. It helps add depth to your relationships. A good memory can reflect where your client was, at a given moment in his journey, and helps you demonstrate progress.

9. **BELIEVABLE.**   Credibility is critical. You never get a second chance to make a first impression. Believability begins at your first meeting with your client. You introduce yourself, and explain exactly what is going to take place during the next 12 weeks. To do that, you must know the Sherpa process inside and out.

Be yourself. Your confidence and comfort with your self speaks loudly to your client. Calm self assurance is the mark of a great coach. Being a Sherpa is a huge responsibility. Show confidence based on your expertise. Communicate your expectations and the ground rules clearly. Then take control and outline how you will contact each other as things arise that shift your schedule.

A client may have a challenge letting their defenses down. Perhaps they're hesitant to share with you, fearing you will report the results of your sessions to their employer. Be honest about the situation and the degree of confidentiality you can guarantee.

If you don't think your sessions are going as you would like, admit it. This increases your believability. Some examples of how to tell your client that things are not going as you think they should:

- "Do you think we are getting to the root of the problem?"
- "Why do you think I might have trouble understanding the story you just told me?"
- "This is not going the way I'd like it to. Let's go back to the beginning of this story."
- "I am sensing you are nervous (uncomfortable, uneasy) about this topic. Is that true?"

Believability comes from being direct, knowing what you know and what you need to know, and acting on it.

10. TRUSTWORTHY. Climbers in the Himalayas trust the Sherpa with their lives. The stakes in executive coaching are nearly as high. Sherpa coaches are trusted with their clients' professional lives. Establishing trust is easier said than done. It's a skill that can be learned, and it requires certain attitudes and actions on the coach's part.

Let's rate your trust factor by turning to Appendix. In assessment SC 1-2, the questions, and your answers, will reveal ways you can be a far more effective coach.

 ## Stories from the Summit

> *Trust is difficult to build, and impossible to force. Suzanne was an exceptional coach. She knew the Sherpa model by heart. She established herself with her clients immediately with her experience and knowledge. Credibility was not a problem, but she couldn't earn that key commodity: trust.*
>
> *Trust means creating a client's "willingness to risk" as they share thoughts, problems, and personal history. Trust is established through consistency and authenticity. It also includes clear, honest communication and respect. If a coach breaks any of these "relationship bonding" issues, trust disappears and your relationship is over. Suzanne lost one client's trust forever, simply by showing up ten minutes late for their first two meetings.*

Let's review, and take a quick assessment. Turn to Appendix, and use evaluation SC 1-3 to measure your potential and find room for growth. No matter how good you are, there's always room for improvement. No matter what basic skills you bring to a task, you can develop well-rounded talent.

Sherpas teach their coaching clients that anything can be overcome. With that in mind, don't be discouraged about any of your evaluations. Everyone needs work, and now you know exactly where to apply your efforts and your intellect toward being a good coach.

Let's move on and find out why coaching works, and who really needs one.

CHAPTER 2

The Case for Coaching

W HY IS COACHING A GOOD TOOL for executive development? Why is coaching the best tool for businesspeople who need to change their approach to their working life?

It's the shortest distance between two points: where a person is and where that person wants to be. A weekly coaching meeting keeps steady focus on areas for growth. Homework and journaling make the process a daily exercise. And, unlike a classroom or a canned seminar, it's highly customized, producing the best results in the fastest possible time frame.

What You'll Find in This Chapter:

- **Why Does Coaching Work?**
- **Who Needs a Coach?**
- **Coaching Tips**
- **Step-by-Step**

WHY DOES COACHING WORK?

Here are six reasons coaching can be so effective.

1. IT'S LONELY AT THE TOP. Management can be a lonely job. You are taught not to fraternize with employees and never to let subordinates get to know you well. You can't share with your superiors how you really feel. Even if you are lucky enough to have a manager interested in your personal well-being and professional growth, that manager's attention span and interest level is still quite limited. Translation: "No one really cares."

Today's leaders are expected to walk in the door and perform. This is the norm for executives everywhere. It generates a lot of stress and isolates leaders from those they are expected to lead. The coach/client relationship is external. The coach has no political agenda, maintains privacy, and allows the manager to admit: "I don't know." That's the starting point for any great idea.

 ## STORIES FROM THE SUMMIT

> *Nora is an executive VP for a health-care conglomerate. She has worked her way up to the position and she's doing exceptionally well. We did two series of 12 weekly meetings, a total of six months' work. Although we'd been through the Sherpa process start to finish, Nora asked if she could continue with her coaching. Why?*
>
> *Nora had no one else to talk to. She couldn't talk to her boss, because he was too busy. She had no peers to whom she was close. She didn't want to talk to her subordinates. Nora wanted to pay for coaching for an extended period of time. This is not the norm, but if it works for the client and the expectations are clear, it can be valuable, as long as the client continues to work on the things you have coached about.*

2. COACHING FORCES CLIENTS TO ADDRESS THEIR WEAKNESSES. In some personal development processes, you're asked to focus on your strengths in order to minimize your weaknesses.

In Sherpa coaching, clients will focus on their weaknesses. The goal is to avoid those situations that "sink the ship." If you can't delegate effectively, you are set up to fail. No matter how caring or charismatic you might be, you'll fail as a leader. Often a client has reached a plateau with their strengths but can't climb the summit because of their weaknesses. They have been avoiding working on their weaknesses, because they often find it more difficult or more painful than maintaining the status quo.

The Sherpa process empowers clients to deal with their weaknesses. This goes against some concepts for development and training. Trainers like to "accentuate the positive." But Sherpas like to look at each client's situation honestly and deal with it openly. The fact is, Sherpas are hired because clients have weaknesses they can't get around and problems they can't solve on their own. Dealing with a client's strength can be a more pleasant exercise, but it's not going to solve their problems.

STORIES FROM THE SUMMIT

Brian is a very skilled administrative assistant who wants to be a project manager. The president of the company has consented to interview Brian for a position that has recently opened. Brian is terrified. He lacks the ability to sell his skills, particularly to an important person like the president of his company.

Confidence and high self-esteem have to be built over time. As a coach, you need rapid results. Brian's Sherpa coach helped him select several affirming statements he could tell himself in the mirror before leaving home, and then again before going into the interview with the president.

"I am a well-educated man."

"I am the perfect individual for this job."

"I can make my case with no fear."

Brian was right for the job. His weaknesses were the only thing standing in the way. Brian overcame them immediately. He decided how to do it. For him, it was effective to pump himself up like an athlete taking the field.

He got the job and gained a much better understanding of himself, too.

3. *COACHING FORCES HONESTY.* In the workplace, employees are allowed to avoid confrontation. They sidestep challenges, procrastinate, and refuse to address matters of importance, because nobody likes confrontation. Problems build up.

Sherpas do not allow clients to avoid the issues. We know our clients, perhaps better than anyone in their organization, because we have really listened to them. We are forced to address their situations.

A coach can go right to the heart of the matter and push a client against the wall, demanding honest, revealing, and thoughtful answers. A coach has the right to ask questions, and the Sherpa process asks the right questions. This can be uncomfortable, but it is the fundamental difference between coaching, training, and just sitting around talking.

Stories from the Summit

Carol has been with her nonprofit for 12 years. She's an expert in a loan product that addresses the needs of senior homeowners. Carol's skills are known all over the region, and she brings in business. The CEO of the company would like Carol to identify and train other team members on this product. It is not good business to have Carol be the only one who knows how to deliver an important service.

I was brought in to facilitate a discussion between Carol and the CEO. There was a lot of nervous energy in the room. I guided the CEO to ask the right questions.

"How can we have other team members trained by the end of the year?"

"Why have you not begun the process?"

"Why is it important to us, to the community, to the seniors, that several people can help them?"

Carol said she just didn't have time for training. I challenged her: Why had it not moved to the top of her priority list? Her CEO had asked her to get it done. Carol finally admitted she was scared to have someone else in the company know what she knows. She thought it gave her job security.

With the truth on the table, solving the problem was straightforward. Honesty and truth work wonders. And sometimes a coach is the best person to get to the truth.

4. COACHING CAN SUPPORT TRANSITIONS. New hires, transfers, and promotions—no matter the transition, it's like getting a brand-new employee. In the hiring process there are trade-offs. It is rare to get everything you want from a new employee. Employers are forced to rank the most important characteristics necessary to successfully perform a job. Then they should commit to developing an employee's skills in everything else.

Often, high performers are task driven and lack the appropriate relational skills to advance in their organizations. The "people person" can be disorganized, even reckless. A Sherpa coach can accelerate the productivity and upward mobility of the manager by creating the proper balance.

Sherpas fit well into transitions: Having a coach can be an incentive to get an existing employee to accept a transfer or promotion. A coach can be a part of the transition package for an employee being downsized or terminated.

5. *WHEN ALL ELSE FAILS.* When is coaching indicated? Under two circumstances: a manager is out of control or is failing as a leader. A coach can change destructive behavior and restore respect for a manager whose personal life spills into the workplace, or whose personal problems become paralyzing. A coach can help fix the weaknesses of a leader who is not up to the demands of the job. Coaching can save an executive's job and maintain continuity in an organization.

6. *ANONYMITY.* The coach is an anonymous entity, working for the success of a company by improving an individual. This gives significant freedom to everyone involved. The coach is not the client's employer. Clients recognize this and understand quite quickly: the coach is there for them and keeps things they say confidential. Sometimes information can be shared with a client's superior or colleague, with the client's consent. When that happens, both the organization and the employee have a sounding board, an outside perspective.

WHO NEEDS A COACH?

The purpose of coaching is to guide rather than to teach. A coach may offer some training but will mainly be an objective observer. As an executive coach, you are not part of the client's organization and his daily life, so once trust has been established, clients will understand you have no ulterior motive.

Your purpose is to zero in on your clients' issues and to enable them to work constructively and purposefully to a positive outcome.

There are three main reasons to coach someone:

- **A promotion is involved.**
- **A job is at stake.**
- **A new perspective is needed.**

In the first two scenarios, the individual needs to change specific behaviors that limit growth or create failure. The client and the employer know these behaviors cause problems, but don't know how to fix them.

> **AMONG EMPLOYERS HIRING COACHES:**
>
> 85 percent want to sharpen the leadership skills of high-potential individuals.
>
> 70 percent need to correct behavioral problems.
>
> 65 percent want to ensure the success of newly promoted managers.
>
> 55 percent seek to provide leadership skills to technically oriented employees.

When a promotion or a job is at stake, the client decides, or is forced by her employer, to develop changes in behavior. The client will be asked to leave, or lose a promotion, if things don't get better.

 ## STORIES FROM THE SUMMIT

> *Andy is a statistician working for a large company. He excels at accounting, but he's horrible in personal dealings with his peers and his staff. His boss approaches a coach for help. "If we can't get Andy to look at things differently with his staff, he can't stay. It's a make or break for Andy."*

We need to address the extreme, the case where an employee's job is in jeopardy. If that is the reason you are brought in to coach, be aware that you are walking into a minefield. There are several possible outcomes and most aren't very pretty.

What if your client's poor behavior or performance continues? Be aware that the client might get fired in the middle of the coaching process. Stay informed about the situation, and stay out of the employee/employer

---

FOR THE PROFESSIONAL COACH

The Danger Zone: You may have been brought in to create a legal defense for the employer, who fully intends to terminate the employee regardless of what happens in your coaching experience. The employer may simply want to say, after the fact, that he did everything possible to help the employee's professional development. In this situation, your reputation with the employer will necessarily suffer. The employer can't say "What a great coach . . ." when he just fired your client. You might be seen as a scapegoat. Look for signs of this scenario in your meeting with the supervisor or executive contact.

---

relationship. Sherpas do not get involved directly in that relationship, especially when serious problems are on the table. It might be impossible to fix the situation, and you could end up in the middle of someone else's war.

When serious problems have been going on for years, it's unlikely that even a Sherpa can fix things in a matter of weeks. If you find yourself in this situation, and decide to take on the client, tell your executive contact you will accept the challenge but should have been called in far earlier.

In the third scenario, when clients need to develop new perspectives, they will hire a coach, or be assigned one to work on personal development, in order to find direction or reach important goals. Often, this will happen when a new executive comes on board with a client company. She'll assess, with the skills she currently possesses, where to go and how to get there. Often, this means working on weaknesses that the coaching process uncovers.

COACHING TIPS

Here's a collection of skills Sherpas develop to create a solid coaching career.

For the new coach, it's important to learn these concepts thoroughly and integrate them in to everything you do. The first three relate directly to the "What Makes a Good Coach?" section in Chapter 1. They are important enough to bear repeating.

1. NEVER GIVE ANSWERS. Be clear about your role, in your own mind and with your client. Clients will often ask their Sherpa to produce the solution to a problem. Your role, as a responsible coach, is to foster independence. To do this, ask your client to find the solution on their own if possible. Your first instinct will tell you to find answers and solve problems. Instead, ask questions, then more questions. Guide, without offering ready-made scenarios. The results will astound you. This is often a difficult area if you, as a coach, are prone to problem solving. Don't go for the quick fix.

The Sherpa resists the urge to solve clients' problems. Your job is to reflect their words back to them, so they can see things objectively. Let them draw their own conclusions and learn their own lessons. When you are tempted to put an answer on the table, ask questions instead. Clients will live by the solutions they come up with on their own.

 ## STORIES FROM THE SUMMIT

> *Jonathan has been a CEO for 19 years in the health-care industry. He is capable and focused on money—bottom-line results. But Jonathan had trouble connecting to his staff. He started a new job and wanted to make his first 90 days memorable.*
>
> *I asked him the key to connecting with his new staff. He couldn't answer. He tried to figure out what his new staff might need, but couldn't get it. He spent 20 minutes trying to figure out the best dialogue for the first meeting with a new staff. He never became frustrated, and he did finally figure it out.*
>
> *Jonathan said, "I'm going to ask them to share something of themselves, their feelings. I'll ask: 'What do you like to do best?' and 'What is the most challenging thing you do?'"*

> *That approach moved him away from the bottom line, and closer to his people. If he hadn't come up with the idea on his own, it wouldn't have meant as much. He ended up being an all-around success.*

2. *ASK QUESTIONS.* In order to make sense of a situation for your client, you need information. Questions are the tool of investigation. They allow you as a coach to help your client find clarity. Questions defuse awkward moments. In person, they provoke an unaltered, truthful response. Your questions enable your clients to sort things out for themselves. They will also teach your clients to ask questions of their own.

3. *FIND THE "UNCLOAKED SELF."* You are helping your clients find out who they are when they are "uncloaked." The client's true identity can only be revealed when you dig deep and search with diligence. Using the phrase "take the armor off" can help a client think more honestly and profoundly. Clients are only coachable if they are willing to put down their defenses and examine themselves. As a coach, you will need to help them get there. Self-examination can be very painful. Your clients must be handled with the greatest of care, yet you cannot allow them to hide their problems.

Our critical skills list continues with policies, ground rules, and ideas that the best Sherpas make second nature.

4. *REVELATIONS.* A revealing of the truth . . . a realization . . . that is what Sherpas look to create. When your client has a revelation about how he has handled—or failed to handle—something, that's when the learning opportunity occurs. Don't be afraid to push. The Sherpa knows when to push, and to be assertive enough to force a client to explain more carefully, in more detail, more honestly. Only when the client's personal "light bulb" goes on can work in that area go forward. The revelations don't have to be profound to be life changing. You can't have a revelation *for* your client. You can help create revelations by asking questions.

5. *THE "THREE-SENTENCE RULE."* One of the most consistent rules for success in communication is the three-sentence rule. As you talk, share three sentences, and then await a response. The first sentence in the

sequence is the introduction: the big-picture idea. The second sentence is the theme: the specific thought you'd like to get across. The third sentence is a question. Eventually, you will teach certain clients this idea. It's a principle every coach should learn and apply.

6. *DON'T MAKE THREATS.*   A coach working with a Disney exec once said: "You better perform, baby, or you're out of here." Don't be condescending. If a client is in trouble, they already know it. Your role is to guide and encourage, not deliver ultimatums. The world is a threatening place for your client. Remember that, and remember why you are called a Sherpa.

7. *SOMETHING NEW.*   Teach your client something new every week. This book offers more than enough material to make that possible. Use everything you can that applies to each client. Do not let your client leave a session without some "gem" for his repertoire. Take it right from the book, but make it yours and make it meaningful. After every session, your client must be satisfied they are learning something new.

8. *YOUR PORTABLE OFFICE.*   Your briefcase is your office. Most of your "working papers" will be in the client's journal. You'll bring progress notes to every client meeting, with a plan for the exercises you'll be using from the journal. You'll also carry any gifts or reminders for your client. Additionally, you'll copy the Sherpa coaching checklist for each client (Appendix, page SC 3-1) and make notes on work completed and planned for each client.

9. *DON'T OVER-PREPARE.*   Study your process diagram before each meeting, but remember: Your client does the climbing while you serve as a guide. All you need are questions that let them direct the flow of conversation. If they have had an eventful week, and need to talk, let it happen, but focus on the events that deal directly with the topics you are working on, and your place in the process. Make sure you evaluate how well you did. In Appendix, page SC 2-1 is a self-evaluation form we recommend you complete the first few times you coach. It helps you determine whether you are on the right track.

10. *WATCH YOUR TIME.*   Make sure you finish your thought process and try to reach specific goals long before your hour is over. Give yourself ten minutes to wrap things up, summarize your meeting, and establish goals and assignments for the next one. Keeping to your allotted time is one of the biggest challenges in coaching.

11. *GIFTS/LITTLE SOMETHINGS/CHARA.* Many times, you will present your client with small gifts that reinforce your message. To describe these gifts, we use the Sherpa's word: chara. People enjoy this, and they come to expect it. Time and time again, clients will ask: "Do I get a present this week?" From CEO on down, your clients will be receptive to presents and candy. Use them as reminders, and as rewards. When your client handles a situation extremely well, give them a Tootsie Pop. While this may seem silly or childish, it is actually a very powerful tool every coach should use. There's more about this in Chapter 7.

12. *RELAX.* Enjoy your work. Enjoy your client. Sit back and listen. Don't think you have to have the answer for everything. Most times, a client will come up with the answers on their own. You are a guide, a facilitator. You are someone they can bounce things off. The more relaxed you are, the more you listen, the better prepared you are to help your clients.

EXECUTIVE COACHING, STEP-BY-STEP

Maybe you are an independent coach hired by an individual. Perhaps an employer has contracted with you. Possibly you're a staff coach employed to coach people within your own organization.

The approach you'll take to coaching is different depending on who's arranged the coaching and who's paying the bills. The distinctions can be extremely important.

On page 32 is a table of the basic steps that define the coaching relationship. In the "Every Client" column, you'll find information about the coaching process in general. This will apply to every relationship, whether you are a staff coach or come from outside the client's organization.

The "Private Client—Private Pay" column deals exclusively with the client who hires a Sherpa on their own and pays for services personally.

The "Corporate Client—Executive Contact Interface" column discusses the corporate client. If you are a staff coach, the client will be employed by the same organization you are. For the coach coming in from the outside, the corporate client is one whose employer arranges and pays for the Sherpa's services.

If you're a staff coach, working with employees of your organization, the first column will be enough to guide you.

In either case, we refer to the person the Sherpa directly reports to at a corporate client as the "executive contact."

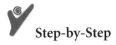 **Step-by-Step**

Startup

In this step, you'll prepare to discuss exactly what you and your client will be working on. You'll find all the questions you need to ask, so you will be ready for the coaching assignment.

Briefing

This is an overview of the Sherpa process. You'll review the Sherpa process diagram with your executive contact and your client, and discuss the work style assessment that gets you started.

Readiness

This step is all about relationships. The relationship between client and coach is established. You will make it clear to the executive contact and the client that they need to be ready to work hard in order to create meaningful progress.

Format

Sherpa coaching is based on person-to-person encounters. Point-to-point videoconferencing is becoming a viable alternative to in-person meetings. Executive contact meetings are discussed and scheduled here, too.

Scope

Establish with your executive contact and your client how often and when you will be meeting. Mention that extensions are available beyond 12 weeks to solve the initial challenge or take on new ones.

Setup

Set a meeting time and place. Offer an overview of what the hour is going to look like from the client's perspective. Inform the executive contact about their role throughout the 12 weeks.

Checkpoints

Checks and balances are key to successful coaching. Don't be afraid of evaluations. You can only learn from them. You are responsible for setting up a midterm evaluation and a final administrative meeting.

Pricing

As part of the preparations of successful coaching, you will want to gather information on costs and pricing in your area. The prices vary as much as the type of coaching.

Contract

The contract is the final step in defining your coaching relationship.

Each step is vital to open and honest communication with your client and your executive contact.

Startup—The Primary Meeting

EVERY CLIENT	PRIVATE CLIENT—PRIVATE PAY	CORPORATE CLIENT—EXECUTIVE CONTACT INTERFACE
Ideally, coaching will take place outside the work environment.	Be extremely clear about your role and the client's right to privacy. Because you are being paid directly by the client, no one else, under any circumstances, will be involved in this process.	This meeting can take place at the client's workplace.
Don't try to establish who you are at your first meeting. You will establish this, as needed, over time. Establish yourself in the context of the coaching process. There will be time during your 12 weeks of meetings to share a little of yourself when it is directly relevant to business behavior.	When you are coaching a corporate client, and are asked by one of their colleagues to conduct private pay coaching, do not inform their employer about the private relationship. Even if his boss knows about it, no information will be shared. Confidentiality must be complete.	Meeting with the executive contact: Request 30 minutes to ask specific questions about the employee. What weaknesses/strengths has she observed? What area of focus does she want you to work on? Get examples and as many details as possible before you begin. This translates to a route, either organizational or relational, later on in the process.
You are not here to be a friend. Coaching will have tough moments. Sherpas communicate and guide in a		

EVERY CLIENT	PRIVATE CLIENT— PRIVATE PAY	CORPORATE CLIENT— EXECUTIVE CONTACT INTERFACE
way that keeps them autonomous. Don't say too much. The hour you spend with your client belongs to them. Your job is to start listening right away. Never talk about coaching when you see a client at a different venue. Loan your client a copy of the movie *Into Thin Air: Death on Everest*. Ask them to view the movie before the next time you meet. This will give them a very clear idea of what a Sherpa is and how important your role is. The movie helps clients understand your role.	This meeting is not considered the "first meeting" in your series of 12. This is the "get to know you" meeting. Make sure you fit each other's profiles and agree that you can succeed with this endeavor before you start the process and the meter. It is important to make sure you "click." Allow your client to tell you that the relationship is good for them. Do not assume you are the perfect coach for that client. Let them choose you.	Do you think the client will accept coaching? If not, why not? What change would you like to see with your employee? What are you really looking for me (as a coach) to do? The more specific you can get, the more quickly you can narrow the routes and paths you'll work on. What is the exec's commitment to this individual? Is it important enough that he will work at it after the coach is gone?

Briefing—Client Overview

EVERY CLIENT	CORPORATE CLIENT
Review the Sherpa coaching process with your client. Go over it briefly, using the diagram on the first page of your client's journal. Do not place too much emphasis on the process. Some clients are motivated by the diagram and enjoy the idea of having a direction. Others are intimidated by the apparent complexity of the diagram. Because, at this point, you don't know your client too well, review the process in abbreviated terms and move on. At any time if your client asks you to see the diagram, bring it out and show them exactly where you are in the process. The first step with your client: Explain that we can make progress in 12 weeks because we "jump start" the process with a personality assessment. DiSC® is the Sherpa coaching assessment of choice. The assessment should be completed prior to the first meeting with your client. Reasons we use DiSC® are listed in Chapter 4. You get a 23-page report from your distributor that is comprehensive. It's mainly for your use as a coach. You can spend as little or as much time as you need explaining the DiSC® to your client. It is a great starting point for your relationship.	Review the Sherpa coaching process with the executive contact. Bring a diagram of the process and a sample DiSC® if you are going to use it for your initial assessment. Review why DiSC® is an effective tool and give them a sample report to review. See Chapter 4 for more details about DiSC®. To set up online DiSC®, email info@sherpacoaching.com.

Readiness

EVERY CLIENT	CORPORATE CLIENT
Make sure your client is ready for coaching. Here are things to examine, to see whether he's ready or not:	Often, your executive contact will be deciding whether or not your client keeps their job. This is a huge responsibility for a coach. Be candid with your executive contact, and be honest about your impressions of the client's abilities to carry on in their current position. If you don't know, don't be afraid to say so.
Your client must be willing to commit. If they will not complete the designated homework or exercises, they'll have an unsuccessful experience. If they are close-minded and do not share truths, you cannot get far with them.	
	Your relationship with the executive contact cannot be hidden from your client. Clients need to know that the executive contact is paying for your services, and a Sherpa has a responsibility to share progress with that contact.
You can tell your client is committed by these traits:	
Always on time Calls if running a little late Responds to your email inquiries Shares good and bad experiences	The environment reinforces change in the client. What does the work environment look like? Who is involved in the success of this coaching? The organization paying the coach has to support your client in any way they can. Can you call their supervisor and get a meeting easily? Does his supervisor take action on things you ask of them? (i.e., will you call your employee once a week to discuss progress)?
It is not unheard of to postpone a coaching appointment with a client because they are not committed. Stick to your guns and clearly state your expectations about commitment. Often, when you postpone meetings, your client will have time to really think about it and will return to the process with more commitment and dedication.	

Format

EVERY CLIENT	CORPORATE CLIENT
Meet personally for one hour per week. With the Sherpa coaching experience, we recommend coaching in person. Here are the reasons to meet face-to-face:	The outline of the 12 weeks for the executive contact look like this:
	Initial meeting to establish expectations
1. When you speak on the phone, you never know if your client is distracted by what is going on in their presence. Are they distracted by all the work that must be accomplished that day? Even if they are dedicated, you cannot really see whether you have their full attention. Too many times, a client's colleague interrupts your phone call and the flow is lost.	Six-week meeting—update and discuss: (midterm evaluation for the executive contact is found in the "Sherpa Toolkit" section in Appendix.)
	1. Are we meeting goals? If not, you will need to know whether or not you should continue with this client.
	2. Is the client committed? If not, you can stop the process or offer another coach in your place.

EVERY CLIENT	CORPORATE CLIENT
2. Email is impersonal. Body language accounts for most of the meaning in a conversation. You lose that, and you lose tone of voice, with email. The only way email or phone would work is in a long-standing relationship, when a client calls or emails with a specific question or concern. You know the client well. In a phone conversation, you know when they are reacting or acting inappropriately, and you know how to deal with that.	3. Have expectations changed since the first time we met? 4. What changes has your executive contact seen with the client in the work setting? 5. If you think it would be valuable, ask the executive contact for a tour of the company, or a chance to stay an hour with your client in their work environment. Unless the executive contact requires a private meeting, include your client in meetings with your executive contact. The more the client and executive contact talk, the better. After 12 weeks, meet with your executive contact to review the action plan you and your client created and discuss continued coaching. Be confident and make a phone call, anytime over the 12-week span, if you need verification of what a client tells you. Last Step: Written evaluation (Appendix, page SC 6-1) completed by your client and your executive contact. Ask for six referrals and a letter of recommendation.

Scope

PRIVATE CLIENT—PRIVATE PAY	CORPORATE CLIENT
We agree to meet, and charge for 12 weeks at a time. This is an easier sell, since it's a limited commitment. A given coaching engagement can last longer, but when it's structured 12 weeks at a time, it's a comfortable arrangement for your client. Extensions can be for an additional 6 or even 12 weeks at a time. If a client starts out by requesting a 6-week coaching experience, trust the process, trust your judgment, and either sell the 12-week engagement or walk away.	Every engagement will be 12 weeks. Meetings with our executive contact will take place prior to the first week, at 6 weeks and 12 weeks. After the 12 weeks are over, meet with the executive contact and decide whether or not they want to renew for 6 more weeks. Limit extensions to 6 weeks.

Setup

EVERY CLIENT	CORPORATE CLIENT
Meetings are best held at the beginning or end of the workday. Taking someone out of their day-to-day routine in the middle of the day can disorient the client. Stick with one hour. You will have a tendency to go longer because your client wants to. Prepare to close the meeting ten minutes prior to when you need to leave, and assign homework for next time.	After you have met with your client the first time, share your schedule with your executive contact.
You'll experience "doorknob syndrome." Frequently, at the end of a meeting, the client discloses a significant piece of information, as your hand is "on the doorknob" and you're ready to leave. You'll hear "I feel like quitting today," "I feel like we have not made one bit of progress together." Be prepared for this by wrapping up ten minutes early.	Be open and approachable to your executive contact. Allow them the availability to contact you if the need arises.
Meet at a regular location, away from the client's office or comfort zone. It is really important to pick a good location. Restaurants can work but have their distractions. Check it out first. Get to know the restaurant and make them aware of your needs.	At this point, you might schedule the 6-week follow-up meeting with your executive contact.

Checkpoints

EVERY CLIENT	CORPORATE CLIENT
Conduct a 6-week mid-term evaluation/review to compare progress with expectations. This helps you get clearer insights on where you are helping and where you need to expend more energy.	Six-week phone or personal meeting with executive contact.
	Twelve-week meeting and a final evaluation you present to your client and to the supervisor. Give a summary of what you worked on with the client to the supervisor. Here is an example of what you should present to the supervisor:
	Dates and number of meetings
	Areas of Focus: List the Route and Path chosen, actions taken, results obtained.
	Successful experiences (client success stories)
	—Recommendations: areas you, as a coach, would like to see the supervisor watch, work on, or help with for client to continue success.
	A sample report is included in the Appendix, page SC 2-3.

When you're hired to coach, these last two steps are important.

Pricing

PRIVATE CLIENT	CORPORATE CLIENT
Review fee scale with the client. Your rates will increase with your experience and reputation. Research prevailing practices in your area.	Review fee scale with the executive contact.

Contract

PRIVATE CLIENT	CORPORATE CLIENT
Make sure you have a signed contract before coaching begins. Include the home billing address of the client in the contract. See Appendix, page SC 2-2 for sample.	Do not begin your coaching without a contract. Make sure the level of detail matches your client's needs, and that your arrangement spells out the executive contact's role. See Appendix, page SC 2-2 for sample.

To get started, we have talked about the characteristics of a successful Sherpa. We have also detailed exactly what happens when you are coaching.

Now, with a road map in place for the working relationship, let's start learning the Sherpa coaching process.

CHAPTER 3

The Process and the Phases

COACHING IS GROWING QUICKLY AS A BUSINESS PHENOMENON. The Harvard Business School sees 40,000 new coaches joining the ranks in the next five years. As far as we can see, 95 percent of them will coach by the seat of their pants. They'll guess, because they don't know what else to do.

Good instincts are useful in coaching, but instinct cannot be the only thing that guides a coach. "Being there" is simply not enough. Knowing exactly where you and your client are going makes good things happen. Sherpas have a plan that includes assessment, milestones, homework, journaling, and an action plan customized for each client.

Any coach will tell you: Every client and every assignment is unique. Many will acknowledge that they don't have any systematic business process designed to produce results from coaching. Their philosophy—"I'll make it up as I go, within a vague framework, and keep the meter running"—is a recipe for failure.

What You'll Find in This Chapter:

- **Why Coaching Needs a Process**
- **The Sherpa Process**
- **Phases in the Sherpa Process**
- **The Sherpa Stance**

WHY COACHING NEEDS A PROCESS

Having analyzed executive coaching for years, we've had a chance to see the results produced by various coaching styles. We've concluded that coaching without a detailed set of conventions and rules is unlikely to benefit the client at all. Here are five principles that the best coaches follow:

1. COACHES WORK ON BUSINESS BEHAVIOR. Coaching seems to be an easy occupation. All you have to do is meet with someone (or even easier, send an email or talk on the phone) and give them your advice. Without a process, what do most coaches do? They may decide that the client needs counseling that borders on therapy: help with "anger management," for instance. Most coaches have never been trained for that. The result? An unqualified advisor, working toward an ill-defined goal with no road map, no documentation, and no deadline.

2. COACHING HAS TO MEET EVERYONE'S NEEDS. A coach, a supervisor, and a client can have very different views on what coaching should accomplish. A coach who wants to talk, instead of listen, can have a very different outlook than the client, who may not want a coach, or the employer who needs immediate results. Without a defining technique like the Sherpa process, everyone is on a different page, looking at a different problem, wanting different results.

3. COACHING NEEDS BOUNDARIES. Without a process that everyone agrees on, there's no road map for coaching and there are no guard rails. The Sherpa process enables you to keep your client focused on areas where coaching is effective. Over time, life will make you respect processes. If you skip phases and steps in a proven process, life will make you go back and revisit them. It's better to follow a structure for coaching from the beginning.

4. COACHING FOLLOWS A PREDICTABLE AGENDA. Having a process does not mean that you always control the agenda. Our process allows "sidebars," interruptions, and detours, but always brings the coach and client back to a route that leads to a chosen destination. There are more opportunities than you can imagine for losing your train of thought or your agenda because of your client's immediate needs or mindset. Your client has a bad week and wants to share stories. If the client brings in a new problem area or problem employee, you are obligated to go in that direction. Without the Sherpa process, you'll never get back to where you left off.

5. *COACHING HAS A "FINISH LINE."* If you don't have a process, you don't know where to start and when to stop. It's hard to sell the concept of coaching, and it's hard to do it well, if it's an open-ended experience with no predictable cost or schedule.

 ## STORIES FROM THE SUMMIT

Louis is CEO of a small janitorial company. He needs help with time management and organization. He has his hands in every pot, and gets more involved than he should at lower levels. Consequently, he can't get his own job done. The things that only he can do? They aren't happening.

One week, Louis came to our meeting, caught up with a customer who doesn't want to pay. He wanted advice on how to handle this situation. A perfect opportunity to tell him: "This is an important issue, but we need to stick to the reason we're here, and stay with our process. If we deviate from this point, we'll go astray, and that is not what we want to do."

I asked him if there was a co-worker he could talk with about this customer. I also asked him to write down the scenario, so when we moved into another area of focus, we could use that experience as a starting point. Louis was satisfied with those options, and we continued climbing the mountain of time management.

We have seen "coaching processes" that simply don't meet the definition of a business process. Here's a simple composite of some of the "process maps" currently in use for executive coaching:

Clarify your situation.

Organize your efforts.

Action planning.

Craft an answer.

Harness your power.

It's very appealing, because it's easy. It's also so vague as to be meaningless. There are multimillion-dollar companies that offer coaching, and don't have any more than a cute catch phrase to define their work.

One of life's basic truths: Anything that seems too simplistic *is* too simplistic. Life is complicated, and coaching is, too. You need to work hard to be good at coaching, or at anything else.

You need detailed maps to reach any destination. You need to know how to proceed, and you need to know when you're finished, too. Any coaching process that doesn't have an "exit strategy" for the coach is a poor process.

> **HOW TO MAXIMIZE THE SHERPA COACHING PROCESS**
>
> **1. Study it and learn it.** You cannot be intuitive about the Sherpa process. You have to learn it, study it, and know it by heart. The more you practice and work through the process, the more you will know what to say and do next. The more confidence you show, the more you'll be seen as an intuitive, perceptive guide—a successful Sherpa.
>
> **2. Work it.** Go through the process. Respect it. Don't be afraid of it. It has been proven in the field. It's systematic. Follow it every time you coach. It works—so work it.
>
> **3. Don't change it.** Skipping phases and steps in the process will prevent you from gaining the outcome you and your client desire. Trust the process. Respect the process.

With all these facts in mind, let's get into the details of the Sherpa coaching process.

We map our coaching across a timeline, and put elements of the Sherpa coaching process into phases. The word "phase" has been defined as "a distinct time period in a sequence of events." In this diagram, starting at the bottom with Phase One, successively higher parts of the mountain represent the six phases of the Sherpa coaching process.

SHERPA EXECUTIVE COACHING

(© Sasha Corporation)

THE SHERPA PROCESS

Intuition is always going to play a role in your work, but coaching must be more than guesswork. With the Sherpa process, there is less speculation and more controlled activity. The Sherpa coaching process is a chain of events, each phase depending on the completion of a previous activity.

The Sherpa coaching process is a consistent way of providing resources and results to your coaching client. We get to the true issues of leadership in a hurry. We offer real answers, rather than off-the-cuff advice. Clients never leave a meeting without a new way of looking at their situation. They gain access to every tool we have developed, and they'll have proven methods to work through each challenge. Progress is measurable.

The Sherpa coaching process leads a coaching client through self-examination and personal planning. We'll systematically create a personal strategic plan. Then we make the plan a reality, creating a list of responsibilities, ways to get things done, personal support mechanisms, and milestones.

Once you have established yourself as your client's coach, review the Sherpa process with them. The previous diagram shows the six-phase process, and the progression toward the top that is the Sherpa philosophy. Your client will find a copy in the beginning of their journal.

The details of the process might be intimidating to some clients. Together, review the process diagram, shaped like a pyramid, using the talking points that follow.

 **PHASES IN THE SHERPA PROCESS**

PHASE ONE. We will be looking at you, the real you (Taking Stock).

PHASE TWO. You'll look at the important people in your life and how they affect and support you (Global View).

PHASE THREE. Then we'll discover your motivations, why people and things affect you the way they do, and how to create and communicate expectations (Destination).

PHASE FOUR. We'll work on specific areas that will affect your day-to-day work life. We'll organize and structure goals that fit your needs. (Charting the Course).

PHASE FIVE. Then we'll make sure it's planned for success, checking that accountability and attitude are right where they should be (Agenda).

PHASE SIX. When we're done, we'll have cause to celebrate (The Summit).

The Sherpa coaching process is patterned after a change management process we developed years ago. There are six phases in the process, leading from analysis in the early rounds to remedial action in the last phases.

Let's examine the phases by sharing questions that will be answered in each area. You'll see a detailed diagram of each phase.

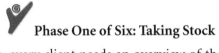

Phase One of Six: Taking Stock

To begin with, every client needs an overview of the Sherpa coaching process. The coach introduces ground rules for the coaching engagement, and prepares the client for the work ahead and the ramifications of the upcoming behavioral changes.

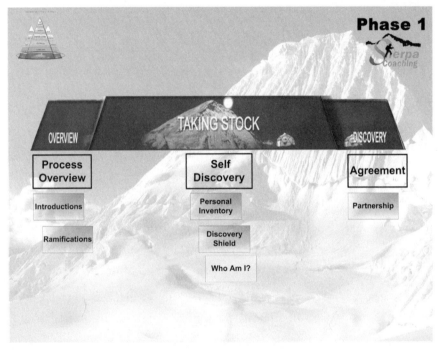

(© Sasha Corporation)

Self-discovery takes the client through a series of evaluations. The Discovery Shield reveals their strengths, weaknesses, gifts, and motivation: "Why it matters." We'll also have the client create a personal inventory. What does your client's work environment look like? How do they perform? What needs to change? The Sherpa and the client reach agreement on what constitutes truth.

Phase One, Taking Stock, helps you understand your clients, but more importantly, it lets them understand themselves. This forms an agreement between the Sherpa and client about who the client truly is and where coaching might take them.

Phase Two of Six: Global View

Phase Two, Global View, takes a detailed look at the world around the client. The focus is on how people, places, and things affect your client. This is a study of their "human environment." We'll look at what keeps your client going, the internal and environmental factors that support their identity. We'll also ask who their true supporters are. Who can they really count on? The Global View involves a reality check dealing with perceptions: How does your client think people view them? What do people really think about them? This involves research, reality, and reconciliation.

A client can't be successful with change unless they look at it head on. Your client's attitude toward change is assessed and discussed; to make

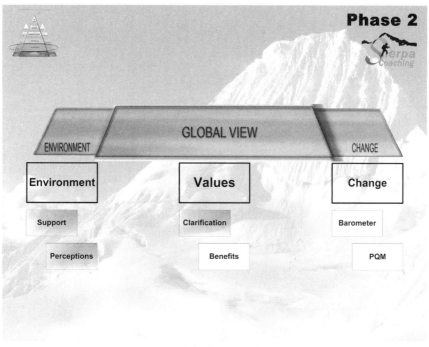

(© Sasha Corporation)

sure they can handle the climb ahead. How well do they handle change? How does change affect the people around them? Why can change be difficult?

What makes your client tick? The Global View explores their values, and what's important to them. Learning what the client defines as important shows the coach why they do what they do.

This exploration of what the client's world looks like is enlightening and sometimes surprising. The Global View is an external assessment.

Phase Three of Six: Destination

Phase Three is where choices are made. Your client knows they have room for improvement. Now that we have examined the client's life and environment in Phases One and Two, we will decide on one of ten paths that will determine how we reach the summit. Those paths are areas

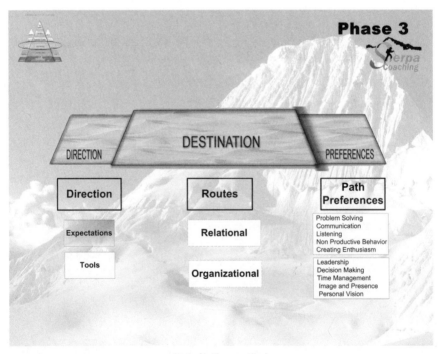

(© Sasha Corporation)

for improvement and development that meet the client's needs. The Sherpa process directs you and your client to one of ten well-defined paths, and to the use of appropriate tools, exercise, and training along each path.

Better communication of business goals produces better leadership. In a Cincinnati Enquirer *article about leadership, Karl Corbett, Sasha Corporation's CEO, shared this:* "The most important thing a leader can communicate is clear expectations. If a leader assumes people know what they're supposed to do but doesn't detail it, people will make up their own course of action, and the expectations will match up only through dumb luck."

As you start this journey, virtually every client will have room for improvement in the way they communicate expectations. The concept of communicating expectations, and a model for doing so, is delivered to every coaching client. After that, the Sherpa decides on direction. Is the client's problem wrapped up in emotion or skills? listening? leadership? time management?

Problems in the business world fall into two general categories: relationship based and organizational. Each has to be taken on independently, and different tools apply to each. In mountain climbing terms, the two categories of problems and solutions are like two faces of a mountain. The client's journey to the summit involves traveling one of those two routes. In the relational route, you will focus on soft skills, areas of improvement centered on the "connecting" and emotions of the client. The organizational route emphasizes the managerial skills of the working person.

Within each route, your client has one of five paths to choose from. The Sherpa has a complete selection of assessments in the client's journal, to help the client decide on which path. Clients will use different tools to reach the summit, depending on the path they choose. *The Sherpa Guide* provides all those tools, and ways to help you to decide how they should be applied. As a Sherpa, you'll know how to offer all the advice and guidance your client needs.

Under the relational route, you and your client may take one of these paths:

- Problem solving
- Communication
- Listening
- Nonproductive behavior
- Creating enthusiasm

If you are following the organizational route, you and your client might choose one of these paths:

- Leadership
- Decision making
- Time management
- Image and presence
- Personal vision

Phase Four of Six: Charting the Course

This is where the hard work takes place. In Phase Four, Charting the Course, we focus on what has to change in your client's business behavior. How do we make necessary changes? What goals are you going to work on?

Drills, training, and homework: Your client's journal includes everything you'll need to guide them to the top. *The Sherpa Guide* has detailed advice, including when and how you might use every assessment and exercise in the journal. You'll find it easy to create a specific action plan for every client, a customized solution that changes their business behavior.

Every client has unique needs, and will have their own personal summit. The process always remains the same. Every client will have to choose one of the ten paths to get to the top of the mountain. Here's a map for each of the paths, and a set of tools you'll be using along the way. For now, do a quick scan to get familiar with it. Later, you'll refer to it as you proceed with each client.

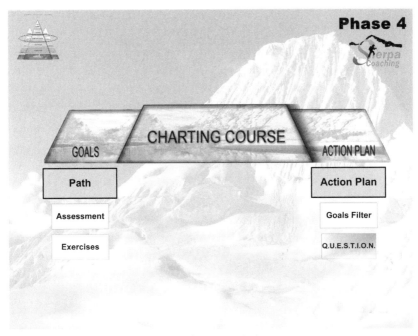

(© Sasha Corporation)

RELATIONAL ROUTE OVERVIEW	ORGANIZATIONAL ROUTE OVERVIEW

Problem-solving Path
  DIG UP
  QTIP
  Separating the person from the issue
	Leadership Path
	  Assessment
	  Leadership analysis
	  Recognizing values

Communication Path
  Assessment
  Communication acronym
  Listen, Think, Then Communicate
	Decision-Making Path
	  Assessment
	  Decision-making mountain
	  Internal/external expectations

Listening Path
  The art of listening
  Body language
  Silence
  Three-sentence rule
	Time Management Path
	  Assessment
	  Personal program
	  Prioritization summary

Nonproductive Behavior Path
  DAPPER
  Anger management
  Intimidation
	Image and Presence Path
	  Why it matters
	  Client connection
	  Helpful hints, tricks, and techniques

Creating Enthusiasm path
  Discovery Shield
  Love bus
  Fuzzy duck theory
	Personal Vision Path
	  Personal quarterly meeting
	  The commercial
	  Finding your talent

Phase Five of Six: Agenda

Your client's commitment to change is solidified here, as we set their course for life beyond coaching. In Phase Five, Agenda, the client figures out what needs to happen for the action plan to become reality. Does the client have the right attitude? The most important factor in personal accountability is their attitude toward it. Is your client accountable for the changes they are working on?

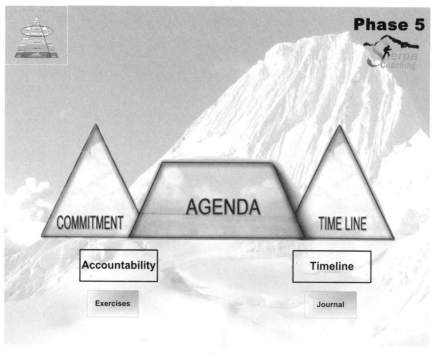

(© Sasha Corporation)

The Sherpa process contains training on what accountability means and how to make it happen. Given the short-term goals, and a proven way to achieve success, the Sherpa and the client look at the long-term goals.

You'll review and discuss the work that you and your client have done in his journal. The results from this discussion will establish your long-term outlook, and help establish a timeline the client will follow on their own.

Phase Six of Six: The Summit

Going the Distance   It's celebration time. You are at the summit. You have gone the distance with your client. There are two things left to cover in this phase: Support and Follow-up.

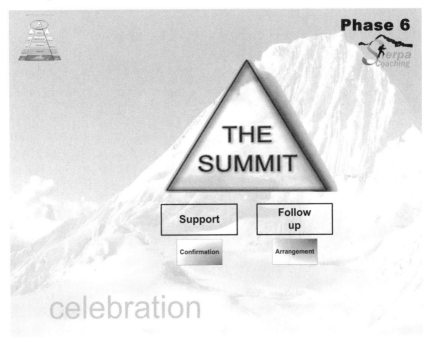

(© Sasha Corporation)

Here's where changes are monitored and documented. Habits are formed. New connections and supports are established. It's time to make sure your work has resulted in a sustainable change. Make sure your client has checks and balances in place. The client has identified their supporters. Revisit those supporters to ensure they are still there, with a role to play when you, the Sherpa, are not there every week.

The other area you will cover in this phase is the follow-up. With accountability partners in place, your client knows what to do. You have reviewed the journal and it's clear what direction the client will take when you are no longer together.

Once a Sherpa, always a Sherpa. Define your expectations for your client and their future connection with you.

The Summit: Your client has reached the goal—a new comfort zone, at the top of the world. You're standing on the summit, and it's time to celebrate. Take some time to "smell the roses." Talk openly and freely about the successes you've shared during your time together. Have your client acknowledge all the hard work and the distance traveled. CELEBRATE!

THE SHERPA STANCE

What a Sherpa coach does, step-by-step, is part of the story. Along with the process, and all the related techniques, there's an attitude every Sherpa carries. We call this attitude the Sherpa Stance. This view of coaching keeps you and your client focused and productive, and puts proper limits on the relationship. The Sherpa Stance sums up the philosophy that keeps us focused on business behavior and measurable results.

In the Sherpa Stance, we ask four "P" questions that determine if a conversation is permitted and whether it's worthwhile:

1. Is it precise? Are we talking about a problem, a symptom, or a feeling? Unless we are talking about a problem, we aren't ready to talk.

2. Is it personal? If it's too personal, we don't continue.

3. Is it present tense? Sherpas live in the moment, not the past.

4. Is it possible? Will a change in your client's behavior actually fix the problem?

The Sherpa Stance is easy to remember. It should be, because it's very important that a good coach work on things that make a difference, and to use every moment effectively.

You, as a Sherpa, control your coaching conversations. You'll always need to be aware of these general rules, so you avoid vague conversations on personal matters that happened a long time ago, in a situation your client had no control over.

As a Sherpa, you are about to embark on an exciting adventure, learning and sharing a powerful process. Your wisdom, guided by the Sherpa process, will lead to outstanding results. In the next chapter, we'll start in with the details: exactly what you'll be doing as you coach each client.

CHAPTER 4

Phase One: Taking Stock

W E HAVE DESCRIBED THE SIX PHASES every coaching assignment will take us through, leading from analysis to action. In Phase One, we'll establish expectations by covering the ground rules for our coaching process. We will introduce the clients' major resource: the personal journal. We'll teach our clients to expect and observe changes in themselves and the people around them. Then we begin our analysis of our clients: their skills, style, and strengths and weaknesses.

Each client is different, but the process will apply to all your Sherpa coaching engagements. Clients will differ in how much they feel a need to understand the process. Some might be interested in the diagram in the front of their journal. Others may ask questions about how their progress relates to the process.

For the most part, the process is for you, the Sherpa. The process is a road map, a reflection of where your journey will take you and a guide to get you there. But coaching is about people and conversation. As you lead that conversation through a natural progression, your client will often have no idea there's a process involved. It's there, but it becomes transparent.

As part of your process, you should complete a quick self-assessment after each client meeting: a checklist that guides you through the Sherpa process. You'll find that checklist in Appendix, page SC 2-1.

Remember, the Sherpa coaching process is divided into six phases:

1. **Taking Stock**

2. **Global View**

3. **Destination**

4. **Charting the Course**

5. **Agenda**

6. **The Summit**

This chapter deals with Phase One, Taking Stock.

What You'll Find in This Chapter:

- **Introductions and Orientation**
- **Process Overview**
- **Ramifications**
- **Self-Discovery**
- **DiSC® Assessment**
- **Personal Inventory**
- **Discovery Shield**
- **Agreement**

Let's explore the details and share exactly what happens in our first phase, Taking Stock.

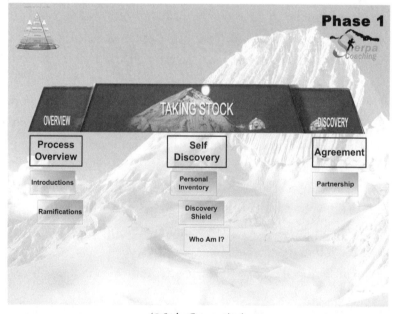

(© Sasha Corporation)

INTRODUCTIONS AND ORIENTATION

In the first meeting, a coach has to establish a relationship based on trust and a clear set of ground rules. Tell your client why we use the term "Sherpa." Explain that you have become their personal Sherpa. Take time to connect. Explain the coaching process and the way you work. Draw your client out, and have them share expectations with you. Make sure your client tells you what they would like to gain from the coaching experience. If this engagement was set up by their employer, be sure they can tell you, in their own words, what the employer expects, too. At the end of Chapter 2, we provided questions you might ask your executive contact.

PROCESS OVERVIEW

To introduce each client to the Sherpa Process, we'll cover two topics: the client's journal and our ground rules for coaching.

First, you'll introduce your client to the journal, which will be used by every client, throughout the Sherpa coaching process. Clients will keep notes, do assessments, and get their homework assignments from this journal.

You'll find a sample of the client journal in the Appendix, along with an order form for them. Every journal you receive will have an order form for additional ones. As soon as you receive your client's journal, remove the order form, to avoid confusing your client, and use it right away to keep journals in stock for upcoming clients. You can also order them with an email to info@sherpacoaching.com or on line at www.sherpacoaching.com.

The journal helps clients, and helps the Sherpa track their progress. It's also a powerful selling tool when you're discussing coaching services with a prospect. Showing a sophisticated and beautiful tool like the journal can close business for you by establishing your credibility as a Sherpa.

Most of all, the journal is about your client. There are a number of reasons why the Sherpa journal creates success for your clients:

1. IT IS A CONSTANT REMINDER THAT COACHING IS MORE THAN AN HOUR A WEEK. It reminds them to work on the assignments you give them.

Once the process starts, it's a way clients prove to themselves they are succeeding.

2. *IT MEASURES PERSONAL GROWTH AND DEVELOPMENT.* It is an accurate measurement of your client's commitment to coaching. If the homework is done, and is done on time, your client is telling you that they want the process to succeed and believe it can.

3. *IT IS A GREAT WAY TO REMEMBER WHAT WAS SAID DURING COACHING.* Client and coach will often write in the journal during a session, so they can revisit the information at a later date. Notes and pictures will serve as reminders of the concepts and revelations you have covered.

STORIES FROM THE SUMMIT

I spoke with one client, Joanna, about her need to have a "kingdom", a comfort zone, walls of defense. In every meeting, she'd set up her planner, her glass of water, her glasses, her pen and her pad surrounding her, like a castle and a moat. I asked for Joanna's journal, turned to a notes page, and drew a picture of what I saw. From that drawing, Joanna realized what her behavior looked like to others. It became apparent that her "wall" put distance between Joanna and her peers.

4. *THE JOURNAL IS A USEFUL PLACE TO ELABORATE ON SPECIFIC SITUA-TIONS.* Often, the homework assigned to the client will be to write about a situation they have shared with their coach, to enable continued discussion next time. It is also used to revisit a situation your client has been through where improved behavior is possible.

STORIES FROM THE SUMMIT

I asked Mary to write about why she thought Kim was "out to get her" at work. Kim was taking over Mary's job, and Mary was moving to another area within the organization. Mary wrote at length and came up with revelations that could never have come out in our coaching meeting. She wrote about Kim's inability to accept her teaching. She came up with the mental picture she had, Kim's fingers stuck in her ears while Mary spoke. We were then able to analyze whether the problem was Mary's manner or Kim's resistance. It was a great place to start working on Mary's perceptions.

5. THE JOURNAL ALLOWS YOUR CLIENTS' OWN WORDS TO SPEAK TO THEM DIRECTLY. A client uses the journal to write responses to situations as they come up. Over time, the client will go back and read those scenarios and clearly determine their success or failure. It is difficult to argue or become defensive with oneself. When faced with their own words, your clients' only choices are to change or accept the way things are. Denial is no longer an option.

6. THE JOURNAL BECOMES A REFERENCE BOOK. Many clients refer to their journal years after coaching is complete. You may even receive a note from a client you have coached quite a while ago telling you their journal is still on their desk.

Using the Journal

When the journal is used to full potential, your client gets full value from coaching. The Sherpa makes each client's journal a central part of the process. Ownership of the journal is important. The more you use it to conduct assessments and identify issues, the more your client will "own" the journal.

A journal takes work. It is one thing to have thoughts in your head, it's another to get them down on paper. Often, the written word represents extra effort and commitment to change. That's hard for all of us. Help your client get past this barrier. Make sure they understand the journal is part of the investment they are making in themselves.

Begin each meeting with a review of what was done for homework. When you ask them to take the journal out and show their homework, clients are forced to relate to it. The more they connect with the journal, the more they will faithfully use it.

The Sherpa's Toolkit

You've already looked into the Appendix when you took the assessment of your listening skills and potential for coaching. In that chapter you'll also find a self-evaluation you can use for every client, every meeting, until the Sherpa process and attitude become intuitive. This evaluation, page SC 2-1, is something you should use from the very beginning. Rate your performance each time you coach, until you're giving yourself straight A's.

Ground Rules

In the second part of your process overview, you'll present ground rules for your relationship. Ground rules will provide mutual expectations:

- This hour is important. Let your client know you are not going to waste it.
- Make sure your client knows that you have everything organized. You are in control.
- Promise your client a total focus on their needs: when you are together, no one else in the world exists.

Ground rules should be the first entry your client makes in the Journal, on page 1-1. Have them write the following list of guidelines in his journal, and discuss each one:

1. BE HONEST.   If a client is not straight with his Sherpa at all times, coaching becomes a useless exercise. Honesty helps coach and client arrive at solutions much faster. Talk with your client about "removing their armor." Remind your client you are paid to be direct and succinct. The two of you work together now.

Talk about the level of commitment you need from your client. Tell them: "This is going to be hard. Do not underestimate the work you will have to do. Every time we meet, you will have to remove your armor. Defensiveness, evasion, and denial are not going to work in this relationship." Honesty will be the norm. Honesty can be hard work, because the truth goes beyond your client's initial perceptions in almost every situation.

2. *DO YOUR HOMEWORK.*   Explain that the work we do away from our meetings may take hours each week. If the client does not do their homework, the two of you will not stay on schedule. Homework reinforces all the information you discuss at every meeting. (*Coaching note:* Homework should be the first thing reviewed at each meeting. You are not "checking up" on them, just making sure the client understands and has agreed to participate. Homework needs to be taken very seriously. You cannot expect your client to find it valuable unless you reinforce its importance.)

3. *THIS IS NOT THERAPY.*   We do not discuss family or personal matters. There are times when the information we provide, the concepts that we teach, will help with personal matters. But we do not discuss problems experienced outside of work. (*Coaching note:* This can be delicate. When a client's personal issues create problems related to the workplace, be careful. Business coaches are not therapists!)

4. *BE ON TIME.*   Your client will be charged for the agreed-on hour, whether they show up or not. If your client wasn't on time for your first meeting, discuss: Did the two of you email, phone, or double-check the time, date, and location? Is this an area you will need to discuss further?

STORIES FROM THE SUMMIT

Being on time is tough for Barry. Barry is the busy CEO of an insurance firm. He didn't show up the first three times we were going to meet. This sent a message. It took a month before we could get to the first ground rule: be there. On our fourth try, he showed up 20 minutes late. We got right down to business and discussed rule one: show up on time. Confronting

> *this issue convinced him that his Sherpa was in control, and he could not avoid participation. Our relationship improved from there.*

Being on time is also a big responsibility for the Sherpa. Timeliness is critical to establishing trust. Being on time shows respect and appreciation for your client. There is nothing more important to your client than you finding them to be the most important person in your life. Being on time shows that. It establishes the "rhythm of the relationship." The rhythm flows throughout all your meetings, and will be reflected in many ways. Timeliness gives Sherpas authority. If you are early to a meeting, here are some of the things you are able to organize:

- At a restaurant, get a table and arrange the settings and seating to your liking.
- If you are at a coffee shop, order coffee and set your paperwork out on the table.
- Pick the right spot, in a corner, not around too many people.
- If you are in a conference room, get rid of the extra chairs.

 ## STORIES FROM THE SUMMIT

> *Linda is the manager of a distribution facility. She is an intense, fast-paced person. Time is extremely important to her. After the third meeting, we were wrapping up and Linda said, "I don't think you realize how much I value you being here and having the table ready for me, without fail. I really appreciate it." In three meetings, Linda had learned new skills, but what she thanked me for was being organized and on time. The Sherpa needs to be on time to show respect for the client, the mission, and the process.*

5. **CONFIDENTIALITY.** This is always an interesting discussion on a number of fronts. Be forthcoming about your relationship (if there is one) with your executive contact. You may even want to show your client, if they are

nervous, the midterm evaluation (Appendix, page SC 6-1). Make sure your client knows that you will limit your conversation to the evaluation form when you meet your executive contact, halfway through the process.

Here are some examples of what a Sherpa might say to an executive contact:

> "Mary has been doing well. We are working on her need to solve her staff's problems. Here are some things I would like you to do to help Mary . . ."

> "Larry is not progressing as quickly as he could. Although both you and Larry think time management is his problem, I am still not quite sure. I am working on his delegation skills and his inability to say 'No.' After we have done this work, I will be able to give you a more precise plan for Larry."

You see, in both these situations, no personal issues are discussed or even hinted at. Executive contacts want the best for your client, not gossip. They'll support your need to keep personal issues strictly private.

To avoid complications in your coaching relationship, stress that confidentiality in coaching is not one-sided. Ask your client to keep the information you talk about confidential as well. This does not mean they should keep everything they learn to themselves. They simply must avoid the temptation to use the coach, and the coaching relationship, as a club or a negotiating stance. The best way to explain this is through an example:

> *The Sherpa tells the client: Darla, you are going to learn to manage your staff very differently, but you also need to learn how to manage your boss better.*

> *Darla leaves and goes back to work: Boss, my Sherpa says I have to manage you in a very different way.*

How's the boss going to react? Not well, probably. He'll see the coaching relationship as destructive, not constructive. Make sure your client does not bring the coaching relationship back into the workplace as a way to control people.

Unless you tell your client to take something outside your meetings, they should assume what you say is confidential. If in any doubt, they should feel comfortable asking you. Don't let the client use you as a weapon. It's happened. Certain clients will try to gain leverage by using your name.

They'll say: "My coach says I need to take a vacation," or "You can't expect me to do that. My coach says I'm not ready," and their boss can't readily contradict them. Make it extremely clear to your clients that they cannot do that. It's part of the trust that goes two ways, between Sherpa and client.

These ground rules are essential to a productive coaching experience. Make them your own by adding things like timing and location. Do not take this lightly. Ground rules set precedent and create a comfort level for your clients, allowing them to put their confidence in you.

Communicate these instructions clearly at the outset. Just as important are the client's instructions for you. Give them the opportunity to set boundaries for their relationship with you by setting expectations. This is usually not difficult for the client, because they know why they're with you. If this seems difficult, then ask your client, as the first homework assignment, to come up with at least four expectations they have of you. Discuss this, first thing, at your next meeting. Remember to refer to these expectations when you have reached the summit.

This is where the foundation of the Sherpa/client relationship is established. Be clear and completely honest with your client. To secure a trusting relationship, you'll need to be honest, even blunt. You and your client should be on the same page from the beginning, so you both understand the direction you are heading.

My Expectations

Give clients a few minutes during your first meeting to sum up their expectations of what they want to work on. This is your first insight into their version of their issues. Good discussion can follow this part of the meeting. This can be written up in the client's Journal, page 1-1.

RAMIFICATIONS

For every action, there is a reaction, a consequence. The word "ramifications" can be used interchangeably with "consequences." Every action in the coaching process will prompt a reaction. It is important for clients to understand that everything they do now, and all the changes they make going forward, are going to have ramifications.

When it comes to a client's business behavior, many things can and will change. It is important for your client to be prepared for those changes and the way they will affect their relationships. As behaviors change, relationships and interactions will change. It takes a lot of courage to step out, knowing things will be different, in unpredictable ways.

Many people abandon their goals and career dreams because the stakes (ramifications) are perceived as too risky. You'll meet clients who know what they want, and what they need to do. They can't explain why they don't make a move. Sometimes people are more afraid of success than failure or the status quo. It's important to help clients understand that changes are coming, and to consciously study their thoughts about the pros and cons of stepping into the unknown in pursuit of a dream.

As we get further into the process and examine expectations, we will revisit ramifications. Mastering expectations will enable your client to communicate clearly and concisely. You might think the ramifications of good communication would be positive, and they may be, but the flip side is this: People around you may not be prepared for that kind of communication. It can derail working relationships when you change philosophies. So it is helpful to explore ramifications often, so your client can make informed choices about their next move.

Every time your client experiences ramifications, have them record in the journal what happens as they move forward, or the results of not making a move (client Journal, page 1-2). They should note how others react to changed behaviors, and how they handle those reactions. They will then be able to review these things honestly and objectively.

 ## *Stories from the Summit*

> *Ramifications are fascinating because you never know how they will play out. I was working with Jerry, who is CEO of a biotech firm. Jerry had a great relationship with Janet, his assistant. He told her everything. One of*

the issues Jerry dealt with was his vice presidents hearing things before he got a chance to tell them himself.

He finally figured out that Janet was the one who told people. The new Jerry stopped speaking to Janet at that level. He no longer brought up anything that could get back to his vice presidents. One day, Janet asked me: "What have you done with Jerry? I want him back." Needless to say, Janet did NOT like being excluded from what was happening in the company.

Your clients will fundamentally change some of the things they are doing in their business and personal life. These changes create ramifications, no matter how great or small the change may be. Often, the people around your client will support the change. Other times, they cannot. Ask clients to record the reactions created by their new behaviors.

Recording events helps us see patterns and trends. When planning on making changes, clients should consider what the ramifications might be before moving forward. Once they have observed ramifications, they can start to predict them more accurately.

Every action, no matter how small, affects your life. Your client could, for instance, record what happens during coffee breaks. What are the repercussions of the things the client says and does? What happens if they stop going on break for a few days? The ramifications page in the client's journal can be used to record responses to two questions:

1. How do people react when you fundamentally change something about your behavior?
2. Record what people see as different about you. What have they said about your changes?

Change is a good thing. Confusion may arise because the people in your client's life do not expect these changes. Let your client know that this is a normal, expected part of the process.

On the ramifications page (client Journal, page 1-2), your client can keep a log of "perceived changes":

- The names of people in their life that have noticed a changed behavior,
- The change they noticed,
- That person's reaction to the change,
- Discussions they've had, and
- How your client feels about the expressed issue.

Acknowledging each change, and understanding the effect it has on others, is critical to the success of the change. Teach your client to be aware of the people in their life who experience the changes with them, and to keep the "ramifications log" throughout the coaching process. Often during your coaching meetings, you'll use the log to work through the effects of the changes that are taking place.

People don't like change, and they don't like to talk about change. Sherpas prepare their clients for open communication with their associates when a change is impending. Often, you'll have to help the client deal with associates' discomfort.

 ## STORIES FROM THE SUMMIT

Margaret worked well, and closely, with three peers in her office. She was a great salesperson. She sold everything she took on and did a spectacular job. Her biggest issue was the general staff in the office. Unlike Margaret's peers, they did not like her. She was intimidating to them.

Margaret worked on a number of changes in her dealings with general staff. One of the most important was increasing eye contact, slowing down, and giving people her full attention. It made a difference, and her relationship with the general staff improved dramatically. The ramification? Her peers began to resent her. They did not like the change. They were always the ones the staff went to for help. Now, all the general staff were coming to Margaret for help and conversation.

Help your client understand the change, and help them share the change with the people who are concerned by asking:

- How do we communicate in advance to others the things they might notice?
- How do you prove the value of the change to a person who's expressed a concern?

Refer back to this journal page often during your weeks together.

SELF-DISCOVERY

Your client understands the coaching process, and is prepared to notice the way people react to changes in their behavior. During Self-Discovery, we'll use three instruments to gather information about your client. A work style assessment will analyze their communications style. The Personal Inventory will allow your client to engage in "big picture" thinking designed to quickly orient the Sherpa coach to what they might need most. The Discovery Shield will reveal their strengths, weaknesses, talents, and motivation.

Self-Discovery—The DiSC® Assessment

A great way to get a running start on your coaching relationship is through a personal assessment. We recommend the DiSC instrument. We call it a "work style" assessment, and think it's the most effective assessment for coaching. There are many personality profiles out there. You may be familiar with one, and want to use it, going forward as a Sherpa. There are a number of reasons why the DiSC assessment works well as you start a coaching relationship.

1. THE ASSESSMENT IS BY FAR THE EASIEST TO UNDERSTAND. It is divided into four behavioral styles. Your client will fit into one pretty comfortably. D represents **Dominance,** I stands for **Influence,** S stands for **Steadiness,** and C is for **Conscientiousness.**

2. THIS ASSESSMENT IS THE EASIEST TO LEARN FOR A COACH. A client's score will be a number in each of the four categories. The category in which they have the highest number is their basic type: High "D," high "S," and so forth. Because this assessment has only four categories, it's easy to remember what the results mean.

3. *IT IS BRIEF.* The test can be taken online in about 10 minutes. Results are available immediately over the Internet. You, the coach, can review them privately and then present and explain them to your client.

4. *THE GRADING SCALE IS BASIC, BUT THE CLIENT REPORT IS COMPREHENSIVE.* The results are packed with information that will quickly take you to the level of honesty and understanding you need.

5. *DISC CAN BE USED FOR BOTH TEAM COACHING AND EXECUTIVE COACHING.* The new coach does not have to learn two different types of assessments. In the team setting, DiSC presents a team report, allows the team to see the big picture, especially as it relates to communication between different behavioral types.

6. *IT IS STRAIGHTFORWARD.* People may have reactions to, or opinions about, colors, animals, or abstract symbols attached to behavioral styles. Those preconceived notions cause people to falsely assign negative or positive value to assessment results. The letter-based scheme of DiSC avoids people's natural inclination to react to colors or icons.

7. *MOST IMPORTANTLY, DISC DEALS WITH BEHAVIOR, NOT PERSONALITY.* That mirrors the goals and scope of executive/business coaching. We are not therapists. We don't discuss personal problems and how they came about. Executive coaches are not expected to work on personality issues. Sherpas change business behavior.

DiSC is effective, easy to understand, and the most appropriate assessment we have found for coaching. Unfortunately, there are many competing products using the DiSC name. To contact the authors about online assessments using the only DiSC the authors recommend, email info@sherpacoaching.com. Make sure you get an assessment on yourself, as a learning and discovery tool.

Self-Discovery—Personal Inventory

Personal Inventory (Journal page 1-3)

In one of your first meetings, assign the **Personal Inventory** as home-work. When you review your client's responses at your next meeting, don't be afraid to push. Make sure the Personal Inventory is complete, and make sure the questions are answered honestly. Don't allow your client to "get by," or take this inventory lightly. This is the beginning of your climb. You will get to know your client very well. Their responses to each question should bring you closer to understanding the path they will need to take in the weeks to come.

At this point, start examining your client's attitude. The following questions will be triggers to help you identify attitude problems:

- How are the questions answered? Quickly? Completely?
- How responsive is the client to difficult questions?
- Does the client understand you have their best interest in mind?
- Does the client think about their responses, or just answer to get finished?
- Has the client identified their problems? developed ideas on how to solve them?

Let's examine the Personal Inventory, (Journal page 1-3), question by question:

1. I want to be _____ in five years.

This leads you to conversational questions such as:

How serious are you about this? What do you want to achieve? What do you expect of yourself along the way? Don't let your client get away with flip-pant answers such as "alive and happy." Make sure the responses are specific. Career transition can be a big part of the way your client answers this question. This can be the basis for your goal setting and prioritization.

Clients often dislike this question. It can be difficult for them to artic-ulate their vision for themselves. "I don't know" is a convenient response, but it's not acceptable. Help kick-start their creativity with conversation about the things they want.

You will handle this question differently depending on whether you are paid privately by the client or by the client's company. Your number-one goal is to honor the best interests of the party paying for your services. If your client is private pay, assure them that if the goal doesn't include their current employer, that's OK. In that scenario, you can focus on what their current job might offer in preparation for a future job. Encourage the client to dream a little. Ask: "If there were no money requirements or time constraints, what would you want to be?"

This will tell you whether your client has a vision for themselves. Are their goals in line with what their employer tells you, in a corporate setting? Do they want to be and to do what their employer has planned?

This question is the very beginning of defining the action plan for your client. This is a very difficult question. Five years, for many, feels so far away when they are having trouble with this week, this day. This question will help you define whether your client is a visionary, a dreamer. Five years is certainly long enough to make extraordinary change. Is your client up to the challenge?

If an employer pays for your services, do not delve further (at this point) into a response like "away from here" or "anywhere but here." You will need more information to be able to deal effectively with that scenario, and we'll cover that in later steps.

Five years can be an eternity if you are afraid to speak about what you really want. However, if your goal is to retire, have a family, or own your own company, it will seem like tomorrow. In either case, help the client focus, detail, and justify their goal. This information gives you the foundation for their strategic path.

> **Why do we ask this question?** We are determining our client's willingness and readiness for coaching. Are they looking for greener pastures, or creating realistic plans? Have they seriously thought about their future, their life, who is in it, why they are doing what they do?

If a client's response gets personal, move on. When Sally said she wanted to be married in five years, a red flag went up. Business coaches deal with business behavior. My response was: "That is a great goal. Now, let's move on to question two."

2. My biggest strength in my business is: _____.

Allow clients to answer this question according to their own criteria. Ask them how they would describe their strength in private, with no one to judge their response. A client may be very humble in describing their strengths. As you get further into your meetings, you will refer back to this question to point out the fact that your client has strengths that can be used to take on difficult challenges. That will serve to encourage and uplift them, should they be discouraged or fearful.

You are going to revisit these strengths throughout your coaching. Take time in conversation to come up with other strengths clients haven't thought of, and make sure those are written down in their journal.

> **Why do we ask this question?** The Sherpa process examines the entire person in their working environment. Clients' ability to identify their biggest strength is vital to identifying how capable they truly are, and how capable they think they are. We discuss this further in the next step with the Discovery Shield. The "Values Clarification" exercises can help clients dig a little deeper in this area. The point here is: Do they know what they do best?

3. My manager says _____ **about the way I do my job.**

This is purely a guess for most coaching clients. Most of them don't know. Even if they think they know, encourage them to interview their manager and get the real answer to this question. This can be a wake-up call for your clients if they are out of touch with what is really going on in their business lives. It can serve as a powerful validation if they know how superiors perceive them. In our next phase, you'll have the opportunity to coach your clients through additional exercises should they need clarification on how others perceive them.

If your client IS the boss, change the question to read:

My board of directors says _____ about the way I do my job, or:

My employees say _____ about the way I do my job, or:

My employees think this about me as their boss: _____.

Those who think they know their boss' mind will mention: responsible, loyal, hard worker, dependable. They probably don't have an accurate picture. In a work environment of limited confrontation and easy lawsuits, many managers hesitate to share their feelings about employees. Many are not willing to be candid, to constructively engage their staff. The Sherpa process allows managers to facilitate, to mentor. It sets them free to talk about what they really need in an employee. It is healthy and helpful for the manager and your client.

This is a very difficult question for many people. Allow your client to take this back as homework, and perhaps discuss this with their direct report. Even with performance appraisal and direct communication, your client might not have a clue as to what their managers think of them. This question reveals strengths, weaknesses, and insecurities that you'll address later, as part of dealing with specific issues.

Nobody likes confrontation. When a client asks the boss: "What do you think of my performance?" it can catch the executive off guard. They'll feel compelled to be positive no matter what. If the boss has talked about a weakness with a coach, that doesn't mean they've talked to the employee about it. You may need to facilitate a conversation, create an environment for the issues and challenges to be put on the table and discussed constructively.

Why do we ask this question? This question goes directly to the need to examine perceptions. If the way your client *thinks* people view them is different from the way people actually do, you have a problem. This disconnect may prevent your client from developing a desire to change. See the "Perception" section in Chapter 5 for more details.

---

4. I am willing to commit _____ hours to my job per week.

This is where we focus on stress and time management. Can your client separate work and home life? This is an area where you might end up spending a lot of your time.

Since the questions prompts for a numeric answer, your clients will usually be very specific. Make sure what they say they are willing to commit matches the number of hours they actually work. You may take the opportunity, if they are working excessive hours, to ask why it takes them so long to get the job done. The client may have a time management problem, tend to procrastinate, or treat the job as their comfort zone while other things in their life suffer.

> **Why do we ask this question?** The client's answer gives us a commitment gauge. This is simply a realistic view of how they perceive their obligation to their work. If someone says "over 55 or 60," we'll delve into that very shortly, under the topic of support cells. We'll find out whether the client is doing this for themselves or under pressure.

5. This really makes me happy (at work): _____.

This question can reveal your client's values and why the work matters to them. It can also give you insight on their level of satisfaction at work. If the answer is success in some aspect of the job, such as closing a deal or delivering a final report, that's good. If the answer involves avoiding a perceived threat (making budget or quotas), that's not good. Later in this book we will discuss this in depth. For now, the question can provide valuable information to help create an action plan directed toward a meaningful, productive work experience. This can also help your client's boss understand how to motivate the employee.

When one client noted that "5:00 p.m. makes me happy," it was an interesting way to say there was nothing at work that gave her any enjoyment. We took a hard look at that and found that she didn't get many positive strokes at work. No one listened to her, and she didn't listen very well herself. That information alone provided a diagnosis, and prescribed a path to the summit.

> **Why do we ask this question?** Happiness is a core competency. What you are looking for here is "Why it matters" to your client. We'll come back to this concept a lot, throughout the Sherpa process. It is a foundational issue. Everyone wants to be happy and successful. This is a starting point to establish, in your mind, what motivates your client.

6. My biggest stress comes from: _____.

This is other side of the "happiness" question. Here, we learn whether employees or their personal issues produce conflict in our clients' lives.

Listen carefully. Ask for clarification. Some people are driven by stress; they actually thrive when they are working "under the gun." Stress may be a positive for some, unless it's extreme.

Be sure to separate stress (negative reaction to pressure in the environment) from fear, centered on future events or consequences.

How does your client handle stress? Where does it come from? Does your client create it, or are there outside factors involved? Is this a positive stress that keeps their adrenaline running and pushes them in the desired direction, or does stress paralyze your client? When is it negative and when is it positive?

> **Why do we ask this question?** Pressure is a fact of life in business. Stress is a negative reaction to pressure, either from other people or from the system. We ask specifically about stress, because the answer to this question can pinpoint a necessary attitude adjustment. Every client wants be happy. This question might reveal what's getting in the way of that.

7. My biggest stumbling block is: _____.

What's getting in the way of good performance? It could be stress, a reaction to an environmental factor. It could be inner conflict, including fear, lack of self-confidence, inability to reach decisions. It could be a relational problem.

A stumbling block can manifest itself in behaviors or in failure to take action. The answer to this question can open a dialogue about giving too much power to people or conditions. There will be many opportunities to revisit this question as your clients focus more on themselves.

> **Why do we ask this question?** Stumbling blocks and stress can be the same, or they can be different. If your client's stumbling block is someone they work with, that's very revealing. That may indicate that your client would rather blame others than make changes themselves. If the stumbling block is a personal weakness, make sure it's clearly identified. "I am too nice to people" is not an acceptable answer.

8. I come to work because: _____.

We continue to get to bottom-line motivation: "Why it matters." Look for agreement with the way they answer the previous question: "What makes me happy?" Is money what they care most about? Status? Power? What about fun, personal enjoyment? If your client does not enjoy life more as he becomes more successful, you've missed a key component of your coaching responsibilities.

> **Why do we ask this question?** The question goes to the heart of motivation. It touches on values, personal mission, and meaning in life. The next exercise, the Discovery Shield, allows for elaboration on the client's sense of purpose. This question opens up the process of self-discovery.

9. Success looks like this to me: _____.

The answer should be work related. There are two other scenarios you may encounter. First, your client may be entirely stumped, unable to come up with an answer. Perhaps they have not allowed themselves to examine what success means to them. In this case, ask what events at work make them feel successful, and go from there. Second, the answer may be larger than work, and include their whole life. After all, it is hard to evaluate success without including one's personal life as well. Allow your client to express their big picture, and then narrow this down to clarify where success at work belongs in his life.

This question can be used to define the client's expectation for the coaching experience.

What are we working toward? If there were no limits, what would you be doing? How does the work you are doing now link to the work you want, in your vision of success? It is a fantastic opportunity to share a client's vision, and enlist the help of others to reach that goal.

> **Why do we ask this question?** Everyone wants to be happy and successful. This question, by allowing the client to define success, tells you a lot about what they make important. This question deals with values, a topic we'll explore further in subsequent meetings.

Self-examination can be difficult for some people. Clients often complete this inventory with little thought. Talk through the inventory. Hold a client accountable for what they say they want, and who they say they are. Be careful not to put words in their mouth. They must express *their own* thoughts. Your job: ask questions that provoke thought and further clarification.

Ask your client to revisit these questions in week nine or ten. Your client's answers to this Personal Inventory may change as your coaching progresses. They will certainly be further refined. This clearer definition of *who I am*, *what I want*, and *why I do what I do* will make your client's action plan easier to accomplish in the workplace. The new clarity may also be reflected in the way the client conducts their personal life as well.

For some clients, this Personal Inventory is extremely valuable. For others, you'll review it for background material and move on. If you're getting honest, well thought-out answers, discussing this won't take too long. Success and happiness are two things that everyone in the world wants to achieve. Without a doubt, this Personal Inventory helps you, as coach, understand what those things mean for your client.

The Personal Inventory is the beginning of the climb. It helps you decide your client's route. Keep coming back to this inventory for insights.

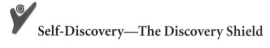

Self-Discovery—The Discovery Shield

The Discovery Shield is another self-assessment tool, one that takes your client to a slightly deeper level. The shield is simple enough to understand. Assign it as homework at your first meeting. Have your client complete the top three sections in advance of your next meeting. You'll find it on page 1-4 in your client's journal.

Ask your client to list three strengths and three weaknesses on the Discovery Shield. This really gets them focused and begins the climb to the summit. The idea here is to get your client to identify their strengths and weaknesses accurately. Many people will skirt around the issues and label them inaccurately. We call this avoidance the "kabuki" dance, after the ritualized Japanese art form. We use it to describe someone dancing around a topic, afraid to talk about it directly. Don't let your client do the kabuki dance.

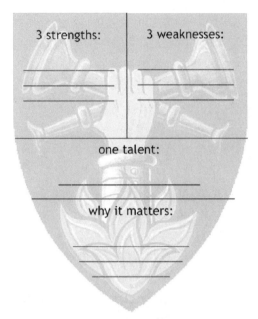

3 strengths:	3 weaknesses:
_____	_____
_____	_____
_____	_____

one talent:

_____

why it matters:

_____

_____

_____

(© Sasha Corporation)

Understanding clients' strengths and weaknesses is crucial. As a coach, you can't move on until you are sure you have accurate answers. Individually, leaders get where they are through their strengths. Because it's lonely at the top, their best ally can be a process-driven executive coach to shore up personal weaknesses. No one else can do that with them.

Some schools of thought in the world of development are based on building strengths. That's not our view. Think about it: The clients we work with are extremely capable. They have gotten where they are because of their strengths and abilities. In fact, their strengths have carried them as far as they can go on their own. Their weaknesses hold them where they are. They don't know how to remove the obstacles caused by their weaknesses. The Sherpa process, in getting rid of weaknesses, unleashes the full potential of their strengths far more effectively than brute force development of their strong points.

Take, for example, an extremely organized and intelligent client who lacks social skills. Offer that client more education and better ways to be organized, and people still won't listen to them. They won't advance. In fact, the client will get even more frustrated, thinking, "I am doing the best

I can." Get the client to acknowledge, observe, and solve their shortcomings, and the intelligence and organization they already have will be a hundred times more appreciated.

 ## Stories from the Summit

> *David said he was impatient. We started talking about what "impatient" really meant to him. "Give me some examples." I said. "Well", he said "I would rather do the work myself than have to explain it to someone." Looking for confirmation of his original answer, I said: "So it's because you are too impatient to explain things that you'd rather do things yourself." He thought, then answered: "No, they just never do the work correctly." This exchange revealed to me and to David that there were issues other than impatience. Given that, we started examining his communication abilities as a development topic.*

Plan on spending a good amount of time with the weakness component. You will be revisiting this area quite a bit in your coaching. If your client's attitude is not right, you will not finish in the ideal 12-week period. You will not be able to redirect your client's behavior until they openly acknowledge they have problems they want to fix. Trust the process. You'll break through, even when you think it's never going to happen. If it takes six weeks to accomplish this first step, connect with your executive contact and suggest a six-week extension.

The talent portion of the Discovery Shield is simple. Can your client identify what they do well? Is this particular talent recognized and rewarded in their corporate culture? What talents are rewarded? Does the client like their corporate culture? Do they fit in? A client may be modest, or not even know their true talent. Be prepared to help them appreciate what their talent is. You may find yourself, weeks later, returning to this section and helping your client provide a better answer.

It's important to recognize gifts and talents. Those basic, positive qualities are what give each person value. The Sherpa will remind every client, in tough moments, the good things they are really made of.

Next is the "Why it matters" portion of the shield. Have your client complete this during your meeting, with ample time to discuss the answers. This is often difficult for your client. Allow them to think out loud and discuss it with you. You can also tell your client that "Why it matters" is the key to creating a great team. That means identifying "Why it matters" for every team member, and constantly reminding them that their work has value.

To illustrate the difference an employee with a mission can make, tell your client the following story. It's important that you memorize it and practice it, so you can share it with style and confidence.

A manager wanted to see how his workers felt about their jobs. He went to his building site to take an informal poll.

He approached the first worker and asked, "What are you doing?" "What, are you blind?" the worker snapped back. "I'm cutting these boulders with primitive tools and putting them together the way the boss tells me. I'm sweating under this blazing sun, it's backbreaking work, and it's boring me to death."

The executive quickly backed off and went looking for another worker. "What are you doing?" he asked, "I'm shaping these boulders into different forms, which are then assembled according to the architect's plan. It's hard work and it sometimes gets repetitive, but I earn a good wage and that supports my family. It's a job. Could be worse."

Somewhat encouraged, he went to a third worker. "What are you doing?" he asked, "Why, can't you see?" beamed the worker as he lifted his arms to the sky. "I'm building a cathedral! I can imagine the steps over there, filled with throngs of people hurrying inside for a wedding. I can hear the bells ringing out on Sunday morning. I can almost see the way the morning sun will shine through the stained glass, creating beautiful patterns. What a great job."

You see three different people, all doing the same job, with three totally different ways of looking at it.

- The first worker focuses on what he is doing . . . breaking stones. He's not at all happy with his job, and he's probably not happy with his life.

- The second worker appreciates why he's doing his job . . . It's part of a plan. He makes a living. He seems more content doing exactly the same job.

- The third worker has a mission and a vision. His focus on "Why it matters" allows him to approach work, and life, with joy and passion. He looks way past the construction and the building; he is looking at what the experience is for the people who will enter. He is thinking about the choir loft, the weddings and funerals that will take place, and the stained glass with the sun shining through.

A leader who understands "Why it matters" can encourage others to share a mission, and to find their work together to be meaningful and satisfying.

We have used the story hundreds of times. No one has ever missed the point. It is a valuable lesson, because everything we do comes down to motivation. You and your client might take an entire hour on this topic alone. *Why does it matter that you (the client) are doing what you do? We are not talking about "making money for my family."* We are talking about why you get up every morning and drive yourself to *your* place of employment, instead of doing something else entirely.

Why do we care about the client's "Why it matters?" If your client has no idea why it matters, that can be the fundamental problem. This discussion forces clients to come to terms with their primary motivators. It can help them recover some of the passion and excitement that has slipped away and provide a boost to their morale. Understanding the bigger picture will help them deal with much of the coaching experience.

"Why it matters" allows the client to delve into the truth . . . the truth of why they do what they do. Here are some questions for your client if they need to dig into this question more deeply:

1. What do you like most about your job?

2. What do you like least about your job?

3. What does your future look like?

4. What do you want to learn? New skills?

"Why it matters" may explain your client's motives for current behavior. It's even more important as a catalyst to making difficult changes. Your client, even if unhappy, is certainly comfortable with the way they behave. It's easy to execute what's familiar. So why should someone make the effort to change at all? Ask your client why it matters: *What's the cost of staying as you are? What's the benefit of working toward a better self?* Sell change as the only alternative, based on your client's own thoughts, words, and values. In the next chapter, we'll delve into change in more depth.

AGREEMENT

Finally in Taking Stock, we summarize what you have discussed in your first or second meeting. Do you have any ideas about a direction to take with your client? It is very early, but use your client's journal to write potential ideas that you would like to work on (Journal, page 1-6).

Ask these questions, and have your client make notes in their journal:

- Based on our discussion, what questions do we need answered?

- What conclusions can we draw?

- What did I (your coach) say that offered a different way of looking at things?

- What do you need to focus on?

Setting specific goals and reaching them will be a big part of the next 12 weeks. Make sure you and your client are on the same page when it comes to identifying needs and deciding where to focus. Continually revisit where they are, what they find important in your discussions. You have to know that you two are in agreement, and verify that agreement at almost every meeting.

Think about this goal for our coaching engagement: closing the gap between where the client is (status quo) and where they want to be (vision). Does your client agree with this definition? From that definition, the next logical step is agreement on where your client is today and where they want to go, with your help.

STORIES FROM THE SUMMIT

> *Greg was an eager coaching client, but starting out, he really wasn't sure what he was going to work on. When we came to "Agreement," he was brutally honest about his life and came up with these ideas:*
>
> I am afraid of success: the responsibility, accountability, and consistency that comes with it.
>
> I am afraid of failure: how will I support my family if I fail?
>
> I resent the way my boss, and others, are judgmental about me.
>
> I lack passion, so I'm disorganized, paralyzed, and in a cycle of despair.
>
> *Given that level of honesty, the Sherpa process gave a clear direction for what we would be working on. The process will always follow a productive path when your client is deeply honest, and when you trust that they have been honest with you.*

From the first day on, follow this principle: *Don't ever leave a meeting without assigning homework.* You can even include something as simple as defining the word "goal." The more your client takes ownership of the things you talk about, the better.

Your assessments have set the tone for your relationship. You and your client have basic information to work from. You've established that the relationship includes ground rules, including homework. You've made it clear that this is more than an academic exercise: the effects of what you're doing ripple out in the real world.

With your client's DiSC® assessment, Personal Inventory, and Discovery Shield, you have everything you need to get started. Here's what you should know about your client at this point:

1. What their biggest issue at work is.
2. The client's corporate culture, and how they fit in.
3. General knowledge of what you and your client are going to work on.
4. What your client needs most from you.

There will be plenty of opportunity to review and update your client's answers to these exercises throughout the process. You may find that their Personal Inventory will change significantly by the end of your 12 sessions.

Phase One, Taking Stock, will generally take up your first two meetings. Once you and your client are in agreement about the general areas you want to work on, we move on to Phase Two, Global View. Don't worry if you take a little longer than that. It's a critical part of your climb. If it takes longer than 12 weeks to get a client through the entire Sherpa Process, it's because Phase One lasts longer than two weeks. If a client gets stuck, if they won't admit they need to change or if they move in an unpredictable direction, you can rely on the process to redirect them. The speed at which the process moves will vary from one client to another.

You will gain all kinds of insight by working the concepts in Phase One very carefully and thoroughly. Going forward, we'll get more specific, and find out how we create positive change.

CHAPTER 5

Phase Two: Global View

IN THE GLOBAL VIEW, we'll learn about your client's personal environment and how others see him. You and your client will analyze the way
he deals with change, including changes he makes in himself. Finally,
we'll focus on the values that motivate your client, and help him relate his
actions to the values that drive them.

What You'll Find in This Chapter:

- **Support**
- **Perception**
- **Change Management**
- **Values Clarification**
- **Benefits Clarification**

From this point forward, you will do your work based directly on your
client's needs, at the pace they set. As long as you direct them through the
Sherpa process, avoiding lengthy tangents, you'll finish up in a standard
12-week engagement. After the Support Mountain, select and use exercises
at your discretion, with each one given the time your client needs. At times,
you might complete an exercise in a few minutes. Others might take
two meetings.

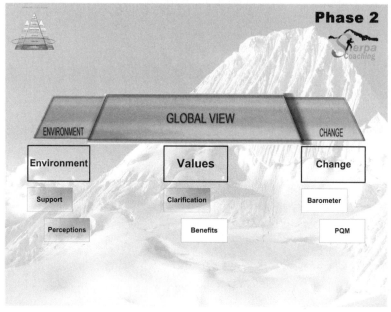

(© Sasha Corporation)

 **SUPPORT MOUNTAIN**

Our first exercise in Phase Two, Global View, addresses people, places, and factors in your clients' lives that serve to guide and strengthen them. Sometimes they take for granted the support systems built into their activities throughout the week. They also forget supporters in their working environment, or think someone supports them who really doesn't. This exercise will help clients identify and appreciate their support systems.

Supports fall into three categories: intrinsic, extrinsic, and environment. We'll define these types of support as we explain the "Support Mountain" exercise in your client's journal. Have your client turn to Journal page 2-1. For each type of support they rely on, they'll write in four people or elements of their environment that provide support:

1. Intrinsic elements in the four boxes at the base of the mountain.

2. Extrinsic supports on the face of the mountain.

3. Environmental supports at the top of the mountain.

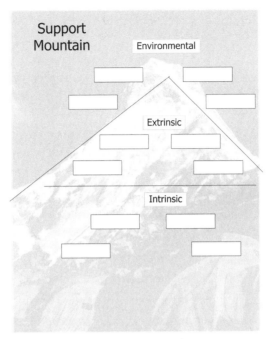

(© Sasha Corporation)

1. INTRINSIC SUPPORT. Your client's built-in strengths.

What is your client doing "from within" to support what they do from day to day? What kinds of sports are they involved in? What activities do they enjoy? What does your client do, just for the sake of doing it? Is your client motivated?

Intrinsic supports include what clients do for themselves, by themselves, for fun. Your client should list personal motivators, things they enjoy, and talents in his journal. If none come to mind, this will have to be explored. Have the client take this on as homework.

Your clients, particularly those who have hired a coach privately, may have focused their attention on the improvement of others. It is a badge of honor for them that they are selfless, so they can't identify things they do for themselves. Help your clients explore the things that give them joy, that offer hope. What are those things that equip them to deal with the natural stresses and demands of work life? Everyone has some of these things in their life.

When you help them take this inventory, their intrinsic motivation can be used to its full potential. The top intrinsic motivators should be placed in the support boxes on their worksheet. Add secondary items as a list, and add to the list as the weeks go on.

STORIES FROM THE SUMMIT

> *Oscar was CEO of a large aluminum processor. He had the hardest time completing the intrinsic portion of his Support Mountain. He did nothing on his own, for himself—nothing. He spent his life worrying and caring for all the people in his life: his staff, his board, his peers, and his family. The one thing we came up with (after much discussion) was the fact that he parked as far as he could from the office and walked to his desk for exercise. I had to spend a lot of time convincing him that doing little things for himself might make him a better person. After much discussion, he committed to walking a half hour per day when he got home. That one thing, he said, gave him time to himself, time to reflect. It changed the way he took on many of the problems in his life, personal and professional.*

2. EXTRINSIC SUPPORT. Support from others.

Who is involved in your client's business life? An inventory of these people helps your client think about who affects their life in a positive way. You'll often spend the most time talking about these extrinsic support systems. Sometimes the support is at work, sometimes at home. Take time to discuss each person and the role they play with your client. Are they really as supportive as your client thinks? Discuss their positive attributes and what they do specifically to support your client.

STORIES FROM THE SUMMIT

> *Greg was the new administrator at his health-care facility; Greg didn't feel like he had a lot of support in his facility. He told me Al, the HR director, was his biggest supporter. I asked: "How do you know?" and Greg told me: "Al always asks me how I am doing and what I am doing." I continued to*

explore this relationship. I asked Greg to see what kind of person Al was before he shared any more information with him. Greg came back the next week and said, "How did you know? Al's notorious for being the biggest gossip at the facility." Greg revisited his extrinsic supports.

In the extrinsic support category, are there people who adversely affect your client? No person has a totally positive or negative effect on those around them. Shades of gray abound in our relationships with those who support us. Someone who is supportive may take up a lot of our time in a nonproductive way. A cost-benefit analysis on those people might reveal some hidden truths. Sherpa clients challenge who really supports them, and know the investment it takes to maintain good working relationships.

3. ENVIRONMENTAL SUPPORT. Outside support from situations and surroundings.

What is happening in the world that supports your client's efforts? What in the environment is affecting them in a positive way? Here are some wide-ranging examples:

"I love my car. It is where I listen to business books. I use driving time for self-development."

"The economy has boosted business. Everything affects me in my business. I get a charge out of reading my stocks and following them on a chart."

"Chamber meetings are a weekly event, and they are very important to me. I have a strong bond with the chamber and I'm involved with several committees."

"Recent changes in tax law enabled me to expand my business. I am very involved with the legislature and know I will become more involved as time goes on. Through my trade association, I lobby for my business and my industry."

When people identify the things they love to do and get involved in them, success is sure to follow. However, you'll meet clients who have not merged the things they are passionate about with what they do for a living. If they haven't, address this: *"What are those extra things that you participate in to enhance your work life? What are the things you long to do?"* Serving in your community allows you to develop skills that may be underutilized at work. Find something and get involved. Create environments for yourself. If this is an area of concern for you or your client, you may want to explore the personal vision path, on the organizational route, to help your client rediscover their passions and vision.

If your client's current support is limited, encourage them to consider the long-term support they've received as a working person. Who was their mentor? What did that person do to become established as a mentor? What did your client bring away from that relationship that directly reflects how they work today? Does your client still keep in touch? Who in the client's current environment has the characteristics that the mentor showed?

Then let's go one step further. We have identified positive influences in our client's life. Another key to understanding in this exercise is being clear about when support is not there. Re-examine all the elements of support and make sure they have a positive influence on your client.

The Support Mountain exercise is eye-opening for many clients. It helps them understand where their resources are, where their comfort comes from, and what is missing in their life. A good Sherpa remembers the truths revealed here. These are truths that will be useful throughout the rest of the coaching process.

PERCEPTION

This topic may be vitally important to some clients, unnecessary for others. Use your judgment, as with all the exercises from here forward, to find the best way to apply it to each client, and to make best use of their time.

What does perception mean for a coaching client? Perception is reality. People around your client will conduct themselves according to their perceptions of your client. As a leader, your client must discover and manage people's perceptions. Incorrect perceptions can have a significant and negative effect on a leader and their team.

We ask clients in their Personal Inventory what their manager thinks of them. It is very important for them to know.

STORIES FROM THE SUMMIT

> *Lynette worked for a company in her youth where she had terrific mentors and encouragement from co-worker to grasp as much of the business as her teenaged mind could handle. As Lynette's career unfolded, this experience shaped the type of work she pursued and formed her style of management.*
>
> *Lynette left her hometown, only to return many years later. She found herself interviewing for a senior management position and found her old mentor on the hiring team. The mentor's perception was that Lynette could do anything. Why? Because he always felt she had enough energy to get the job done and enough savvy to ask when she needed additional help. You might think: "It's magnificent to have someone place that much confidence in you." It didn't work for Lynette. It was lonely at the top, and she often needed someone to help her, guide her, and tell her what to do.*
>
> *That perception led her down a dangerous path.*

Often, our clients will depend on individuals, extrinsic supports, to help them gain specific truths about the way people perceive them in the workplace. Later, you may discuss image and presence, two elements that contribute to the way those around you form their perceptions of you.

Managing Perceptions

Take your client through the perception exercise on Journal page 2-2. Let's examine what people really think of your client. Prepare your client by getting an idea of who the key people are in their working life. You may start a list from the Support Mountain worksheet, and add names of those who are dependent on, or supported by, your client.

STORIES FROM THE SUMMIT

> *Sarah is an engineer and Daniel is her boss. Sarah is extremely helpful in the office. She has no problem getting tea for Daniel in the morning, or*

> *making sure Daniel's dry cleaning gets sent out. Sarah is very good at what she does. She is qualified to get a promotion and a raise. Daniel's perception of Sarah? He finds her helpful and willing to do anything, but thinks she spends too much time running other people's errands and not enough time with her engineering duties. The way Sarah has allowed Daniel to perceive her is all wrong, and it will hurt her chances for promotion.*

Let's fill out the worksheet using these instructions:

FIRST COLUMN. Begin by asking your client to identify people whose opinion is important, using names taken from the Support Mountain exercise.

SECOND COLUMN. Write the number of years that person has known your client. This is significant because it helps the coach identify a new pattern versus one that has been going on for years.

THIRD COLUMN. What do they think I am all about? Have your client answer this question about each significant person. Do not have your client ask for input quite yet. It is important for them to see whether they can clearly identify the perception.

FOURTH COLUMN. Contains a minus sign, part of an equation you are going to examine later.

FIFTH COLUMN. What do I want them to think about me? Sometimes this is hard for the client. What does he really want others to see on a day-to-day basis? What are the critical traits he feels are important for others to recognize?

SIXTH COLUMN. An equal sign, part of the equation you'll discuss.

SEVENTH COLUMN. The heart of the matter, the answer to your equation: What people see in your client minus what the client wants people to see. That's the difference between reality and perception. If your client's boss sees them in a certain way and the client disagrees, the equation tells him what's missing or what needs to be eliminated. Identifying the difference is the starting point to getting where your client needs to be.

EIGHTH COLUMN. How to get from where your clients are to where they want to be.

Remember, perception is reality to those who see it. Offer plenty of feedback to make sure your clients have a realistic idea of how people see them.

STORIES FROM THE SUMMIT

Janet worked in accounting at a large manufacturing plant. She was always worried about being taken seriously. It showed. How? By walking quickly from place to place in the office, carrying a stack of papers, never smiling, Janet unconsciously tried to create an impression. At home, she was a jovial, lighthearted person. At work, the perception she created was intimidating. To plant workers and her colleagues in the office, Janet was not warm or welcoming. The result: Janet was lonely at work. She had no idea this perception flowed through the plant. We started with the Perception exercise, and she discovered, after doing her homework, that everyone around her found her unwelcoming. That was Janet's starting point for changing people's perception of her.

This Perception exercise can help your client control and manage perceptions. Often, a client will not have given much thought to what others think or expect. Once investigated, it can be quite a revelation for the client, one of those moments a coach tries to achieve in every meeting. This exercise helps your client recognize the paths they might choose in the coaching process and the changes they will need to make, either in themselves or in the way people view them.

CHANGE MANAGEMENT

Some clients are fluent in managing change. Some revel in change and have no problems with it. If you have already figured out that your client deals well with change, skip ahead a few pages to "Values Clarification."

If you doubt your client's ability in any way, or if you know change is difficult for them, you will want to spend some time in this section.

What choice do any of us have, honestly, with things changing around us every day? We all have to change. If your client needs to think this over, we tackle the issue of change by doing an assessment called the Change Barometer.

Give your client the Change Barometer on page 2-5 in his journal. Ask them to carefully answer just one question per day. Here are the questions and our commentary on each one:

1. Is change easy for you?

After your client has answered this question, you may want to ask why (or why not). It may give you helpful insight about what has brought them to their current state.

2. Have you experienced any big changes within the past year? Describe.

This question seems simple enough. If your client plans less than they should, and reacts more, this may be a difficult assignment. This might also be difficult for the client who is not very reflective. In either case, clients may move through situations without acknowledging how big the changes they experience actually are. Being oblivious about change can be a method of coping.

These questions require that a client think deeply about the past year. What happened? Talk about it with your client. If possible, you or your client can ask a person from their list of extrinsic supporters to share their observations of your client over the last year. Your client may be too close to their own journey to acknowledge changes, both positive and negative. This question presents an opportunity for you, the coach, to gain more insight into your client, and offers your client an opportunity to understand himself better.

3. Did you feel you handled major changes effectively?

Using the information from question #2, give an example of a change in the past year and how you handled it. If this is difficult for your client, have them ask someone in their extrinsic support system.

4. Did you feel you handled the change independently? Where did you seek assistance?

No one does their best when they're doing it all alone. If your client handles change independently, they might be prompted to ask: "Is it possible that I could get better results if I solicit help or use a sounding board?" As a coach, use this as an opportunity to refer back to those supports and consider where the client sought assistance and where they should have.

5. Did you feel you handled the change with a positive attitude? If not, what were your fears?

Any time you talk to someone about their fears, it will be hard to break through to an open and frank discussion, but it will be valuable when you do. One discussion could be: "Are these fears related to your weaknesses, or are we talking about something different?"

6. Could you identify your personal weakness throughout the change?

Refer to the Discovery Shield from Phase One, Taking Stock. Did the weakness your client identified there show up here? How did this weakness affect the way your client handled the change? Did their fear or weakness prevent them from taking actions they knew were necessary?

7. Are you being honest? How do you know?

As a coach, do not hesitate to discuss inconsistency or lack of depth in your client's answers. This is a tough topic. Your clients should not be allowed to bluff their way through anything. Be observant. Pay close attention to body language, vocal inflection, things that tell you whether they are being honest about this, or whether there is something blocking their ability to think these things through.

Change Management—The Ability to Change

We are evaluating our clients' ability to change. Change might be very hard for them. In their need to justify failures or stagnation, some clients might talk about "trying." Trying, or convincing oneself that one is trying, is quite different than actually doing something. Once a decision to change is reached, action follows immediately. That doesn't suggest that it's easy, but it does remind our clients that it's all within their control. Change is a mindset. It is a decision to be made.

If a decision to avoid change is made on any level, nothing will happen. I call it the Paul Fredrik Theory. A man I once knew smoked two packs of cigarettes a day. One day, as he finished a tremendous bout of coughing and choking, I asked him, "Paul, why do you smoke, if it bothers you so much?" and he calmly replied, "This smoke is me, and I am this smoke."

That was profound. He truly did not believe he was Paul Fredrik if he did not smoke. He thought he would lose who he was if he quit. When we believe our own behavior constitutes who we are, we have no motivation to change. Self-image can be an incredible obstacle to change. That's why the Perception exercise and the Change Barometer combine to produce powerful action signals for your client.

 ## STORIES FROM THE SUMMIT

> *My client Kim was in the long-term care business. She was unbelievably kind, and very dependent on others for approval. She simply had to be nice, regardless of the situation. Needless to say, people abused her and took her for granted. They talked down to her. I suggested she be more direct and assertive. Kim said: "I can't, it's not me. Being nice and being walked all over . . . that's me." Different person, same theory.*

We are not spectators in life. Clients need to be reminded that they live the life they choose. People have a hard time understanding that they'll still be who they are after a change is made . . . the same person with better character, behavior, and results.

How does your client relate to, and process, change? Can your client clearly identify what they are striving for and what it will take to get there? Can they "get their arms around" change? If change is a "hot button" for your client, use the following exercise to spur discussion: Pull out your client's journal and put the word **"change"** on the top of a page. Assign this homework:

Drive a different way to work and write in your journal about the way you react to the difference, the emotions you experience. Once you have started writing, fill the page with whatever comes to mind.

Change Management—The Personal Quarterly Meeting (PQM)

This is a one-person "meeting" that you might recommend to a client who needs to share or clarify their thoughts about change, and could use time away from his office. You can recommend a day trip, a picnic, or a visit to the library. No cell phones, no beepers, and no communication with their office for the entire day.

The PQM is an introspective exercise. You can review the exercise with your client, starting on page 2-6 in the client Journal, and explain the questions individually. It's a personal journey you can assign as homework. Since your client will want to do this quarterly, they should photocopy the exercise each time they use it.

When your client has finished the PQM, the answers to the assessment will provide tremendous opportunities for discussion about where your coaching journey should take the two of you.

There are two ways you can handle the PQM. The first is to dissect each section of it. Review the questions and answers and see if your client had any revelations. The second way is the overview—what did you learn from this exercise? What have you come away with that is different from before? Both ways can be successful. You choose.

STORIES FROM THE SUMMIT

Derek enjoyed working for a high-profile law firm. I was asked to coach him because the partners in the company wanted to promote him into a partner's role. Derek hated change. He was afraid he would lose his "personal touch"' as a lawyer if he became a partner. He thought he would get caught up with all the "red tape" and miss his calling.

> *Needless to say, we worked on change for a long time. He took a day off to complete the PQM about change. Derek came back the next week and said "My favorite place in the world is down by the water watching the boats, so I sat by the water for three and a half hours and completed this project. This was the best thing in the world for me. It made me face my worst fears, and understand why my fears drive me in all my decisions. Thank you."*

VALUES CLARIFICATION

Your client's values will drive their decisions and behavior. They are what enables your client to get up in the morning and go to work. We're about to define what really matters for your Sherpa client.

In the client Journal, page 2-3, there's a worksheet about values. Give this to your client as homework. Before you send them off, make sure you go over the form. Discuss definitions for each of the values and ask them, before your next meeting, to prioritize their personal values. Your client's top five values can direct you to profound discussion. As mentioned on the journal page, it is easier to go through the list, crossing out items that are not top values for your client, and work from there. When your client reviews the list of values, the best question they can ask is: "How important is (this value) to me?"

When you assign this page as homework, review each value with your client, asking for their personal definition of each word. Why? Because, no matter how *you* might define a word, your client will act upon their own definition. If your definitions and his differ, that can set up a shaky foundation for communication between the two of you. If your client does not understand what a given word means, have some definitions at hand and discuss those words in detail.

The purpose of this exercise is varied. The client has to think deeply about what motivates them. The client has to think about creating clear definitions.

STORIES FROM THE SUMMIT

Janice is a CEO of a delivery service. She says her number-one value is integrity. She has defined integrity as "Doing what is right, even when no one is looking." I prompted her: "Now, let's look at this more closely. If integrity is important to you, then why do you keep Fred on staff, who has twice stolen from you?" Janice sat back in her chair and her jaw dropped. She really didn't know how to answer that question. Often, people believe they are motivated by a guiding principle. Then they find out that they do not live by the values they claim to. This part of the Sherpa coaching process makes it possible to bring beliefs and actions into alignment.

Here are a description and some talking points for one of the values your client will prioritize: Accomplishment means a sense of mastery and achievement. Does your client feel that "getting things done" is more important than anything else? Does your client like to see a task or project completed? If so, they rank this value highly. If "accomplishment" is a client's number-one value, then "friendship" and "pleasure" might not be. This could lead them to treat people and relationships as a secondary consideration.

Clients live and die by their values. The purpose of this exercise, more than anything else, is to get a commitment from your clients to clearly state what is important, what motivates them, and what they hold dear.

STORIES FROM THE SUMMIT

Angie owned her own company. She said "family balance" was her number-one value. I challenged her: "Angie, you just told me you worked until 9:00 p.m. every night this week. If your number-one value is family balance, you are certainly not living it out." Angie said to me: "It is important. I just feel trapped. I really do have to start living it. I just don't have a clue how to leave my work and go home." Based on that, we started work on priorities and time management.

> *Unless she had told me what was really important to her, I would have assumed Angie was happy being a workhorse. Knowing your client's values can clear up a lot of misunderstandings.*

A situation like Angie's presents a perfect scenario for the following exercise related to your client's values: Benefits Clarification (Journal page 2-4). Angie needed to look at her values a little more closely, because there was a clear disconnect between her motivators and her behavior. If it seems this exercise might be valuable to your client, use it. Trust your judgment.

Defining the benefits of your clients' expressed values will help them get to some deeper truths. The truth will help them establish what really matters to them. Let's find out how these "top values" benefit your client when they are lived out in day-to day life. Your client has chosen their top five. Have them transfer those to the Benefits Clarification sheet, page 2-4 in his journal. Elaborate on what these questions mean to clarify the type of answer you expect.

Why do you want to get there? What is it about this value that makes it so important for you? If this particular value is emphasized, made more important than your everyday external pressures, what do you gain?

How do you get there? What's been holding you back? How do you eliminate that factor or make it less important? What changes in your behavior, or the results you get, would demonstrate that you are living this value more fully? Living out values is all about prioritization. Does your client understand what that really means?

Here, in Phase Two of the Sherpa process, we narrow down what we need to work on with our client. When this is done well, we avoid wasted time, pointless discussion, and action without purpose. Knowing what motivates your client will also help the two of you work toward appropriate behavioral changes.

The way we define and identify progress and attainment of goals is our next step. We have to connect problems and solutions directly to things the client feels are important. That's how we get results: by making it matter.

You need to know why your client does the things they do. Don't rush: Take time with the values and benefits worksheets. Allow your client to discuss their interpretation of what they find important and how they act out their values.

Bonus Exercise: Who Am I?

As with every exercise, you, as a coach, will decide when to pull this out of your hat. You don't have to use everything in this manual. Use what will work for each client. See page 1-5 in the journal to review "Who Am I?" with your client.

If you have enough information to define who your client is, and what motivates them, you can skip this exercise. If you want a little more depth before you move on, here it is. This is an introspective look at oneself. You can use it if there are serious disconnects between what your client wants to be and their work persona. If you and your client are having trouble figuring out what to work on, this exercise can be used now. Here's what you do:

Your client will identify six positive personality traits and six areas of challenge or weakness. Have them put a few of their positive traits in the circles on the top half of the page, negative ones in the figures on the bottom half. Use the Discovery Shield as a starting point if your client can't remember all their strengths and weaknesses.

(The list is included to help you offer examples. Your client should come up with their own answers.)

Positive Traits:

Adventurous	Excitable	Intelligent
Ambitious	Expert	Leader
Cheerful	Fun-loving	Neat/Orderly
Compassionate	Gentle/Kind	Respectful
Consistent	Hard-working	Responsible
Courageous	Helpful	Self-confident
Creative	Honest	Serious
Daring	Independent	Successful

You get the idea—this is an endless list that can be created by the client. Clients know themselves best and can easily complete the top section.

The bottom section lists "pitfalls," your client's weaknesses—areas that they will work on with your help. **Negative traits** might include words such as:

Apathetic	Lazy	Stubborn
Conflict/Crisis	Loud	Tired
Crazy	Perfectionist	Uncooperative
Disorganized	Procrastinator	Uncreative
Impulsive	Reserved	Unhappy
Lack vision	Serious/Angry	Unsupportive

Your client has listed six exceptional character traits and six pitfalls.

Next, we will get to the important part of this exercise. We will try to match areas of strength that can be used to address areas of weakness. ("Driven to succeed" might counteract "Lazy," for instance.)

Have your client draw lines between negative traits and the positive traits that can counterbalance each one. Have the client dig deep, to find and explain how these traits might relate to each other.

Next comes the issue of using these insights in a practical way. How do you help your client understand what to do when negative personality traits come to the fore? Here's an example:

Your client is hard-working and has a lot of support. How does that relate to the fact that they are disorganized? What does "hard-working" have to do with being disorganized? Here is the key to coaching: You don't have to know the answer for every question you pose. You are responsible for asking the right questions. When your clients find *their* answers, respond with more questions. Bring your clients to a meaningful understanding of why they act the way they do, and why they are like they are. When they have their own answers, they'll take action.

- Are you working too hard and "can't see the forest for the trees"?
- Does your disorganization prevent you from accomplishing everything you want?

- Are you disorganized because you work so hard?
- Could one of your supporters help you overcome your disorganization?

Looking at oneself objectively, as this exercise facilitates, helps your client to center in on areas that need the most work and to see exactly what can be done. It helps narrow down your discussions. You now know exactly what the client sees as their strengths, and what they see as their pitfalls. You even have the beginnings of a plan to overcome those weaknesses and negative traits.

When your client tells you how their strengths can counter his weaknesses, you will have the beginning of an action plan. You are ready to conquer the rest of the mountain.

CHAPTER 6

Phase Three: The Destination

YOUR CLIENT KNOWS CHANGE IS COMING, and that it's for the best. We looked at your client's life and environment in the first two phases. In Phase Three, we'll choose a specific course for each client. Before Sherpa and client set out on a unique path, however, a few common elements remain to be shared.

Realistically, a manager's ability to lead is kept in check by their weaknesses. As your client corrects weaknesses, they will think and act differently, and generate more respect among those they lead. We'll address a personal weakness first, on the side of a slope called the Weakness Mountain.

Second, we'll teach the process of delivering expectations, a universal shortcoming of managers and executives. If ever the phrase "room for improvement" applied, it does when it comes to the way people express, or fail to express, their expectations. As our climb takes us higher, client and Sherpa will ascend Expectations Mountain.

Then we will decide on one of ten paths that will determine how we reach the summit. Those paths are areas of improvement, development, and progress that encompass what your client must learn. We start with a choice of paths and then use appropriate tools, exercises, and training along the chosen path.

You are approaching the halfway point in this 12-week process. The halfway point prompts the Sherpa client's evaluation (Journal page 3-4) for the first six weeks. Ask your client to do this as homework before your next meeting. Don't be afraid to have them evaluate what you've done together so far. It might be difficult at first, having your client put you on the spot, but it is valuable to know how involved they are, what exercises and information have made a difference to them, and how much more you need to do.

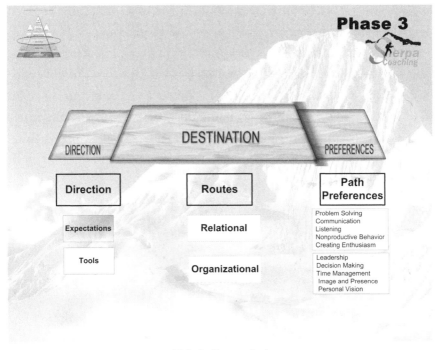

(© Sasha Corporation)

What You'll Find in This Chapter:

Choices:
- **Logistics**
- **Weakness Mountain**
- **Expectations Mountain**
- **Narrowing Your Focus**
- **Decision-Making Tools**

Routes:
- **Relational**
- **Organizational**
- **Path Preferences**

LOGISTICS: MIDTERM MEETINGS

Schedule a meeting with your executive contact, if you have one. Ask your client whether or not you can share the evaluation they have completed. If they agree, go through the evaluation with your executive contact. If not, prepare for this executive meeting with a progress report of your own.

When you meet your executive contact midterm, know exactly what you want to say going in. Sometimes, you'll want to have the executive contact evaluate progress, too. The feedback can help you and your client. To capture that evaluation, use the form in Appendix, page SC 6-1. You can either send the form in advance or have it completed after your meeting, based on your judgment and your contact's wishes.

STORIES FROM THE SUMMIT

Jonathan is a brilliant VP for a software company. He was not very motivated to complete his assigned homework. I asked him to do the midpoint evaluation as homework, but he came back with the work undone.

Jonathan enjoyed and benefited from coaching, but didn't have time to do much outside our meetings. Knowing that, we did it his way. It was much easier to fill out the evaluation along with him, during a meeting. He did this willingly and openly. We got all the answers he felt he needed to share.

Your meetings with your client may have revealed information that's confidential, and that's OK. The goal you are trying to achieve is not confidential. The client's _progress_ is not confidential. Ask your contact what they've been seeing. Their perception of progress is their reality, after all. Shape that perception with positive examples.

Having your client and your executive contact in the same room can be valuable. Use it to your advantage. If you feel it will be helpful, facilitate a meeting that allows everyone to express themselves freely. Creating an atmosphere of candor may take a few minutes, if people are reserved or cautious. The executive contact sometimes wants to avoid confrontation. You must be prepared to ask the right questions to promote discussion.

Rusty, a confident, experienced designer, had been hired a year back. In the beginning, Rusty would have claimed that he really didn't need to be coached. He was good at his job and everything was going well. This was very frustrating for his Sherpa, because it can be hard to travel a path your client does not want to follow. The coach used the midterm evaluation to allow Donald, the executive contact, to state the problem. It went something like this . . .

COACH: "Donald, how would you rate Rusty's performance on a scale of 1 to 10?"

DONALD: "A five (5)."

COACH: "Rusty, are you surprised at that response?"

RUSTY (completely stunned): "Yes."

This is the kind of revelation a Sherpa needs to get a client ready to work. Without the meeting, Donald would have never delivered his blunt assessment straight to Rusty's face. Rusty never would have believed the poor performance evaluation unless he'd heard it straight from his boss. This midterm evaluation set the stage for the real work to begin.

LOGISTICS: THE FIRST SIX WEEKS

Often, the coach will think the client has made tremendous progress, yet the executive contact or manager has not seen it. The midterm evaluation is the perfect place to identify that discrepancy, so you can help your client make their changed behavior more obvious to the appropriate people.

You may be a little frustrated that you are not farther along with your client. Here is why you need to be exactly where you are in the process:

During the period of self-discovery, your client is learning, and acknowledging behaviors that simply don't work. They're building the confidence to tackle weaknesses that impede their progress. The more clients knows about themselves, the more equipped they will be to deal with ch.. .enges and obstacles in the future. Each client will eventually change, improve, and follow a path of their own choosing. The more they know about themselves, the more willing they'll be to work on their own. The time you spend on the front end, learning about the client and helping them discover themselves, will make success possible in the end. After you're done, your client will continue to work on problems independently. They'll discover new things to address on their own.

Your client has to trust you implicitly. Sherpa clients should say: "Whatever my coach says, I will try." That is why "rushing it" will not produce the results the two of you need. Only with time and care will that happen. If this was quick and easy, anyone could do it. It takes time and patience on your part. Trust is not immediate, but your relationship requires it.

You are meeting issues head-on with your client that no one else talks about. Emotions run high, but when trust is at the core of your relationship, your client will blossom in ways that you can only imagine. They will remember the things the Sherpa teaches. Even when they temporarily revert to bad habits clients will recognize that, and correct their behavior going forward. So our relationship and our process unfold over time. To speed things up, you will be tempted to "problem solve" instead of coach. Answers may seem obvious to you. After all, you have an aerial view. Clients are in the daily grind, and often cannot step outside themselves to gain a different perspective. Restrain yourself. Be patient. A client will only use what comes as a personal revelation. Your revelation is not their revelation.

The lessons learned in our most challenging moments are the fabric of success. This is why the Sherpa works on creating an "Aha!" moment every meeting. With each realization comes more confidence that your client can tackle absolutely anything in their business life.

There are two areas that every Sherpa coaching client will work through. Dealing with expectations is one skill we have consistently found lacking in all our clients. No matter what his role in his organization, your client has to successfully share, receive, teach, and communicate expectations to others. A second area of difficulty is accountability. There are very few givens in Sherpa coaching, but we teach every client how to communicate expectations and what personal accountability means.

We'll cover accountability in Phase Five, Agenda, in Chapter 10. Here we'll take on the topic of expectations. Expectations are task definitions. When a task must be done by someone else, you communicate what must be done, when, how, by whom. Those things make up our expectations.

STORIES FROM THE SUMMIT

> *Diane, an executive director for a nonprofit, was a BIG talker. She could talk her way into, or out of, any situation. She could always explain to her funders how much money they needed and why. She could always explain to her people what their goals were for bringing in contributions. What Diane could not do was clearly explain how her people could reach their goals, how to be successful.*
>
> *They understood that they needed more money, but they had no idea how she wanted to solve this problem. Diane was unable to clearly communicate her expectations in this area. She would say things like: "We need more money. Let's go out and get more money." She did not realize that her people did not understand how to do it, when to do it, what to do. Expectations were her problem. Their failure was her fault.*

So what gets in the way of expressing clear expectations? A weakness, usually in the area of communication.

A manager's weaknesses will limit their ability to lead. As your client identifies and corrects their weaknesses, they will think and act differently. As that happens, they'll adjust the way they express expectations. The manager's subordinates and peers will listen more attentively, with more intention to act. The quality of results improves geometrically. That's why we are going to address weaknesses, particularly communications weaknesses, before we start "Dealing with Expectations."

One client, a visionary leader, can see what needs to happen, and knows it's possible. She'll outline the vision in broad terms for her staff, and then tell them to "go off and get it done." She will sometimes fail to give clear instructions, time frames, and rules of engagement. Her weakness:

She assumes that everyone thinks like she does. She doesn't realize that talking is one thing and communicating another.

Another client is a detail person. He's very specific, very precise in the way he expresses himself. That's not necessarily a weakness when explaining something to his staff. When your client is talking with a big-picture, visionary person, that level of detail will be a turn-off. You can't express expectations clearly to a person who is not listening.

The Sherpa's client should learn to be versatile enough to create good communication with everyone. Why? Common wisdom says that good leaders surround themselves with staff that complement their skills, people to handle those things they typically don't do well. A great concept, but it creates a challenge in team communication: the manager will need to motivate others in ways that do not come naturally. A visionary has to give a detail-oriented staffer enough direction to be successful: strict definitions, parameters, and time frames. A "data head" manager has to explain the big picture, the vision, to those who want to know how everything fits together. Learning to communicate well with everyone is a skill that can't be hired on, nor delegated out.

THE WEAKNESS MOUNTAIN

In Chapter 4, we used the Discovery Shield to help our client examine weaknesses. Let's bring that out for review and re-identify the weaknesses. Discuss it, and make sure you and your client have reached the same understanding about their weaknesses. Let's work on one of those, selecting the one that has the most to do with communication or with things that prevent clear communication. Push your client to identify exactly what weakness is holding them back from communicating effectively.

It is extremely important to get this right. If you don't, you will have to revisit it with your client over and over. Follow the Sherpa Stance to clearly define a relevant weakness to be addressed:

- Is it precise? Are we talking about a problem, a symptom, or a feeling? Unless we are talking about a problem, we aren't ready to continue.

- Is it personal? If it's too personal, we don't go on.

- Is it present tense? Sherpas work on the future, not the past.
- Is it possible? Will a change in your client's behavior actually fix the problem?

Next we'll share four steps that enable clients to overcome the weaknesses that get in the way of good communication. This is the "Weakness Mountain." You will revisit this mountain on a number of different occasions. This will be a very good place to start any time clients find themselves in a problem of their own making. Your client will have a basic diagram of Weakness Mountain in their Journal on page 3-1. This exercise will require at least two meetings, with homework in-between, and continued effort on your client's part, even after you have gone further into the coaching process.

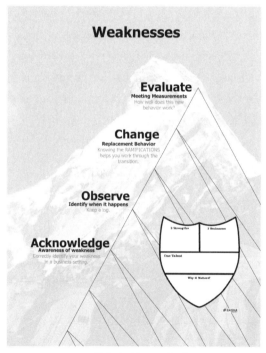

(© Sasha Corporation)

Your clients were setting expectations long before you came along. They're capable of managing a company, looking after a manufacturing plant, or whatever they are doing. They simply don't know which of their behaviors is not working. Weakness Mountain dissects this issue. In every case, those weaknesses, less-than-perfect behaviors, affect the way your client communicates.

Weakness Mountain: Step 1—Acknowledge

The Discovery Shield gave your client a chance to look at their major weaknesses (Journal page 1-4). Before we take the next step, let's review those weaknesses, and what has happened since you first began meeting. Is your client really prepared to do the work? When their weaknesses influence their behavior, are they aware of it? Do they know how this affects their business life? Have they changed since your preliminary discussions?

This conversation is groundwork. Once you're ready to take your client up Weakness Mountain, here's exactly how you'll lead them, coach to client. The Sherpa will say: *The first step in the process is to acknowledge your weaknesses. You can't begin to improve if you are not aware of them. Let's select the one weakness that has the most adverse effect on your communications with subordinates, and write it on the top of page 3-1 in your Journal.*

Acknowledgment is critical to starting this exercise. This weakness must be tangible. It must be something that you can put your arms around. You must absolutely believe that the weakness, as stated, is in fact a weakness for you. Do not go any further until you acknowledge that the weakness we are going to work on causes you "professional pain."

Coaching Note: Discussing examples and situations can create some breakthroughs. Once you have worked this through with your client, don't forget to ask, *What does that mean?* Each time your client thinks they have their weakness correctly identified, be prepared to challenge. Unless your client is totally comfortable with the definition of their weakness, they cannot move up the mountain.

Weakness Mountain: Step 2—Observe

Continue with your client:

Notice when your weakness shows itself. Almost anything to do with the weakness itself is advanced by writing or journaling about it. Write down in your Journal (page 3-1) the times this weakness is shown at work. You can also do your writing at home if you like. This requires that you go through your business day consciously. Observe what goes on each day and under what circumstances your weakness occurs. Writing this information in your journal gives you the opportunity to take the first step to correct it.

Ask yourself these questions about this weakness, the five W's:

1. *When does it happen most?*
2. *Where? In what situations do you notice your weakness?*
3. *Who? Does someone/or a type of person provoke it?*
4. *What motivates you to handle things using that weakness?*
5. *Why? What situations or circumstances provoke it? Why does it happen?*

Take notes. Remember the specifics. Keep track, so you can identify trends and patterns. As soon as you are conscious of this one weakness, at the moment it comes into play, you are able to change your gut reaction into a reasoned decision. If you need to create a grid, or a table to record the times something happens, go ahead. Don't be afraid to measure it. Maybe we can design something in your notes pages to help with this.

Coaching Note: Help your client create situations where they can observe their weakness, such as taking the journal to staff meetings. Your job here is to help establish an easy way to observe when "it" happens.

Weakness Mountain : Step 3—Change

Why is change so hard? Sometimes, you know you have a weakness you want to change, and yet you can't. Weight loss ... nail biting ... smoking ... bad habits are hard to break. You have to answer the paramount question for yourself: Why it matters.

Remember the Discovery Shield? We talked about "Why it matters" that we do our type of work, why we have chosen this place of employment. Here we identify "Why it matters" that we change our behavior, overcome our weakness. Once we've identified a meaningful motive, we constantly bring it back to mind as we break our habits.

Commitment: It is not enough to simply know why it matters. That's a start. Change requires commitment and effort. Most people know their weakness. They have not made up their minds that it matters enough. Does it matter enough for you to make a change? If you want to lose weight, you probably have to give up a food you like. If you want to be self-employed, you'll need to sacrifice and save more aggressively, so you'll have money to live on while you build up your business. Perhaps you have to return to school to be further educated. Positive change always requires sacrifice, in one way or another.

Modeling: The best way to change is to be a role model for yourself. Just do it. It takes 21 days to change a habit, and this weakness is a habit. You need to realize that and work on it. Be aware when the old behavior appears. Be aware of what you want to do, instead of responding the way you are accustomed to. The weakness will fade, and new habits will form if you model the appropriate response. It is going to hurt the first few times. Then you will be able to observe, be motivated (because you'll see how well people react to a different approach), and you will "role model" yourself into the new way of doing things.

The Weakness Mountain: Step 4—Evaluation

So we have replacement behavior that builds new habits and overcomes weaknesses. Look at the new ways you are dealing with your weakness: How is it going? How well are you handling it? Is it better than the old way? How do you feel about yourself? Is it too difficult? Too easy? Hard to remember? Too stressful?

Expect some lapses. Celebrate your victories. Don't give up as you build new habits. When you succeed, reward yourself. Give yourself something that you want, need, or desire. Keep up the good work.

That's how you lead a client through the process of changing behaviors—the Weakness Mountain. Look how far you've come. Your client's weaknesses have been identified and reviewed. Like a great Sherpa guide, you have provided the necessary tools, tips, and tricks to meet the challenge. Your client is facing their weaknesses and moving toward positive change.

So, as we said, getting rid of weaknesses is a prerequisite to progress. Remove the number-one stumbling block to achieving a goal; then tackle the goal itself.

Our client has now identified weaknesses. When a leader makes a positive change by addressing a personal weakness, several things happen. The leader models by example that anyone can change for the better.

- The leader shores up good relationships and repairs bad ones.
- The leader earns new respect. People start listening to them.

So what does climbing Weakness Mountain have to do with setting clear expectations? Everything. That weakness, the one related to communication dictates how well your client will communicate their expectations. So we conquer the first mountain, Weakness, before heading up the second, Expectations. Given all that, it's time for the leader to work on the quality of communication, and capitalize on this newfound willingness to listen to the people around them.

EXPECTATIONS MOUNTAIN

Let's work on something that few leaders are consistently good at: communicating expectations clearly. Why is this important? As you know, when it doesn't happen, people make up their own course of action, one that may only match expectations through dumb luck.

The most important thing a leader can communicate is clear expectations. That's going to happen through four steps:

- Communication
- Commitment
- Consequences
- Coaching

Before the climb begins, ask whether the view from the top is worth it. Not everything is top priority. Deciding what is most important; it's a primary role of leaders. Your client should answer the five W's (who, what, when, where, and why) before setting any process in motion. That is a prerequisite to identifying and then explaining any expectation.

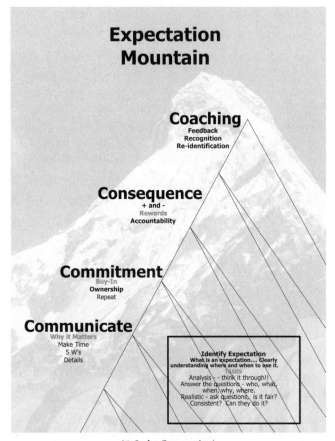

(© Sasha Corporation)

Remember that you can't always expect positive results from the positive changes your client makes. For every action, there's an equal and opposite reaction. Remember ramifications? You can't always predict what that "equal but opposite" reaction will be. Remind your client to use Journal page 1-2 to record unexpected outcomes of the actions he takes. If he uses this page regularly, he'll start to see patterns that might shatter some assumptions he's made about the people around him.

 ## STORIES FROM THE SUMMIT

Helen is a vice president of housing in a social service agency. She is tenaciously committed to her people and her job. She is a great problem solver,

one of the best. Over the years, however, this burden started to wear on her. Tired of carrying everyone on her back, she empowered her people, and started giving clear and defined expectations about resolving their own problems.

Work still got done, as well as ever, but Helen's staff began to fight with each other. Up to now, Helen had stepped in whenever something went wrong. Now they had to confront and reprimand each other, once Helen's sole jurisdiction. This development, conflict created by empowerment, was unexpected but easy to deal with. Helen's staff took courses in communication and developed the skills they had never needed in the past.

Here's how a Sherpa proceeds with a client:

There are important, specific questions you have to address before asking others to accomplish something. Memorize these questions or carry them in your pocket until it is second nature to bring them to mind. Think them through for any project that calls for you to lead a team:

Who's involved?

How do their strengths and weaknesses come into play?

With what will you need help?

When do you need results?

Is this realistic, fair, and consistent? Can they do it?

Using this as a guideline, decide exactly what needs to be done. That's the first step. We'll talk in detail, in just a minute, about how we communicate all this. Start at the baseline and answer the question: "What are we going to do?"

While you are planning your communication, and while you are delivering it, use the five W's as a checklist. Your expectation may not require an answer to all five questions, but mentally addressing each one will add consistency to your approach.

1. Who will be involved in executing the expectation? Who will be affected by the work being done? Who requested the work? How much feedback and involvement do they want along the way?

2. What needs to happen? What steps will there be along the way? What resources will be required? What's our end result? How do we know we've achieved it?

3. When do we start? When must we be finished? Think about time frames for the whole project.

4. Where does the work happen? In the office? On a customer's site? How do travel time and cost relate to where we decide to work?

5. Why are we doing this? Reinforce the link between each person's "piece of the action" and the end result. Discuss the purpose of the assignment in global terms. Talk about the benefits we'll realize as a department or company. Then connect all this with "Why it matters" for that one person.

Given this groundwork, when your client has defined what has to be done, have them check the steps in the Expectations Mountain. The client will have this diagram in their Journal, page 3-2, and can use it for reference and notes as you continue.

As you and your client approach Expectations Mountain, you will share four steps that make your expectations become reality. This is a training piece, material that the Sherpa must know extremely well and pass on to every client. Make Expectations Mountain your own, so you can talk a client through it with eloquence. Use Journal pages 3-2 and 3-3 to further your discussions. Have your client make notes, draw pictures, and journal in-between meetings.

Expectations Mountain:
Step 1—Communicate Your Expectations

Here's how you'll explain it to your client:

Make time with the person you're communicating expectations to.

Don't take your people or your conversations for granted. Organize your time so you're not rushed. Plan ahead and prepare for every conversation. Figure out how much time a meeting might take and set an appointment. If you need an immediate conversation, stay out of "fire-fighting" mode and be professional. Allow the person whose time you need to adjust any scheduled business in a professional manner.

STORIES FROM THE SUMMIT

Jeff leads a fast-growing tech company. He's just come out of an exciting meeting about his new strategic plan. He runs into David, a manager who was not asked to be a part of this meeting. Jeff tells David: "I need you to think about expanding your quality project to include our other plant. I'll want to talk about that next week. Please inform your team about this. I'm on the run. Talk to you later."

Jeff really expects David to take this bit of information and run with it, do research and analysis in advance of an unspecified meeting sometime next week. David has never seen the overall plan. He's not sure what Jeff's goal is, why Jeff thinks the quality project will work in a very different environment. David engages, goes through the motions, simply to appease Jeff. Nothing substantial comes of it, and David doesn't get his meeting until three weeks later.

Keep your meeting focused: no distractions. Don't multitask. Part of that focus will be choosing a location that adds weight to the conversation. Do not communicate your expectations in the hallway when you can arrange a conference room.

STORIES FROM THE SUMMIT

Kate is an assertive business executive. She is working diligently on her weakness. Her problem? She has a difficult time putting aside her work when she is at her desk and someone walks in. While she's talking, Kate does two or three things at once. She answers email while she is assigning someone a report. Sometimes she's asking someone to do something fairly important, and she's not even looking at him.

The result? She has no idea if her staff even hears what she says. Instead of the few seconds it would cost her to look people in the eye and give them full attention, Kate is spending hours fighting fires and doing cleanup duty. Her solution was very simple yet very difficult. She's now

> *extremely aware when someone walks into her office. She sets everything aside and concentrates solely on the person she's with. In the middle of conversations, she's still tempted to check email, but she's learning. And her entire department is more productive.*

In short: if you can't set up the right attitude, time, and place in which to express your expectations, stay quiet until you can. This is the opportunity to use the 5 W's you have identified.

"Why it matters" is one component of the "why" question. It's so important that it deserves more discussion. Communicating an expectation offers an opportunity to share your vision of the organization, where it's going, and how the matter at hand relates to the big picture. That's all fine. Don't forget to refocus on the employee and discuss why it matters to the person you are giving the expectation to, something directly related to that person's motivation for coming to work every day.

Getting things done comes down to your employees. Understanding their "Why it matters" will change the way you deliver the expectation. Why does it matter in their worldview? Answer that question correctly and you have provided the motivation to get things done—correctly.

STORIES FROM THE SUMMIT

> *Larry has just been named president of a mid-sized company after working as a senior manager for many years. Over the years, Iris has worked side-by-side with him. As a production line supervisor, Iris spent 12 years learning the products and equipment and focuses on how to get the job done one day at a time.*
>
> *The company is growing. Larry sits down with Iris to share expectations about growth and long-term plans for their people and systems. Larry, always the visionary, delivers his expectation in big-picture terms. He is excited, animated.*
>
> *Iris listens and sorts out Larry's message in her own terms. Her feedback to him is precise, mentioning tasks, checklists, and databases. Larry is*

> *frustrated. He does not understand why Iris doesn't see the big picture. After all, he talked with such clarity and enthusiasm.*
>
> *Larry needs to see that Iris does understand, in her own terms. To be a good leader, he has to start communicating in her language, based on her definition of success. Larry has to understand "Why it matters" to Iris and move forward on that basis.*

Here are a few things you should learn about your employees:

- *Why do they work in this industry?*
- *Why do they wake up every day to work for you?*
- *Why did they choose this company?*
- *What career goals do they have for themselves?*
- *How do they define success?*

Moving forward, be specific about details, time frames, and standards.
Don't deliver an expectation until you have details. Your task-focused people will want the details. Your "big thinkers" will need the details, whether they know it or not. Determine checkpoints for completion. Note responsible parties for each task. Give everyone all the information they need. Don't allow assumptions that might differ from your expectations.

Cincinnati Bengals football coach Marvin Lewis set just such a tone at the end of his first season. He gave each player an individualized sheet of expectations for the off-season. It flagged critical days, key meetings, when camps would start and end, as well as how the physicals, therapy, and personal workouts would occur. Every player had a road map of what they needed to do, every day, over the next six months. There were no surprises.

 **Expectations Mountain: Step 2—Commitment**

The Sherpa coach continues training the client:

The second step in the Expectations Mountain is to inspire mutual commitment.

You have already posed these questions to yourself: Is this realistic to ask? Is it fair? Can they do it? Relying on your own answers to these questions, there is a temptation to skip the details and go straight from Step 1, Communication, to Step 3, Consequences. An autocratic leader will view rewards and punishment, or perhaps a paycheck or a pink slip, as all the motivation people need. That's an egocentric point of view. The most productive people are those who've had a part in shaping the work they do, and who believe in what they're doing.

Respect the logical rhythm inherent in Expectations Mountain. Step 2 is commitment. Respect your own time as well. Actually, it takes longer to skip a step than to go through it as it's written. If you assume buy-in, you might find to your surprise, when the due date arrives, that there was none.

You may be eloquent in your delivery of expectations, but that doesn't guarantee that you've been effective. When you're delivering an expectation, make sure you are completely understood. Ask the person to repeat what you've told him in their own words.

Someone who's a "note-taker" might read it back to you in your words, not their own. Listening to them repeat your expectation in their own words will confirm the quality of your communication and help you pace your discussion according to the listener's needs.

So you've been understood. Does this prove that someone has taken ownership of your expectation? Not yet. Look for the message in their body language. Are they interested? Did they ask questions, clarify or verify your expectation? Ask for comments with a neutral phrase such as: "What do you think?" "Can you do it?" Then stop for as long as it takes to get a response. "Fair enough?" says just enough. It lets your employee know that you are interested in creating a situation that they feel is fair, whatever that might mean to them.

To make sure you're on track, force an objection. Sales professionals will tell you that an objection is not a problem, it's an open door to opportunity. You can overcome any objection you know about, so invite an objection. This may take a little work. You will have to trust your instincts about your employee. You want them to be able to express themselves freely, with no repercussions.

Their knowledge becomes your knowledge, and communicating your expectations has become a two-way street. Do not move on without "buy-in." When you're sure you have it, it's time to move to the next step.

Expectations Mountain: Step 3—Consequences

Here's what your client needs to hear in the next step:

What happens when consequences are overlooked while an expectation is being carried out? The person acting on the expectation will have no boundaries and no sense of urgency.

Talk all you want about deals and deadlines, if you forget to set up "guardrails" that keep everyone on track, very little will happen. In this step, we set up a personal accountability system. Set up time frames and reminders for yourself. Build checkpoints along the way. If you aren't the person who monitors progress, get the responsible party on track.

Perhaps people react negatively to positive change because they are afraid of consequences. A great boss will make consequences a positive word. Create an environment where people expect positive outcomes, instead of thinking "he'll be fired" or "she'll be in trouble."

Rewards are a fabulous way to motivate your employee to get a task done. This is often so overlooked. The reward can be as simple as your staff being gratified to please you, or knowing they'll get recognition from the CEO or the board of directors. As people communicate their progress, offer recognition. Review their "Why it matters" and acknowledge them in a way that's meaningful for them. Some people get gratification from within themselves. Others need it from you. The objective is to notice their work. Tell them they are doing a good job as many times as they need to hear it.

Knowing all the ways your people might look at a situation, you're prepared for the fourth step on Expectations Mountain: Coaching Through the Expectation.

Expectations Mountain: Step 4—Coaching

The Sherpa continues with the client:

As a leader, you can't leave people alone to "sink or swim." To guarantee your results, stay involved. Coaching is not problem solving, it's not prodding, and it's not scolding. Coaching is listening and watching and asking the right questions.

Feedback:

Once you have communicated your expectation, then what? Stay involved. Follow up. Ask questions. Check the status of work in progress. Ask more questions. Why stay involved? So you can look for opportunities to help people get better, to save them from failure, to let them know you care.

Coaching comes through example as much as from instruction. You, as the boss, will have to know who is doing what, at all times. This is as good for you as it is for your people. It is your own personal follow-up process.

Re-identification:

As work progresses, make sure everything stays *achievable and fair. As you gain feedback, if you find someone can't achieve the desired result, talk it over and either fix the expectation or re-assign it in a way that maintains everyone's dignity.*

You, the Sherpa, can work through an expectation with your client, using the assessment called the Verification of Expectations (Journal page 3-3). If your client has a current or upcoming project, allow them to practice discussing expectations while you, the Sherpa, rate how well they are doing.

We teach every client to climb Expectations Mountain, because everyone has room for improvement in that area. It's going to be essential for the rest of your client's working life. It sets your relationship on solid ground as well.

This recap is a good way to review Expectations Mountain with your client:

- Communicate: Discover "Why it matters" to the person who'll act on your expectation.
- Commitment: Do you have buy-in?
- Consequences: Do they know what to expect when they succeed?
- Coaching: Are you making sure this expectation is being carried out?

COACHING NOTE

Self-assessment can be tough for your client. It's tough for anyone. As a Sherpa coach, you should address your own weaknesses in order to successfully help clients address theirs. After your coaching sessions, evaluate each client and the way you performed. How did your own attitudes, fears, or weaknesses affect the way you guided your client or avoided confronting your client?

Know yourself and the assumptions you impose on relationships. Perhaps you like to figure things out for yourself, so you'll offer little in the way of instruction. Maybe you're a good listener. If your client has a short attention span, you'll have to adjust to what works for them, not what's natural for you.

Your feelings are irrelevant when you're coaching with the Sherpa process. Perhaps you hate to push or confront others. Coaching will force you out of your comfort zone. You'll have to deal with that and get past it.

Your client's feelings aren't that important, either. Pushing your clients might make them feel uncomfortable. Whether it does or not, it's necessary. Challenges and confrontations add value to your coaching. Without some push, a coaching relationship cannot move quickly enough.

NARROWING YOUR FOCUS

The Sherpa process takes us to choices now: Which route, relational or organizational, will your client take? Which of the ten paths will they follow? It's an important choice. Whatever route and path you take, you and your client will follow it all the way to the summit.

Sometime, the Sherpa has an obvious answer such as: This client is not an effective communicator. Naturally you will continue on with the relational route, and the path of effective communication.

If you and your client are already in agreement on a route and the path from the lists below, you can skip ahead to either Chapter 7 or 8 to continue the process.

Relational Route (Chapter 7)

- Problem-Solving Path
- Communication Path

- Listening Path
- Nonproductive Behavior Path
- Creating Enthusiasm Path

Organizational Route (Chapter 8)

- Leadership Path
- Decision-Making Path
- Time Management Path
- Image and Presence Path
- Personal Vision Path

If you're learning the process, or working with a client whose path is not obvious, read ahead.

DECISION-MAKING TOOLS

The Sherpa has three ways to help a client pick a path:

1. Assessments
2. Interviews
3. The Sherpa's Recommendation

Look over all three, and pick one of the three to start with.

First, the Sherpa has assessments that reveal more about client's issues. You'll find these in the Sherpa coaching client Journal, on these pages:

Attitude	5-3
Time Management	4-12
Anger Assessment	4-6
Listening Skills	4-3
Communication	4-2
Leadership	4-8
Image and Presence	4-15

These assessments should be applied directly to your client's needs. If they don't have anger issues, don't have them complete the anger test. If your client has image issues, complete the related assessment. The assessments you use will tell you and your client where you will be going next.

Second, the Sherpa can conduct an interview. We'll ask several "Why" questions simply to make sure we work on and discuss the right issues: "Why do you feel and behave the way you do? Why do you respond to life the way you do? Why do you behave in certain ways with certain people?"

Here are some examples of responses you are likely to get, and the tools and approaches they might dictate:

I have always done it that way.

> Organizational route, Leadership path
>
> *Leadership assessment for path confirmation (4-8)*

I have no idea how else to say the things I do.

> Relational route, Communication path
>
> *Communication assessments to confirm the path (4-2)*

It is easier to do it myself.

> Organizational route, Decision-Making path, or
>
> Relational route, Problem-Solving path
>
> *Time Management assessment (4-12)*

Because I say so.

> Relational route, Listening path
>
> *Listening or Attitude assessments (4-3, 5-3)*

That's a short list, examples of the answers your client might give to your "Why" questions, and the assessments or path choices that might relate. Encourage your client to participate in choosing the path. Sherpa coaching is not an exact science, so your choice will probably not be any better than theirs, unless they're avoiding the obvious.

An additional way to choose the path: The Sherpa's recommendation.

At the end of Chapter 13, starting on page SC 6-2, we ask a number of questions about your client. Your answers will narrow down the number of paths that might benefit the client the most. Think carefully about each issue and see where it fits in the total picture: the client, their job, and the people around them. Ask yourself: Should I start here? Make a copy of this survey, and circle where you think your client needs the most work. Your path recommendation will come to you by visually seeing where your client falls.

You are now ready to get the process moving by selecting a route and a path for your client. You will be presented with issues, struggles, and problems that constantly change. The authors' newsletter, *Sherpa Strength*, will continually offer new tools, assessments, and approaches you can use with your clients. Email info@sherpacoaching.com for details.

Each route has a choice of five paths. Each path comes with climbing tools. The climbing tools are resources, tricks, and techniques that guide your client's steps along each path.

The overall route you choose—relational or organizational—will depend on the results from the assessments you've done with your client, conversations with your executive contact, and your own judgment.

You might find, following the Communication path, that your client has other issues. Continue work on communication. Avoid going off on tangents. Follow the process. Work the chosen path all the way through to Phase Five, The Agenda. Then revisit, and loop back again, to begin again with route and path selection.

Sometimes deciding is not easy. Don't worry, there is nothing you can do but help your client with any path you choose. If you choose communication and the real weakness is listening, it will not hurt anything. You will succeed in the path you choose, and the Sherpa process always allows you to pick up a higher priority path later in the coaching process. Once you have produced positive results, you can always go back.

A coach and client's "must do," at this point in the Sherpa process, is to make a decision.

Under the relational route, you and your client will take one of these paths:

- Problem Solving
- Communication

- Listening
- Nonproductive Behavior
- Creating Enthusiasm

If you have decided on the organizational route, you and your client will now choose one of these paths:

- Leadership
- Decision Making
- Time Management
- Image and Presence
- Personal Vision

If you've chosen a path on the relational route, move on to Chapter 7. If your path is on the organizational route, the process will take you to Chapter 8. Once you have followed a path with your client, you'll continue to Chapter 9, where we consolidate the gains made in each and every path, and continue to the summit.

We've made every effort to build all our experience into *The Sherpa Guide*. Given the broad range of human experience, every client will be different. Active coaches who use the Sherpa process can connect with the authors via email at info@sherpacoaching.com.

CHAPTER 7

Phase Four: Charting the Course—The Relational Route

THE NUMBER OF PEOPLE who buy self-help books is staggering. Of all the self-help books purchased, perhaps 1 in 20 is actually read and acted on. That is why coaching is so much in demand. Coaches force attention on the areas of one's life that need work. Effective coaches spend time making their clients do the difficult work on their "rough edges." A Sherpa holds clients accountable. As a coach, your job is to have your client acknowledge that no one else can be blamed for their weaknesses, and that solutions, although they may be simple, take work.

We've arrived here, on a chosen path, based on our work in Phase Three, Destination. You and your client have decided on a relational route and one of its five paths.

Now, how do you know what steps you'll take to get to the summit? In each path, the Sherpa process details the steps you'll take in the form of training and self-discovery exercises.

What You'll Find in This Chapter:

- **Problem-Solving Path**
- **Communication Path**
- **Listening Path**
- **Nonproductive Behavior Path**
- **Creating Enthusiasm Path**

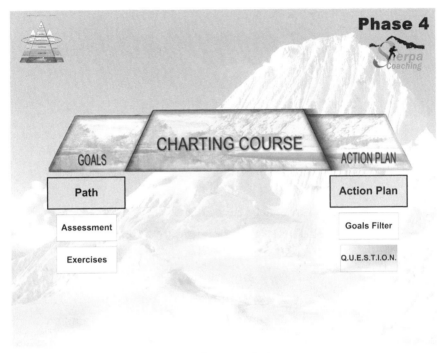

(© Sasha Corporation)

Here's a list of the tools you will offer for each of the paths:

Problem-Solving Path

- DIG UP
- QTIP
- Separating the Person from the Issue

Communication Path

- Assessment
- COMMUNICATION Acronym
- Listen, Think, Then Communicate

Listening Path

- Assessment
- Body Language
- Silence
- Three-Sentence Rule

Nonproductive Behavior Path

- DAPPER
- Anger Management
- Intimidation

Creating Enthusiasm Path

- Discovery Shield
- Love Bus
- Fuzzy Duck Theory

Leading a client along each one of these paths, the Sherpa will know these tools, decide which ones to recommend to the client as valuable, and then allow the client to accept or reject each recommendation.

What we have done here is provide you with tools and techniques, the most effective we have developed, to get to the crux of the matter. These exercises are designed to break down your client's habits and build new ones. There is a wealth of other material on all the areas we are about to discuss. Use the best and most appropriate material for each client, from this book, your own experience, or even from a client's favorite business book. Whether the client struggles with time management, communication, or problem solving, answers are available.

Recall the information you gathered in the Weakness Mountain (client Journal page 3-1). It's a valuable way to revisit your client's weaknesses. Get comfortable with this exercise. You will refer back to it during your trip to the summit.

The biggest obstacle you may face is getting your client to acknowledge that they have tremendous room for improvement. You'll hear the usual rationale for staying in a comfort zone:

- "I have been getting along fine all these years."
- "I get hurt because nobody listens to me."
- "I don't know why people say I am angry all the time. This is just how I talk."
- "Why doesn't anyone understand me?"
- "Why do they all act like that?"

For any area of weakness, there are readily available answers. So you have to ask the question: Why has your client not figured this out, and fixed it, before you came along? People want quick fixes. They don't want to be bothered with the hard work involved in self-improvement.

For both routes, the relational and the organizational, and for all ten paths, you'll find both training and facilitation we have developed as part of the Sherpa coaching process. All of this is designed to make your client understand their particular issue more clearly, and to take action that produces quick results.

For example, if your client's issue is anger management, you'll use related assessments in their journal and work on the exercises we provide. You'll know when they have taken the materials to heart and when further reading and study on their part is necessary.

What you are about to read are tips, tricks, and techniques to get to the bottom of virtually any client's issue. There is a lot of material here. Our recommendation? Read it all the way through to learn the scope of the resources you now have available. Then, as you apply the material with individual clients, you will find it becomes second nature for you. Keep this book close by for reference. Using the individual tests, exercises, and training materials, you'll find you have a fairly complete solution for just about any situation.

One of the unique features of Sherpa coaching is the success we have experienced with giving out small gifts, tokens, and prizes to our clients. These little gifts are called "charas." The word chara is from the native language of the Sherpa guides in Tibet. The definition used in the Sherpa coaching process is "a small token of appreciation given as a gift." We will use this term for gifts we give our clients as they make breakthroughs in thought and action.

Although not all paths have a chara, we'll suggest a specific chara for most paths. Clients love their charas. They become permanent fixtures on their desks. You may have clients you don't think will be big "gift people." But you'll be surprised to find even they will love to receive a chara. One chara that can be used throughout your sessions is the Tootsie Pop. Use it to reward a revelation, a new idea, or an acknowledgement. They are a fun way to assure your client that they're doing good work. Clients seem to treasure them.

STORIES FROM THE SUMMIT

> *I worked with Jana for a long time. She is the brilliant executive director of a nonprofit organization. She found our relationship invaluable because there was no one else, staff or peer, in whom she could confide. Her spouse and friends had little interest in her work.*
>
> *Jana had trouble putting her arms around expectations. She just didn't "get it." She fought it. Then one day she tried going through the expectations process with her Sherpa, as we talked about an extremely difficult employee. The results were remarkable. I handed her a Tootsie Pop as a reward when she figured out her situation. She said: "It has been at least a month since I was this good. Finally!" That is what charas and treats are all about: putting a little fun in life and adding something special to the coaching relationship.*

THE RELATIONAL ROUTE

Relational paths encompass the "soft skills," the client's interpersonal relationships at work. This is the nontechnical side of your client's job. Relational skills are the ways that we get things done, and done correctly, through and with other people.

The relational route will involve the client taking one or more of these paths:

- **Problem Solving**
- **Communication**
- **Listening**
- **Nonproductive Behavior**
- **Creating Enthusiasm**

Like a mountain guide, the Sherpa Coach provides all kinds of guidance and information for clients. Some of the things we offer, they will use.

Some they will leave by the side of the trail. Some of the concepts will be as crystal clear as a mountain stream. Others they might not understand or want to acknowledge as valuable. The Sherpa offers the opportunity to choose. This gives your clients the ability to make decisions and create changes they are committed to making.

If you are reading this book for the first time, read everything: five paths on the relational route, here in Chapter 7, and five paths on the organizational route, in Chapter 8. You'll get familiar with a wide range of training and development exercises.

A Sherpa who is following the process with a specific client will read the material for the client's chosen path, and then skip ahead to Chapter 9, where all the paths rejoin on the way to the summit.

PROBLEM-SOLVING—PATH 1 OF 5, THE RELATIONAL ROUTE

Some of the questions that may have led you to select this path:

- Does the client put off solving problems?
- Does the client have trouble dealing with conflict?
- Does the client solve all the problems of their staff and peers?
- Does the client take things personally?

If your client can't deal well with problems, you are going to follow this path on the relational route. Some clients have difficulty with problem solving because they don't empower, never give their staff the authority to solve a problem. They prefer to solve every problem themselves. Others avoid solving problems because they don't deal well with consequences and risk. They don't believe in their own ability to make a good decision. To sort this out, consider:

- Would your client rather solve a problem than coach their staff on how to reach a solution?
- Does your client feel good about solving problems that are not work related?

- Does your client have a long line of employees outside their office asking questions?

- Does your client fail to solve problems altogether?

- Does your client feel that every problem is a personal affront?

- How about dealing with problems head on? Can your client handle that?

These questions will help you decide the steps you'll need to take on the Problem-Solving path. There are several tools we offer on this path, explained and detailed below.

 ## STORIES FROM THE SUMMIT

> *Bill is a brilliant engineer in manufacturing. He has solved problems all his business life. He always got a charge out of solving all his staff's problems. After working with his Sherpa for well over 12 weeks, he had a revelation. He found coaching his staff through their problems was more fulfilling than actually solving the problem. Bill was able to experience a true paradigm shift, a new way of looking at his business world. He became a great manager, with a different method for handling problems.*

Here are the tools and techniques we use on the Problem-Solving path:

- **DIG UP**

- **QTIP**

- **Separating the Person from the Issue**

 ### DIG UP (Problem Solving—the first of three tools)

The letters in DIG UP serve to remind our client of a method for solving problems. These steps, in sequence, constitute a way to allow team effort in a difficult situation. Walk your client through this acronym, allowing questions, discussions, and role-plays with each letter. You can use page 4-1 in the journal to walk through this with them.

Here's how you'd teach this concept, beginning with a case study:

Case Study ABC Industries is a garment distribution center. Terry has worked at ABC for 10 years. On the other hand, Dorothy has been there just 18 months. Right now, deliveries to customers are running late. There's enough capacity to get things done on time, but scheduling is a real problem. The dispatch team takes care of everything efficiently, but there's a bottleneck causing delays in the flow of authorizations and information. Terry, the veteran, blames Dorothy.

D STANDS FOR DEFINE.   Define your problem. Write down specifically what the problem is. When your client uses this technique, a flip chart in their office can be valuable. When a problem, scenario, or issue is written on the flip chart, it becomes something abstract, removed from the personalities involved. The goal: narrow the definition of the problem down to one sentence.

Don't accept a statement like this:

"Terry is having problems with Dorothy."

Definition is probably the most important step, and it's also the most difficult. Sometimes it's hard to establish exactly what the problem is. So look into things, brainstorm, before you write down your summary description.

Ask specific questions to get to the underlying sentence you are looking for: When you are told something like, *"Terry is having problems with Dorothy,"* determine:

- What exactly is the problem?
- Is everyone experiencing the problem?
- Can each employee summarize the problem in the same way?
- Can everyone agree on a one-sentence description?

Define the problem. You might conclude with a statement like this:

"Dorothy is not getting her paperwork done on time, which causes scheduling problems for Terry."

Or better yet:

"There are paperwork delays, which causes scheduling problems."

Defining the problem accurately is only the beginning.

I STANDS FOR IDENTIFY. Identify possible causes. Write down every idea you come up with. Write everything down.

Now, let's get back to Dorothy and see how we can identify possible causes for this problem: Dorothy is not getting her paperwork done on time.

Possible causes identified:

- Dorothy is personally unable to handle a reasonable workload.
- She's been sick lately, and will improve on her own.
- Dorothy has too much paperwork for one person to do.
- Dorothy wastes her time making personal phone calls.
- Does Dorothy really want to be here? Is this an attitude problem?

Make sure you think big as well:

- What can cause paperwork problems in Dorothy's job?
- Is there a better way to route this paperwork?

It's important to identify all your possibilities. You may have heard the story of three blind men who are asked to describe an elephant. The first blind man touched the elephant's leg and described an elephant as a tall pillar. The second touched its side and said: "An elephant is like a wall." The third blind man, holding on to its tail, described the elephant as a piece of rope. All of them were right, but none of them had a complete answer.

Look at your problem as a whole. Be creative. You'll be surprised at what you come up with. You may find you don't really have a problem at all. Maybe you'll find you're trying to solve the wrong problem. In our example with the paperwork that's always late, you'll first need to make sure Dorothy is really late with her work. Answer questions that are specifically directed at the problem:

- What paperwork is Dorothy late with?
- Does she have all the tools needed to be successful?
- What does "late" mean? Is it late according to her boss or just her peers' perception?
- Does she understand what she has to do? Is it in her job description?
- Does she have the training to do it well?
- Is she given specific time and dates to have her work complete?

G STANDS FOR GATHER.   Now that you have defined the problem and its possible causes, gather every possible fact about the situation. Gather possible solutions from anyone who is able to provide you with information. Share the list of suggested solutions with your team. Cross impractical solutions off your list. What's left is a list of workable solutions and information that will support any decision you make.

In our case study, we find that Dorothy gets hit with a blizzard of paperwork at the end of the day, including changes to orders that must go out the next morning. It's a teamwork issue, not a Dorothy issue. We can't penalize customers for last-minute changes and still remain competitive, so our solution has to come from within.

U STANDS FOR UMPIRE.   Webster's dictionary defines an umpire as "a person who has authority to decide a controversy or question between parties." You have taken the time to list reasonable options. Now evaluate your choices. Consider all the options at this point. Review the situation in detail. Pick one answer. Make the call and stick with it. Don't be afraid to make a DECISION. (Sherpa, please refer to our decision-making route if your client has trouble in this area.)

In our case study, we add some duties for the dispatch team, and have them finish each day, during their slow time, by handling some of the paperwork they'll need to get things moving first thing the next morning.

P STANDS FOR PUT INTO EFFECT.   Be confident of your solution. Because it was arrived at with the DIG UP process, your solution is based on input from everyone involved. You have spent time with the problem. You've decided on the solution you are going to apply. Make it measurable. Make sure you have a start date and an evaluation method. Be content with your solution and your staff will be, too. "Put it into effect" is the implementation of your plan.

Make sure that changes in duties for the dispatch team are clearly laid out. Expectations must be clear across the team: times, workspaces, authorities granted. Measurements of success have to be easy to produce and widely disseminated on a timely basis. Rewards and consequences have to be spelled out in advance.

᾿s a coach, you might want to wrap up this piece of training by handing the client a toy dump truck or "excavator" with the words "DIG UP" on the hood or on top of the vehicle. The toy truck is the chara for this concept. Ask your client to keep this on their desk as a reminder of the DIG UP concept. Continue the exercise by asking your client to go through the acronym with a problem they are currently dealing with.

Why use this technique for a client who has difficulty solving problems? Most of the time, leaders and managers let problems continue to pile up because it takes too long to sort things out, or they are afraid they will make the wrong decision. Don't let your clients look at this as too time consuming. It will take a little time to learn the technique, but they end up with a clear method for solving intricate problems. A clear process, like the DIG UP technique, forces a quick and reasonable decision that everyone can abide by. It also provides consistency in management techniques; if your client always follows this acronym, they will never miss a step in solving problems efficiently. It works wonders for people, increasing their ability to lead in profound ways.

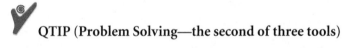

QTIP (Problem Solving—the second of three tools)

The chara is the key to this tool. The cotton swab (Q-tip) that you can purchase at your local pharmacy is all you need. Always keep a few in your briefcase. QTIP stands for "quit taking it personally." Q-tips are an effective reminder anytime your client starts taking things personally.

When you take things personally, it creates obstacles to communication. This is the most important skill you can learn in business. Remind your client to keep the Q-tip on their desk. The message it sends: Stop thinking with your feelings.

STORIES FROM THE SUMMIT

Alexa is a district manager at a Fortune 100 company. She is emotional, to say the least. She thinks with her feelings on every level. I said to her one day, "I don't care about your feelings." She sat back in her chair in disbelief. I continued: "I care about you, but I do not care about your feelings. Your feelings are related to things that happened a long time ago, some association you've made, or an emotion you experienced last weekend. Perhaps your feelings are related to what you had for lunch today. Your feelings are not what you are thinking about on this issue." That simple lesson paved the way for tremendous progress, and opened up Alex's career path to the top.

We have applied this technique with most of our clients. Almost everyone can relate to it. Ninety percent of arguments are based on emotions. Negative emotions should not be part of business life. Now that's a whole lot easier to say than it is to live by. It takes conscious practice, lots of it, but your clients need to do it. Not taking things personally can go a long way toward making your clients stronger managers and motivators.

Your client will argue: "Look, they're saying these things *to* me, *about* me and I'm not supposed to get angry?" Your client should understand this: Most of the time, this has nothing to do with them *as a person*. They just happen to be there at the right place, at the right time, to catch the abuse.

Tell your client: Whenever you hold a Q-tip from this day forward, you will see it differently. Faced with someone who is upset, when you find your negative emotions starting to drive your actions, think of the Q-tip. Your customer has had a very bad day. You are the first person to see them after some disaster has occurred. QTIP will help you stay in the moment and not take things personally.

Use the Q-tip when your teammates are fussing and fuming. A service rep comes in ranting about a problem with a delivery. Guess what? It's not about you. They have just been yelled at, screamed at, barraged by their customer. Whatever they may say, they are not mad at you, even if the ranting is directed at you.

We have taught this concept for years, and it's proven to be very effective. We just went back to a hospital and encountered a nurse we taught this concept to a year earlier. She pulled a Q-tip out of her pocket and waved to us: "I still have my Q-tip."

Everyone is responsible for their own behavior. Everyone can control their behavior by not taking things personally.

Separate the Person from the Issue
(Problem Solving—the third of three tools)

When problems come up, people can go after each other to the point they forget what the original problem was. The issue, not personalities, should always be the center of a business discussion. Repeatedly, as a coach, you will help your clients deal with employee issues. When your client leads a group in discussing an issue, it's pretty easy to get tangled up in people and forget to work on the issue at all. When your client develops the skill of separating the issue from the person, they'll go from playing defense to playing offense. A flip chart is a very good tool to create focus.

STORIES FROM THE SUMMIT

> *Cody is a CEO of a company of 70 employees. He is a hard-driving leader. When his team "butts heads," he has to get past their feelings and find answers they are searching for. One of the biggest assets in his working environment has been a flip chart. In meetings, the flip chart changes the focus from the people in the room to what they see and share: defining and diagnosing problems. His working environment has totally changed just because of that flip chart.*

The chara we recommend is a desktop flip chart that can be purchased at an office supply store. Using a flip chart is a habit your clients should develop to remind everyone that it is not about the person, it is about the issue. The flip chart will help them get there.

It is often human nature to emote first and sort second. What does it mean to separate the person from the issue? Here's an example you may wish to share with your client:

Dan, our client, has to confront two employees for not getting a paint job done on time. Dan is nonconfrontational. He hates to make waves. His choices might be: (1) Let things slide, and see when the project will be finished; or (2) step out of character and yell at his employees to get the job done.

Letting people slide does not work. They'll do what's demanded of them—that's all. The autocratic, over-forceful style? Employees become defensive and usually choose to "slack off" even more.

Here is what we recommend: Separate the person from the issue. Talk about the matter at hand.

DAN'S QUESTION TO EMPLOYEES: "What is your schedule for this paint job?"

PAINTERS: "We are supposed to have it done already, but we have run into . . . . etc., etc."

DAN: "Let's review what needs to be completed. How many days will it take you to finish the lobby?"

PAINTERS: "Onc day."

DAN: "The storage areas?"

PAINTERS: "Two days."

DAN: "So, what you are saying is, in three days this should be completed?"

PAINTERS: "Yep."

DAN: "Since this is Tuesday, you can have the entire project completed by Friday."

PAINTERS: *"No problem."*

In this scenario, nothing personal is exchanged. No negative emotions come to the surface. Nobody gets defensive, because conversation stays focused on the issue. The scenario does not get complicated. Dan was very clear with his pursuit of the issue, and the painters are equally clear with their answers.

Your client is looking for a behavior change. Separating the person from the issue allows people to let their guard down and work together. Even if you have to dig deep, find the issue and separate it from the person sharing the issue with you.

This takes practice. Work with your client on specific situations they are dealing with and have them separate the person from the issue.

That's the end of the Problem-Solving path. If you are working with a client, you can move to Chapter 9 and continue the Sherpa process. Otherwise, read on to learn more.

COMMUNICATION—PATH 2 OF 5, THE RELATIONAL ROUTE

Some of the questions that may have led you to select this path:

- Does your client get their message across?
- Does your client know how important it is to communicate effectively?
- Does your client work well with others?

The tools you may want to offer:

- Assessment
- COMMUNICATION Acronym
- Listen, Think, Then Communicate

To begin with, your role as a coach mandates special rules about the way you work. Coaches create an environment that allows focus. In most cases, you will meet your client at a public place. Choose carefully. Think about whether this location is conducive to your relationship with this particular client. Be centered. Prior to a meeting, arrange enough time to wind down your own thoughts, so you can be attentive to the needs of your client. This can mean arriving ten minutes early to your meeting site.

WHEN YOU ASK YOUR CLIENT A QUESTION, WAIT FOR THE ANSWER. Uncomfortable with silence, they will start talking to fill the space, and get practice in stepping out and saying what's on their mind.

BE CAREFUL WHEN SHARING AN UNINVITED OPINION. Mirror the thoughts of your client. Repeat their words out loud, and then stay quiet.

USE SHORT WORDS AND PHRASES. Examples include "Stop," "So what?", and "What does that mean, exactly?" Challenging, short phrases are magic! They force your client to immediately reflect on what they are saying. Know your client; don't use these challenging phrases without first establishing trust.

YOUR CLIENT MAY RAMBLE. If they go off on a tangent, use words or effective body language such as a stop signal with your hand. Every client will need to vent, but the coach must use expert judgment on the health of the conversation, reflecting the Sherpa Stance and how to achieve the goals for that meeting. The coach will be vigilant about redirecting the conversation to focus on business matters.

POUND THE ISSUE. Your client will always be more comfortable sharing how they feel rather than how they think. Keep an issue on the table. Repeat it. Draw a picture of it. Redirect irrelevant conversation.

COMMUNICATION IS YOUR CONNECTION. Be brilliant.

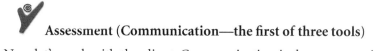

Assessment (Communication—the first of three tools)

Now let's work with the client. Communication is the most consistent challenge for our clients, personally and professionally. Those who think they are great communicators will find it difficult to name a weakness in this wide-ranging aspect of human behavior. This is a very broad area of focus that must be narrowed to specifics.

Begin with our quiz on communication (client Journal page 4-2). This helps clients find specific room for improvement in communication skills. This quiz can be given on paper or verbally. It's designed to guide a conversation, so a discussion of each answer is best as soon as the answer is given. It's pretty easy for your client to choose the best answer, even if it doesn't accurately describe their behavior. Emphasize that truthful answers will ensure that your client takes advantage of the room for improvement they and everyone else have.

1. When conversing with others,

    ___ a. I usually do most of the talking.

    ___ b. I usually let the other person do most of the talking.

    ___ c. I try to equalize my participation in the conversation.

BEST ANSWER: **c.**   Conversations should be a balanced two-way flow of dialogue. Sometimes clients simply don't realize that they do all the talking. More information on this issue can be found in the "Listen, Think, Then Communicate" section of this chapter.

2. While conversing,

___ a.   I hold my head still at all times.
___ b.   I nod my head at appropriate times.
___ c.   I nod my head constantly.

BEST ANSWER: **b.**   When you nod, you are communicating that you've received someone's point and are still listening. You're responding appropriately to what they say. You can work on body language if this is an issue.

3. When I first meet someone,

___ a.   I wait for the other person to make the introduction first.
___ b.   I introduce myself with a smile and offer a handshake.
___ c.   I usually hug the person.

BEST ANSWER: **b.**   It's a positive, rapport-building move to initiate the introduction with a handshake and smile. This will bring on discussions of networking and comfort with people they do not know. If this is an issue, refer to the Image and Presence path, in the organizational routes, Chapter 8.

4. While listening to other people talk,

___ a.   I tend to be distracted.
___ b.   I listen for meaning and ask questions.
___ c.   I watch the person speak, but often don't hear everything.

BEST ANSWER: **b.**   If you're a good listener, you keep mentally busy searching for meaning in the message, and you ask questions. We all experience emotional deafness on occasion. If you get easily distracted, try taking notes. More discussion and a further assessment can be found in the Listening path.

5. In a brief business conversation,

___a.   I often stand while talking to a person who is sitting.
___b.   I often sit while talking to a person who is standing.

_____c.   I follow the lead of the person I am speaking with, and do as they do.

BEST ANSWER: **c.**   Communicating at eye level helps build rapport. So, if the person is sitting and a chair is available, take a seat! When you walk into a colleague's or a superior's office, ask if you can sit down. Even better, wait for an invitation to sit.

6. As a general rule,

_____ a.   I tend to be serious and don't smile often while conversing.

_____ b.   I smile all the time while conversing.

_____ c.   I smile at appropriate times while conversing.

BEST ANSWER: **c.**   Smiling when greeting people and at appropriate times builds rapport. Don't smile all the time, or at inappropriate times. Know that when you smile, you're communicating in a very special way.

7. In conversation with someone I don't know well,

_____ a.   I usually make eye contact.

_____ b.   I sometimes make eye contact.

_____ c.   I never make eye contact.

BEST ANSWER: **a.**   Eye contact is important for building bonds. It gives the impression you're interested and engaged in the conversation, and you have self-confidence. Eye contact should be broken periodically to avoid the appearance of staring.

8. When I cross my leg in a seated conversation,

_____ a.   I cross my leg facing the speaker.

_____ b.   I cross my leg away from the speaker.

_____ c.   I bob my foot.

BEST ANSWER: **a.**   For homework, create a spreadsheet and have your client record the way they and other people use body language. There's more on this topic later in this chapter.

9. In normal conversation, face to face,

_____ a.   I stand less than two feet away from the person.

_____ b.   I stand two to three feet away.

_____ c.   I stand four or more feet away.

BEST ANSWER: **b.**   Arm's length is the appropriate distance (two to three feet). Standing closer makes the other person feel uncomfortable (or threatened). Standing further creates emotional distance. You can help clients understand personal space by having them walk toward you and noting when it's comfortable for them to stop and talk. Have them note whether there are people in their life who invade their personal space.

10. In business meetings and gatherings,

____ a.   I make an effort to remember and use people's names.

____ b.   I don't pay attention to names as I tend to forget them.

____ c.   I only learn the names of important people.

BEST ANSWER: **a.**   It's wise to call people by name whenever possible. It makes a good, lasting impression, and it makes the other person feel important. When someone tells you his or her name, immediately use it several times in the conversation.

11. To end a conversation,

____ a.   I often just cut it off, say thanks, and leave.

____ b.   I begin to look impatient, hoping the person will get the hint.

____ c.   I wrap up with a closing statement.

BEST ANSWER: **c.**   Closing summaries confirm you and your listener are on the same page. Summaries allow you to validate, verify, and prove that you are an effective communicator.

12 . When I'm listening,

____ a.   I often cross my arms over my chest.

____ b.   I often lean back and relax.

____ c.   I often lean slightly forward and face my body toward the speaker.

BEST ANSWER: **c.**   Leaning slightly forward and facing the speaker shows you're interested. Sitting with your arms crossed over your chest sends a defensive message. Leaning back or turning your body away from the speaker gives the message that you are bored, uninterested, or feel in charge.

146

13. When I have a negative opinion or comment,

    ____ a. I just come out with it.

    ____ b. I lead in with a positive comment first.

    ____ c. I say nothing, to avoid appearing disagreeable.

BEST ANSWER: **b.** It's best to say something positive first and then express a negative opinion or comment in a tactful way. How important is it for your client to be positive? It depends on how many people work for them and how they connect with people. This question might reveal whether your client is intimidating, impatient, or even being manipulated.

14. When dealing with team members at work,

    ____ a. I usually warm up conversations with small talk.

    ____ b. I usually avoid small talk and get to the point.

    ____ c. I usually avoid starting conversations.

BEST ANSWER: **a.** It's good to initiate conversations with small talk. Topics to warm up the conversation might include a chat about the weather, news of interest, or impressions about the current activity. How good is your client at small talk? Does your client need it to get further in their job? Role-plays might help this area if they are uncomfortable making small talk.

If you don't finish this during a meeting, or you sense your client is getting restless, assign the rest of the questions as homework. You can discuss the answers next meeting. When you identify an area that needs more discussion, go for it. If you see a question that your client has no issues with, just move on. Take this as the foundation for your communication discussion. It covers a lot of areas that you might otherwise never discuss.

Communication Acronym
(Communication—the second of three tools)

Using an acronym helps your clients define the importance of communication, and improves their commitment to examine their communication skills. With this process, they can work through problems on their own.

Acronyms relay memorable concepts that are vital to reliable and effective communication. Additionally, an acronym can help your client form a complete view of a situation or circumstance. Your client's acronym will be based on a *word* the two of you choose to reinforce work on their communication weaknesses.

The chara is a bracelet or necklace with the letters your client chose for their acronym. You'll find "letter" jewelry pieces available in gift shops. This is a great way for your clients to keep their word fresh in their minds. Many clients continue to wear their bracelets long after the coaching is over.

Good communication is by far the most vital function of a successful working environment. It can also be the most neglected. If your client has trouble talking to people effectively, bring out this exercise on communication. This could take more than one meeting. You and your client will delve into the basics of communication and the key elements of effective interaction. Assigning this as homework can be a good way to begin.

In our exercise, your client will develop an acronym to help them communicate more clearly. A base word will be selected, such as TALK or MESSAGE or even COMMUNICATION. The chosen acronym should be a perfect match to your client's "issues."

Allow your client to decide what each letter stands for in the importance of communication. The exercise becomes a basis for conversation, whether you do it in a meeting or as homework. Each time your client suggests a word, discuss how the two of you can measure the client's ability in that aspect of communication.

STORIES FROM THE SUMMIT

> *Bill, the CEO of a 65-employee company, was a father of six. He loved toys, especially stuffed animals, and had at least a dozen in his office. So I used the acronym "CURIOUS GEORGE" for his communication exercise. At the end of the exercise (which took us about three meetings), I presented him with a CURIOUS GEORGE stuffed monkey. To this day, he doesn't forget his own personal acronym for communication.*

Here are some ideas based on one client's intimidation issues. He was extremely curt and unfriendly with his employees. He came up with the word "CALM" as his acronym, and related the qualities of good communication suggested by each letter to his particular challenges. This is only a short example: the choice of word should be your client's, whatever the length.

C: COMMITMENT. Interact with your staff. Make a time commitment. Listen when they tell you about their jobs. Be open to feedback. Record the amount of time you spend outside your office, walking and talking. Are you getting useful ideas and comments from your staff? Are you using them? Let your staff know when you use an idea they have suggested.

A: ASK QUESTIONS. Create a cycle of communication. Keep the feedback process going by asking questions. If you want to clarify, don't ask "yes or no" questions. You want your employees to talk to you. Don't wait for the performance appraisal to give feedback. That's going to throw some unpleasant surprises at your employees at a critical time.

L: LENGTHY. Give people details. When you're sick and tired of communicating, you probably haven't communicated enough. We've got to do that every day. Go overboard with communication. Repetition creates understanding.

M: MAKE IT POSITIVE. You know there are better and worse places to work. You have so much here and know that there is no perfect place to work. Every place has issues. Don't be the issue maker—be the issue breaker. Don't say anything you wouldn't want to hear about yourself.

The point of this exercise is to get your client thinking of what they're missing when they're communicating. If they don't acknowledge and take responsibility for their weakness in communication, you can't convince them they need to change. This exercise will help you get that ownership.

Listen, Think, Then Communicate
(Communication—the third of three tools)

The chara handed to the client when you begin explaining this tool is a Band-Aid you will prepare with a printed label on each side: "Listen, Think, Then Communicate" on one side and "Open in case of emergency" on the other.

Well-reasoned words are the most effective. Here's another key to successful relationships and conversations, especially in times of stress. When you catch your client trying to defend themselves, time after time, share the Listen, Think, then Communicate exercise with them. What does that mean? It's a three-step process that reminds your client to control what they say and retain a leadership position by setting an example. Here's the way we teach this to our clients:

LISTEN: *Listening is defined in the dictionary as the conscious effort to hear. Listening is a skill. Listening takes practice. Listening takes effort. To really hear what people say to you, listen to their words. Give them your full attention. Connect with them. Look at their body language; listen to their tone of their voice.*

THINK: *Thinking is judgment. Your natural tendency is to respond to what people say right away. Don't. Take the time to think through what the person is trying to say. Remember, if you are consciously hearing, you haven't planned your response while someone is still talking. Give yourself time to process the things you are hearing.*

Have you ever thought to yourself: "That didn't come out right. I should not have said that. I put way too much emotion behind those words." We all have. Once words leave your mouth, you can't take them back. You can be sorry. You can offer further explanation, but you can't take words back.

Thinking allows you to communicate with confidence and purpose. Reflect. Make sure this becomes a habit.

COMMUNICATE: *Communication is everyone's responsibility. Don't expect that the person you're talking to will pay the same amount of attention as you do. The important thing is for you to hold up your end of business communication. First, clarify that what you heard is what they meant. Then deliver a clear and well-reasoned response. Repetition is important. It will clarify your message.*

With certain clients, we have spent an entire meeting just on the concept of "reflecting" and "taking time" before communicating, the thinking part of this three-step process. If your client speaks too quickly, without thinking through issues and situations, complete this discussion with the band aid you've prepared in advance. That should serve as a reminder of this lesson.

When your clients get into the habit of Listen, Think, then Communicate, the dynamics of their conversations change. Impulsive words disappear, and clients start to engage in "phrase mapping." They have the ability to change part of sentence in midstream, to deliver a message they *should* deliver instead of the message they "feel" like delivering.

STORIES FROM THE SUMMIT

Amy is a senior manager at a paper converting facility. She tends to say exactly what she thinks. After Amy learned "Listen, Think, Communicate," she started phrase mapping, changing a sentence in midstream to create more positive communication. She came to a coaching session with this story: "I was in the middle of a controversy with my maintenance supervisor. He said he had to leave, and couldn't get back until after second shift to repair a motor. I said 'You'd better . . .' Then, I stopped in midsentence, thought about it, and continued 'You'd better know how much I appreciate you, and all you do around here.' Jerry responded by putting out his hand and thanking me for saying that. He hadn't heard a compliment in a long time. Of course, I was going to say, 'You'd better not leave here till you get it done.' That would have made things worse, not better. That proved it to me. Thinking about my words and phrase mapping was making a difference."

That's the end of the Communication path. If you are working with a client, you can move to Chapter 9 and continue the Sherpa process. Otherwise, read on to learn more.

LISTENING—PATH 3 OF 5, THE RELATIONAL ROUTE

Every Sherpa client should understand: The fact that they don't talk *too much* doesn't prove they're a good listener. Your client must "tune in" to the words that are said, and to messages that are delivered without words.

Some of the questions that may have led you to this path:

- Can my client read body language well?
- Does my client really hear their staff, boss, and peers?
- Does my client know when to stop talking?

The exercises you may use to help your client:

- Assessment
- Body Language
- Silence
- Three-Sentence Rule

From the Sherpa's point of view, listening carefully deepens the relationship between coach and client. Listening carefully, and knowing a great deal about the client, enables the Sherpa to hold clients accountable for the things they say, for their goals, and for their actions.

Assessment (Listening—the first of four tools)

Listening is something very few people do well, yet it's vitally important. People are screaming to be heard. As a result, a good listener gets immense respect. Listening requires our full attention. It is very hard. When we fail to work at it, we miss important opportunities. It's the other side of communication, but listening has its own path because it's so important, and a problem for so many clients.

Your client has to think about listening constantly. The reminder chara here is a sponge. A small sponge that fits in the palm of the hand is perfect. Hand your client their gift, and ask them to become a sponge with their staff and peers, paying attention to every nuance of their conversations.

Let's review your client's listening skills, with the assessment in their Journal on page 4-3. It's the same assessment you took, as a coach, in the early chapters of this guide.

Giving this assessment for homework allows your client time to think about their answers. When you look over the completed assessment, review the low scores, areas of weakness in listening. Listening is tricky. You will want to assign independent study, research, and reading if your client is a poor listener. Here are some basics you may share with your client:

- Being a good listener takes practice.
- With practice, good listening becomes a habit.
- Commit yourself to being a good listener, picture yourself as a good listener, and you will be.

Until you get to that point, you'll need to remember techniques, and act like you are listening well. Will people believe you? Yes . . . people believe what you show them. If you're striving for something, act like the person you want to be, and people will buy in to you and your goal. Picture yourself listening well, and you'll be a good listener.

A study was done recently with 40 high school basketball players. Twenty of the students practiced daily and played their games every week, as they always did. The other 20 were asked, whenever they sat on the bench, to mentally play through the games and practices they were watching, to picture themselves playing basketball. The 20 who were asked to visualize while they sat on the bench also carried around a basketball all day during school, carried it at home, even going to sleep with it. Who do you think played a better game by the end of the study? It just makes sense: the 20 who visualized and mentally played basketball around the clock.

Practice. Concentrate on your listening skills. Visualize yourself listening as you consider an upcoming conversation. That helps create habits. Make yourself better by thinking about being better. Be a sponge; soak up what people tell you. Give your client his chara, the sponge, as you go over this. It's a great reminder of their need to "soak up" what people are saying.

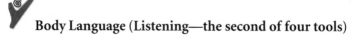

Body Language (Listening—the second of four tools)

Sherpa, you will know if your clients have body language issues. How do they sit while talking with you? Are they looking at you? Does someone walking by easily distract them? Are they clearly interested in what you are saying? By this point, you know your client well, and know if there are issues in this area. Review these concepts with your client, and practice them during your meetings, too:

MAKE EYE CONTACT. Look the speaker in the eye. An actor friend of mine told me this: Even if you don't want to look someone right in the eyes, you can make the right impression. Look at the bridge of their nose, between their eyebrows. Then you don't get so nervous. Always look when you listen; people really appreciate it.

TALK FACE TO FACE. At work, ask yourself how you are going to set up your office or your work area to make conversation open and straightforward. Avoid putting a desk between you and the person you want to communicate with. Make sure there are no obstacles in your view.

DON'T LOOK AROUND. When you are listening to someone, give them your undivided attention. Don't let your eyes wander. Avoid distractions–keep your hands still and keep them empty. Focus your mind on the person who is speaking and make sure they know they have your undivided attention.

Stay focused. Don't look like you have something to say, and don't interrupt. Don't you hate it when you talk to someone and you know they want to interrupt you? Give the speaker your full attention and don't say a word until they're done.

LEAN INTO THE SPEAKER. Don't look bored. Appearing bored shows disrespect. If you catch yourself not listening, change positions. Lean into the speaker slightly to show interest.

DON'T CROSS YOUR ARMS OR LEGS. When you cross your arms or legs, you are giving off a very strong message. It makes the person on the receiving end feel you are defensive, even angry, or that you're shutting yourself off from them.

NOD YOUR HEAD SLIGHTLY AS EACH POINT IS MADE. When you nod, you are communicating that you've received their point and are listening. You're responding appropriately to what they're saying. As they finish a point, agree with your body language. Nod slightly.

AVOID MIXED MESSAGES. Don't let your body say something different than your words. Give clear signals. Match your body language with your words.

SMILE. Smiling is like nodding your head. Don't smile at inappropriate times. Know that when you smile, you're truly communicating and the speaker knows you are listening.

 ## STORIES FROM THE SUMMIT

Myles is interviewing for a job that I am helping a client fill. He didn't make eye contact. Now, I know my client well, and he would hate this type of behavior. I almost wrote Myles off. But I didn't, and Myles came up with the best answers of any of the candidates. Asked about motivating his people, he said: "I'd make sure they understood why it mattered to them personally."

At one point Myles asked, "Why has it taken two years for me to get a job?" I shared my initial impression about his lack of eye contact, and told him that lots of people can't deal with that. Myles protested: "Well, I have bifocals, well I have..." I stopped him: "Myles, none of that matters. This is an interview. You are responsible for connecting to me and with me. You can't do that unless you look at me." Myles said as he was leaving: "You know, I want to thank you for being honest. You've given me something to work on."

Body language makes up most of the communication you share with someone. Examine this with your client. The following exercise will help you show them how easily their body says things they want to say. It is very simple exercise that stimulates discussion.

Use the worksheet in your client's Journal page 4-4. You, as the coach, will observe your client and evaluate their body language. For your first conversation, bring up a simple topic about the weather or innocuous current events. Rate them, based on the scoring system from the journal. Stop and discuss what you have seen. Then repeat the exercise. This time, bring up one of your client's most difficult employees or a tough situation you know about. Record their body language for this second conversation; note and discuss the differences. You might even go as far as video recording your client, so they can see what others see.

Silence (Listening—the third of four tools)

For tragic personal reasons, poet Maya Angelou lived in self-imposed silence for four years. During this period in her childhood, she was a voracious reader, memorizing Shakespeare and reveling in great literature. Had she lived differently, she might never have had so much inside her to share with the world. We advocate self-imposed silence to our clients for the same reason, but of course not nearly to such lengths.

The chara, your client's gift, is a book of Maya Angelou's poems to which they can refer anytime.

Silence is an important technique that should be used more often than words. Some of the strongest managers you will coach have not mastered the art of silence and the power of using words at strategic times.

These guidelines could change the way your client listens:

1. Present your idea, thought, or information completely, and then close your mouth. In a team discussion, let the other team members speak. Wait for someone to ask your opinion.

2. While a discussion is taking place, use all your senses and skills. Watch for body language, inflection, and opportunities to have valuable verbal input.

If your client has trouble staying quiet, they may need to examine their motive for talking. Here's a homework assignment that might challenge them:

Practice being silent. Listen carefully. Using a notes page in your journal, record your conversations at work, as soon after the fact as you can.

Record your cravings to talk. Record how you handled those urges. Think about why it matters or whether it matters that you speak. Note your feelings about this, and any realizations you've made.

As a coach, you'll find that being blunt gets a point across. We'd even recommend, in certain situations, telling a client to just "shut up." Now in no way are we trying to be rude. You have a relationship with your client by now. When you suggest to them that the best solution to this problem is to shut up, you may be surprised at how well they accept this idea. This is an effective way to make your client aware that speaking is not always the solution. Saying "shut up" might bother some coaches. We have not found another phrase that is quite as effective, at least in the U.S. Be gentle. Use this advice carefully. Know your client and be prepared for amazing results.

This can also be a valuable lesson for you, Sherpa. Examine your need to talk during your coaching meetings and journal for yourself. What were the ramifications of your speaking at a given moment? What happened as a result? What might have been the benefit had you been silent?

STORIES FROM THE SUMMIT

Sherry is a brilliant woman. When she was first hired, she was a superstar. She got bonuses and a promotion within her first year of employment. Five years later, her future has flatlined. Still, Sherry takes managing others seriously. She works hard at learning her craft. She's driven in other ways, too: She is the first one to speak, the first to volunteer, the first to confront, the first to protect, the first to fix. She feels this is necessary to be a valued employee.

The problem: Her colleagues dislike her. They are intimidated by her knowledge, frustrated by her aggressive behavior. They no longer notice the good work she performs. Her Sherpa recommended that she practice being quiet, and make a return visit to Weakness Mountain: observe, change, and evaluate. After many, many sessions, Sherry discovered her motive had been to gain recognition. The more she tried, though, the more she pushed people away.

Silence was the only way to reverse this scenario, and silence worked for Sherry.

Silence is a wonderful listening tool. It lets you truly give your attention to someone. You show you are listening with your eyes, your gestures, and your silence.

Let's go back to the basics. The definition of listening is "a conscious effort to hear." That won't work when you are preoccupied, with your attention drawn in more than one direction. Any time you have a conversation, you are pulled between listening and deciding what to say next. When you make a conscious effort, you will decide when to talk and when to be quiet. Most people experience some discomfort with quiet spaces in a conversation. It's very tough for most of us to be silent. Most people will say anything to fill up those quiet spaces.

People get nervous because they don't know what will happen next, and they don't know when it's going to happen. Use this to your advantage, to get information when you need it. You're talking with an employee who is upset. Keep in mind that they need to vent, to be heard. Give them a chance to do just that. Participate in the conversation, of course, but once you have said your piece, be quiet. Do whatever you have to do in order to be quiet. Close your eyes, bite your tongue, and remember the old adage: "Once you have said what you have to say, be quiet. The first person who talks . . . loses."

Some people get their energy from listening to themselves talk. We've had clients who literally can't stop talking. They have never given silence a try. If your client finds silence difficult, have them write about it in their journal. Why is it so difficult? Why the desperate need to hear themselves talk? This often has to do with intelligence. Your client may be so smart that their mind feels like a dam, holding back a flood. They have an unending amount of information to pass on.

Your client should review the weakness exercise and examine exactly how their weakness comes into play: talking too much, talking about useless things, and interrupting. Acknowledging their weakness in the area of silence is the first step to overcoming it. Silence can also simply mean responding without overwhelming the listener with words.

Here is an example of using silence in an awkward conversation:

JOHN (SUPERVISOR): "Mary, can you work this weekend?"

MARY: "(agitated) What? Work this weekend? They told me when I was hired I wouldn't have to work weekends. They said that working weekends was rare . . . and . . . it just shouldn't happen. (calmer now) I don't want to work this weekend. I can't believe you asked me."

JOHN: "I asked you."

MARY: "(almost subdued) Why ask ME to work this weekend? What about Linda and Susan, did you ask them? . . . No, of course not. Ask Mary, Mary never says no. Well, this time I am saying no. (still calm) No. (pause) NO."

JOHN: "Mary, do you have a problem working this weekend? Some family commitments?"

MARY: "Yes, I promised my cousin to help her move to a new apartment."

JOHN: "Mary, thank you for telling me that. Any chance you could work around that?"

MARY: "Yes, John. I think I can, I will be here."

Every time your employee talks without encountering resistance, the calmer they get, as long as they know you are listening. Let them vent. Sometimes they just need to be heard. If they haven't solved the problem themselves by the time they've finished speaking, it's time to sort out the details.

Silence defused this situation. Your staff is going to follow your lead when they know you're listening and trying to understand. Silence is golden. Your client may feel compelled to talk, at times. Maya Angelou's life proves that when we stop talking, our life doesn't stop. It usually gets better.

 **Three-Sentence Rule (Listening—fourth of four tools)**

Simply stated, this rule requires that your client speak in three-sentence increments. The first sentence in the sequence is the introduction: the big-picture idea. The second is the theme: the specific thought you'd like to get across. The third is a question. Here is an example:

"I have a new dog at home. I'm taking him to obedience training tonight. Is it a problem if I leave a few minutes early?"

The chara for this tool is a pyramid, representing the three rules: introduction, theme, and question. Any desk decoration in this shape will work.

Your clients need to involve the people they talk to. It seems like a simple thing to do, but tends to be the most difficult for clients who have a tendency to go into too much detail or like to hear themselves talk.

The purpose of the three-sentence rule is to force your client to stop talking and connect with the person they're speaking with. When they stop talking and ask a question, they create an opportunity to connect. The three-sentence rule helps in meetings and in presentations as well. Your client stops, looks around, checks the body language, and becomes aware of who is listening and who is not.

The most amazing part of this concept is that it can be used for a variety of issues your client is dealing with. If they are detail oriented, this stops them from going on and on with people who are not interested. If your client never stops talking, this forces them to stop and listen. If your client is passionate, this forces them to be less intimidating by allowing someone else into the conversation. And finally, if your client is too quiet, this forces them to communicate the entire thought without giving up and giving in. It is a concept we teach most of our clients, whatever their main issue might be.

 ## STORIES FROM THE SUMMIT

Paul, a dynamic sales executive, has been working on talking less for some time now. He really wants to succeed with it, and I've given Paul the three-sentence rule in our previous meeting.

Here is the email he sent me: "Just have to tell you, this one-sentence speaking is quite boring. I did not have a lot of conversation on Saturday."

> *I wrote back: "Paul, it's not one sentence—you are allowed three sentences in a row . . . Aren't I nice?"*
>
> *Paul's reply: "Three! I thought it was just one. You owe me two sentences now, so I'm going with five sentences tomorrow. Now maybe my neighbors will stop looking at me funny. Thanks. Paul."*

Here's a more specific application of the three-sentence rule:

1. FIRST SENTENCE. We call this the INTRO. Grab your audience. Make sure they know that what you are about to say is important. Get their attention. This is called the "effective introduction."

- "I think this project will make you more valuable to the company."
- "Your opinion on this is make or break for me."

2. SECOND SENTENCE. We call this the THEME. State the goal. Validate what you just said with some data, facts, or important information. Make it simple and straightforward.

- "The design process is straightforward and by completing it by yourself, you will be adding value to everything else you do."
- "We are looking to revamp the customer service program, with you in the lead."

3. ASK A QUESTION AND THEN STOP. Wait as long as you have to for a response.

- "How do you see us proceeding?"
- "What do you think?"

Then stop, and do not proceed until you have heard a response from the person you are communicating with. The reality is, almost everyone can benefit from using this technique. People have to be taught to stop and think about how they are communicating. Don't be afraid to tell your client that this technique takes work and time to perfect. It has fundamentally changed the life of more than one client. The pyramid chara reinforces the three-sentence rule: Intro, Theme, Question.

STORIES FROM THE SUMMIT

Frank is a plant manager who sometimes struggles to get his point across. He is using the three-sentence rule to get to his point. He needed to really practice this concept. We worked on role-plays together. He wanted to ask his boss to extend our work together for another six weeks, and came up with this:

1. *Boss, I have had amazing successes working with my coach. (introduction)*
2. *She has helped me with empowerment, problem solving, and effective management techniques. (theme, state the goal, or in this case, progress toward the goal)*
3. *Are you okay with renewing the contract for another six weeks? (question)*

Frank fulfilled his boss' need to know in a minimum number of words and then asked his question directly and succinctly. It worked.

That's the end of the Listening path. If you are working with a client, you can move to Chapter 9 and continue the Sherpa process. Otherwise, read on to learn more.

NONPRODUCTIVE BEHAVIOR—PATH 4 OF 5, THE RELATIONAL ROUTE

You know you are dealing with unproductive behavior when your client's leadership brings to mind Einstein's definition of insanity: "Doing the same thing over and over again, expecting different results."

There will be days that are not as productive as others, but what do you do when those days multiply into something more than a passing phase? The answer depends on the causes of unproductive behavior, and whether the behavior is that of your client or of their subordinates.

Some of the questions that may have led you to this path:

- Does your client feel "surrounded by incompetence"?
- Is your client too involved in details?

- Does your client have to be in charge of everything?
- Does the word "manipulation" come into conversations? (either being manipulated by or manipulating others)

There are three tools to the Nonproductive Behavior path:

1. The DAPPER technique
2. Anger Management
   - Assessment
   - Evaluation
   - Simple Questions
3. Intimidation
   - Busy Feet
   - Delete "want" and "need."
   - "I am right but I am wrong."
   - Intimidation Through Passion

Nonproductive behavior is sometimes hard to detect. An employee *satisfaction* survey won't uncover it, as long as people are happy working at less than their full potential. An employee *attitude* survey is more likely to point out this kind of problem.

Questions to ask about nonproductive behavior:

- Are we complacent as a company?
- Have we stalled in the continuous improvement of our company and its people?
- Are we running around in circles with little success?
- Do our employees avoid change?
- Are we fighting fires every day? The same fires? If you are dealing with the same problems now that you had a year ago, you're in a nonproductive environment.
- Are some people seemingly angry all the time? Am I angry all the time?
- Is your client being taken for a ride by their employees?

Dealing with nonproductive behavior can be a huge stumbling block for any executive. They cannot get their employees to pull their weight. They have trouble getting buy-in and commitment. Ask yourself some questions:

- Is your client able to identify their nonproductive people?
- Is your client nonproductive?
- What does your client do when confronted with nonproductive behavior?
- Does your client add to the problem in any way?

Your client cannot run away. Ignoring a situation usually makes it worse. With the techniques that follow, they can create profound change faster than they believe possible.

What kinds of things can lead to nonproductive behavior? Here are four key factors:

1. UNCLEAR EXPECTATIONS. Your client must be able to execute each component of the Sherpa Expectations Mountain: communication, commitment, consequences, and coaching (Journal page 3-2). Missing a step may lead to a level of frustration that creates unproductive behavior.

2. AN ATMOSPHERE OF NONPRODUCTIVITY. If your client does not develop a nonproductive employee, that employee will limit the success of the productive team. The lowest common denominator becomes corporate culture. For anyone to be productive, everyone has to carry their own weight.

 STORIES FROM THE SUMMIT

In an example one Sherpa client shared, her team was given an assignment and a time frame in which to show results. Everyone had been assigned a role. Gary did not like the project, so he avoided it by extending his lunch breaks to the allowable maximum.

As Jill told it, she attempted to complete Gary's unfinished work. Upset with his behavior, she screamed orders at her colleagues in a vain attempt

> *to "rally the troops." Needless to say, the work was not finished on time, and morale collapsed. One person's nonproductive behavior affected the entire project.*

3. LACK OF STRUCTURED TIME MANAGEMENT. Successful leaders will manage their own time, and define their team's time frame. When employees are not provided with a time framework in which to work, they often flounder and become nonproductive; which refers us back to Expectations Mountain.

4. EXAGGERATED FORMS OF MANAGEMENT, BOTH MICRO AND MACRO. Your client needs to be aware of their personal management style and evaluate whether it is the kind of leadership that works for the team. For clients unable to assess themselves, refer to the Leadership path in Chapter 8 for some exercises and development materials.

The first technique we'll share is the use of the acronym DAPPER. It will help to handle any nonproductive behavior.

DAPPER (Nonproductive Behavior—the first of three tools)

Often, executives hesitate to address nonproductive behavior because it involves confrontation. Some executives will do anything they can to avoid that. This tool offers your client a clear method for dealing with reprimands or confrontation.

STORIES FROM THE SUMMIT

> *Mary, a brilliant manager, was afraid of confrontation. She stated she was so afraid that if she saw someone she had to reprimand, she would duck into the nearest office. She did not want to be caught unprepared to deal with such a situation. She used the DAPPER technique with great success, and it boosted her confidence. This method helped her deal effectively with discipline and correction.*

Sherpa, sit back and review this with your client. It could make them look at their life quite differently. The process will take the focus off the employee and direct it to the behavior itself. It removes emotion from the discussion.

What does DAPPER mean? Webster's definition is, "neat and trim in appearance, stylish." Stylish and classy—that's how we want our client to act when it comes to dealing with nonproductive behavior. Ask them to go to page 4-5 in their Journal. Then share the following, as your client takes notes.

D STANDS FOR DON'T FIGHT IT. DON'T IGNORE IT.   Never argue with an employee, no matter how profoundly wrong you think they are. You're the boss. You can't start fights; you are supposed to stop them. Handle everything gracefully, and don't reprimand employees in front of anyone. When you have a potential conflict or a difference of opinion, use your energy to coach and to mentor.

Never let a problem go by failing to deal with it. There are some people who put off difficult situations. Our recommendation is "just do it." It is amazing how the mind can make an issue seem bigger than it actually is. Create a simple mantra for yourself, "Let's get this done," and then act on that phrase.

A STANDS FOR APPOINTMENT.   Dealing with someone who's caused a problem might unleash negative emotions. When people are pressured or angry, they're seldom in control of what they say. You are responsible for creating win-win situations in your workplace. If it's possible, tell your employee that you would like to meet with them on break, or ten minutes from now. Setting an appointment allows you time to prepare an effective strategy for dealing with the situation, and it allows the person in error to think about what they've done and to cool down.

THE FIRST *P* STANDS FOR POSITIVE.   Sometimes you have to correct people, keep them on track. When you're reprimanding an employee, use the "*sandwich*" technique. This means sandwiching your reprimand with praise. Think of two things that the employee in question does well, like getting to work on time or being a hard worker. The reprimand should be placed in-between these two points of praise.

For example: "Nora, you know, I can set my clock by you in the morning. I appreciate you getting in and getting things set up every day. But I've noticed you're taking a little too much time on your breaks, and that causes problems for me. We have a lot to do, and barely enough time to get it all done, so I need your help with this. You know, some of the new people really look up to you. I'm going to trust you to set a good example."

Nora knows now that you dislike her *behavior,* not her as a person. I've proven that I notice good things about Nora, and I've given her a good reason to improve, because I trust her.

THE SECOND *P* STANDS FOR *"PERHAPS YOU DIDN'T KNOW."* Use this phrase if you think it might help an employee save face, especially if you think they might not be aware their actions are off track. Most people who exhibit difficult behaviors don't even know they are being difficult. They may have been told a hundred times by people around them, but they never get it. It just doesn't sink in. "Perhaps you didn't know" gracefully lets you get your point across.

E STANDS FOR EXAMPLE. When you're solving a nonproductive "people problem," be specific, and be prepared for your discussion. Know the facts. Support your statements with examples of the person's behavior you have witnessed yourself. Do not use other people to prove your point, either as bad examples or as sources of information. Hard as it may be, you have an obligation to show respect to every employee, every time. If you think a third party needs to be involved, make sure to include that person in the appointment. Don't involve anyone who was not there, EVER.

R STANDS FOR REPEAT, REPEAT, REPEAT. Your best defense working with nonproductive behavior is *no defense.* Say what you have to say, and then say it again. Repeat yourself. Make the same point in as many ways as needed to solve the situation. Summarize the situation and summarize the solution. Make sure this repetition is simply designed to handle the situation at hand. Never talk down to an employee. Don't mention any other problems, concerns, or questions. Keep your discussion on the situation at hand. Repeat as often as you see fit; then ask the employee to repeat what you have said. Make sure the employee is clear about the situation and the solution.

After you have repeated what you have to say a couple of times, use the silence technique and let them respond. Communication is much more effective if both parties agree about what is going wrong and how it can be fixed. Don't let people get you off track or put you on the defensive. Practice this concept with your client, use examples, and have them practice at work and report back to you the following week.

For supporting material on this step, you may want to refer back to the Expectations process in Chapter 6. Setting clear expectations and handling nonproductive behavior directly and appropriately are critical to your client's success.

Anger Management
(Nonproductive Behavior—the second of three tools)

Many executives have issues related to anger. This can easily make them nonproductive. When anger becomes counterproductive, the Sherpa will focus on the issue and start suggesting alternative behaviors.

Anger is often related to stress. Use a stress ball as your client's chara. Hand a stress ball to your client when you begin this discussion. It will help them stay focused in difficult situations and create better habits.

If it feels better to be happy than to be angry, why are we ever unhappy? Anger just happens, and it takes some control, some energy, to stop. Sometimes we just run with our emotions, and that's a mistake in business.

STORIES FROM THE SUMMIT

Jerry works in the world of law. He is brilliant at what he does. Jerry has no support at his work. People stay away from him. They avoid him like the plague and he has no idea why. We examine how he handles situations, problems, and projects. We come to the conclusion that if he doesn't get what he wants, he gets angry. He has for 30 years. We are not about to delve into why he gets angry. We will help him discover how unproductive it is for him to behave like that. This behavior is hurting Jerry's career.

Jerry agrees that anger is his problem. He uses two of the techniques we offer him, and sees positive changes in his working relationships. Based on better communication and trust, Jerry starts building the teamwork that's always been missing in his working life. Jerry emailed just last week and said: "I miss my Sherpa. It has been over six months, but I still remember everything you told me. Thank you for calming me down. Life is much better."

Anger is a natural emotion, and a Sherpa will discuss it openly and handle it constructively. People often get angry because there's some truth being revealed about their shortcomings or failures. Anger is often an emotional defense against vulnerability.

There are three tools we use on this path to help clients acknowledge, channel, and overcome anger in their business setting. The first is an assessment used to explore anger issues and reveal what you should work on. The second allows for introspection. It's an evaluation—answering the who, what, where, when, and why about anger. The third section involves questions you can ask, a great beginning to really dig into the work anger issue.

Anger is a reaction, a negative reaction. It is important to learn how to put anger aside, because it takes so much energy. With your help, your client *can* learn how to put their anger aside. Learning something new can be hard, but this is definitely worthwhile.

This is probably a good time to reiterate that you are not a therapist. Make sure you don't allow conversations that could be viewed as therapy. If conversation strays in that direction, redirect the dialogue with questions such as: "What happens at work?" or "How does it affect you at work?"

Anger can be rooted in past life experiences. We don't work on ancient causative factors. We change business behavior.

Remember to guide your conversations by using the Sherpa Stance:

- Is it **precise**? Are we talking about a problem, a symptom, or a feeling? Unless we are talking about a problem, we aren't ready to continue.

- Is it **personal**? If it's too personal, we don't go on.

- Is it **present** tense? Sherpas work on the future, not the past.

- Is it **possible**? Will a change in your client's behavior actually fix the problem?

This information will help you narrow down your area of focus. There's quite a bit of material available on this topic in your bookstore or library. The more you know, the better you will handle your client.

Assessment The Anger Assessment is a great way to get conversation started, especially if your client does not want to face the fact that anger is driving their behavior. Have your client turn to page 4-6 in their Sherpa client Journal and complete the series of true or false questions that make up the quiz.

1. People tell you that you need to calm down.
2. You feel tense much of the time.
3. At work, you find yourself not saying what is on your mind.
4. When you are upset, you block the world out by watching TV, reading, or sleeping.
5. You drink or use drugs almost daily to help you calm down.
6. You have trouble going to sleep.
7. You feel misunderstood or ignored much of the time.
8. People ask you not to yell or curse so much.
9. Your loved ones keep saying that you are hurting them.
10. Friends do not seek you out as much as they used to.

The numbers of "true" responses indicate:

0–2 = MANAGEABLE: You could benefit from relaxation training.

3–5 = MODERATE: You need to understand more about what stresses you, and learn stress management techniques.

6 + = OUT OF CONTROL: You could benefit from learning anger management techniques.

Your client will need to reflect, and answer honestly as each question relates to their business behavior. You should judge the honesty of their answers. To help make that happen, have your client read the questions aloud. Watch for body language and get a feeling which questions are borderline. You will be amazed at the revelations your client might have, just by reading these questions out loud. They may begin in a defensive mood and finish on the tenth question with open and honest emotion.

No one wants to be angry; it is just hard to redirect oneself. Sharing these emotions is vital to getting past the anger. Again, the main focus for your client is that you care. Listen attentively and act appropriately. With that, you'll change your client's opinions and behavior.

Evaluation   This next step will help answer the who, what, where, when, and why of anger, the 5 W's. Begin with your client and ask them to think about the last time they were angry. Let's take a long, hard look at that last time. Examine these questions with your client.

Refer your client to page 4-7 in their client Journal, and have them complete this tool after an episode of being angry. Your client must take this seriously. They need to be honest about the level of anger they have.

If your client has a recent episode they'd like to discuss, you can walk them through these questions, which parallel what they'll write in their journal after an upsetting episode.

- WHO were you angry with? Is that person in your life most of the time, some of the time, or hardly ever?
- WHEN did it happen? Was it something that happened recently, or something brought up from the past?

- WHAT was the source? Was it something you did or something they did? Explain.
- WHY did it happen? Was it an accident? Or did somebody push you by doing something deliberate?
- What is this really about?
- Why did that push your button?
- Is there any truth to it?

If your client is not quite ready to answer these questions, direct them like this:

Every time you feel yourself getting angry, pull out your journal, turn to a notes page, and record the circumstance and the environment in which you are working. Anger is very physical, so don't concern yourself with proper grammar, legibility, or whether it makes sense. Just let your anger roll out onto the paper.

Why? Well, the minute you observe your anger, or start writing about it, you stop being angry. You might be observing the fact that you were angry a few seconds earlier, but the distance that observation creates can be profound. Many times, when you are experiencing anger at work, you just need to do something different. Journaling is a safe and immediate solution.

You can also use what ends up in your journal to further investigate the answers to the questions on pages 4-6 and 4-7. When finished talking through those journal pages, your may feel free to tear them out and throw them away. The idea is not to make a permanent record but to create a temporary tool, a catalyst that makes honesty easier.

STORIES FROM THE SUMMIT

I encouraged Mamie to keep a journal, to sort out her thoughts and ideas. Intellectually, she knew it was a good idea, but she found it difficult to write consistently. However, it seemed that she always wrote something in her journal when she was angry.

Even though she didn't find herself to be angry often, she would write about it every time. She used her writing to release and redirect. One day, several months later, she gathered the courage to read her journal. Her handwriting was barely recognizable. She was shocked to find a pattern. Even though each event seemed unique, Mamie realized they were all really the same. She learned that she kept putting herself in the same situations, and creating the same emotions, over and over. For Mamie, nothing could have been more profound than to get that lesson in her own words, from her own handwriting. It's a lesson she never forgot.

Simple Questions   After you have had the opportunity to fully examine the cause and course of the anger, ask your client if this is something they can just let go of. Tell your client: "Examine how much energy it takes to carry anger. Set your anger down. Examine it from a distance and see how it looks, as seen through a different lens." Ask your client: "Do you really want to pick it back up, or should you leave it right where it is and move on? Why respond that way? What is in it for you? Why do you bother? What do you get from it? What are you proving?" Question the anger and its purpose for each and every episode, and you may open your client's eyes.

Intimidation
(Nonproductive Behavior—the third of three tools)

This topic has become an ongoing research project for us. The notion of intimidation just keeps rearing its ugly head with many of our clients. Intimidation is defined in the dictionary as "being made to feel afraid or timid," or "the feeling of discouragement in the face of someone's superior status."

Intimidation has as many faces as there are people. We are going to examine several types of intimidation, to discover some general rules and archetypes.

1. INTIMIDATION THROUGH ACTIVITY.   This type of intimidation comes from ignoring one's subordinates. Ignoring people makes effective leadership impossible. The best way to remind your client of this issue is to share the following story and a rabbit's foot as a chara. The rabbit's foot will remind them to slow down and be more aware of the people around them.

STORIES FROM THE SUMMIT

Leana is a supervisor in an insurance agency. She is task focused, but she tries to be attentive to her staff. Leana had one very bad habit. No matter where she was going, she would carry with her a stack of papers and binders. Leana was giving off a very strong signal that even her bosses noticed: Leana had busy feet. She was communicating to her staff that she was extremely busy and had NO time for any of them. This was a barrier between her and her staff that she wasn't even aware of.

Explain this to your client:

Acknowledging people with a smile or nod, even when you have things on your mind, will communicate something important about you as a leader. When you think of yourself walking through the office, how do you walk? Are you sending a message that you're not aware of? Take a look at the way you walk through your office area or department.

Do you smile at your employees? Do you make eye contact? Or do you put your head down and ignore everyone? Take the time to notice those around you, because after all, they're the ones who help you get it done. (Sherpa's note: This is also a good opportunity to revisit the "Body Language" discussion found in the "Listening Path", earlier in this chapter.)

You have to allow your client to figure out why this is personally important to them. Remind them to put their stack of paperwork on their desk before walking through the office. Remind them to stop, make eye contact, and talk to their staff. Have them try this for a week, and watch the way people respond.

2. INTIMIDATION BY DEMAND.   Every boss wants things done, and needs things done. The intimidator goes straight to the point, and uses the words "want" and "need" without qualification. Those words offer no possibility for discussion. They do not allow the listener to own even a small part of the conversation.

STORIES FROM THE SUMMIT

Scott is a vice president at a midsized equipment manufacturer. He has a lot to get done, and as a result, he is demanding of his staff. Scott was very aware that he needed coaching. At an early meeting, I stopped him and said: "Scott, do you know you have used the word 'need' 12 times since we started?" "NO way!" he said. That was Scott's revelation of the day. He could not believe that he used that word so many times. From that day on, he consciously counted how many times he used the word "need." By the following week he said he had cut the word usage by half, and his people didn't see him as quite so demanding.

Follow the process we revealed in the "Weakness Mountain" section in Chapter 6: acknowledge, observe, change, evaluate. Make sure your client acknowledges they use the words "want" and "need" in an intimidating way. Second, have them observe and count the number of times those words appear in their vocabulary. Then ask your client to *stop* using those words. Draw the two words on a notes page in your client's journal and then put a big X mark through the words.

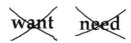

Explain that when people hear the words "I want" or "I need" something, they feel they have lost power. They are intimidated by those words. Each week, your client should evaluate the way they use these words, and the frequency with which they use them.

3. *INTIMIDATION THROUGH KNOWLEDGE* In most cases, your client is extremely knowledgeable about their position. They know more about their job than anyone else at the company. There is no argument about their expertise.

The problem comes in the way your client shares that knowledge with their people. Are they capable of instructing people? Can they teach, coach, and train? What are they doing to pass on the information? Most folks who have an "intimidation through knowledge" issue don't share their knowledge very well.

The most common issue we have seen with the "intimidation by knowledge" client is their assumption that everyone knows, or should know, as much as they do. They set unrealistic standards and goals for others. People are afraid to ask questions, so they make up their own interpretation of what the manager really meant to happen.

You have taught your client to set expectations, through communication, commitment, consequences, and coaching. If they remember these steps, their employees will perform much better. Expectations can and should be reviewed and repeated. The Expectations Mountain can change most managers' lives. This will especially help intimidating managers by bringing their people much closer to them.

So your client knows a lot. We also agree your client has trouble grasping that not everyone thinks the way they do. Therefore we teach your client this sentence: "I am right, but I am wrong." We consider it a mantra for this individual.

Coach your client on the sentence "I am right, but I am wrong" because it always seems to put them at ease. The fact is, the client is right about the information they have to pass along. They're right about the need for their employee to understand this information, but they are wrong in the way they are passing it along.

Allow your client to hold onto being right, while at the same time admitting to being wrong in the method they use to communicate. That will enable powerful and positive changes without hurting the client's pride.

Stories from the Summit

> *Vera is an office manager. She has knowledge of her job like no one else. She thinks she has one weakness. She explains it: "I am impatient with stupid and incompetent people." You see, she considers people who don't know as much as she does as stupid and incompetent. What Vera thinks is not the issue. The way she treats other people in a business environment does matter. Vera is intimidating, authoritarian, and impatient.*
>
> *We taught Vera the mantra "I am right, but I am wrong" and her world changed. She would always ask herself: "How can I get this across a different way than my instincts tell me? How can I tell people what I need from them in a different way?" She often said her coach was "haunting" her. That is exactly what we are looking for. It's as if we were on Vera's shoulder all the time, reminding her to get better.*

4. INTIMIDATION THROUGH PASSION   Your client is packed with passion about their job. They love it. They're good at what they do and believe their love for the job cures all. Your client believes that the way they act is enthusiastic, energetic—exactly as it should be.

Don't subdue your client's passion. Redirect it. We want to make sure that passion is appropriate and understood by all involved. The chara we give this client is a small STOP sign that fits on their desk. They'll be constantly reminded to stop and think about whether the people they communicate with understand and welcome their passion and intensity.

Some of the people around your client don't appreciate this passion. It makes people worry that they aren't good enough, they don't work hard enough, they are somehow inadequate. As a result, those people can fall out of the team.

Use these questions to get to the foundation of the client's passion:

- Do you feel on fire about the work that you do?
- Does it energize you?
- Does it make you feel alive?
- Do you communicate your passion for the company's mission?

There's a right way and a wrong way for leaders to express or exude enthusiasm about the organization's work. They can be a source of inspiration, or they can intimidate people with their passion. If there's a problem, explore alternate ways for you client to show their enthusiasm in a way that has a positive effect on those around them.

 ## STORIES FROM THE SUMMIT

> *Donald is production manager in a plastics shop. He is passionate and knowledgeable about his job. He is accurate and thorough when it comes to the paperwork.*
>
> *One day, Delores, one of his front-line workers, came into his office and said she had completed a spreadsheet in a different way. Don was ecstatic. He almost jumped up and down. He was thrilled that she had thought of changing something, and he told her so, sincerely and enthusiastically. Delores went to a colleague and said that Don's reaction was "scary." She did not understand his passion for her involvement.*

Remember the Paul Fredrik theory from Chapter 5. He smoked two packs of cigarettes a day and thought that if he quit, he would lose his identity. It's simply not true that you lose yourself as a person when you lose a negative behavior. The best way to explain this to your client is to ask: "What would your work life be like without that 'over the top' passion, the energy that frightens people? If you were calmer, what would happen?"

Everyone should have someone in their professional life, a support person who will always tell the truth, even when it hurts. Ask your client to name the person who could truly tell them to stop when this is necessary. Then have your client connect with that person and ask for a little help: a reminder when his colleague sees too much passion. A verbal stop sign, along with the right words, can change an old habit into a new, well thought-out behavior pattern.

Teach your client to revisit "why it matters" for the person they're talking to. Everyone can have a different "why it matters." No matter how important your client's motive is in their own mind, it might fall flat, or repel someone else.

Ask your client these seven questions:

1. Do people know you are sincere?

2. Are you a role model for passion in your company, or do you just make people uncomfortable?

3. What does your body language say? Are you bringing people into your circle or shutting them out?

4. When you display passion, do you make your role the most enjoyable and/or important? Do your subordinates have jobs with meaning and value?

5. Does your passion help uncover hidden talents and reward individuals who find satisfaction in their work?

6. Are you passionate enough to provide opportunities for your people to grow and advance?

7. How do you encourage creativity and passion in your people?

More food for thought, and topics for conversation.

That's the end of the Nonproductive Behavior path. If you are working with a client, you can move to Chapter 9 and continue the Sherpa process. Otherwise, read on to learn more.

CREATING ENTHUSIASM—PATH 5 OF 5, THE RELATIONAL ROUTE

Some people lack enthusiasm about work and life. They appear flat, listless, drab. This is a difficult thing to change. Your responsibility, as a Sherpa, is to help the client think about enthusiasm in a different way, to help them understand the positives of passion and enthusiasm.

STORIES FROM THE SUMMIT

Larry, a top IT guy, liked the word "despair." For some reason, he connected to this word and described himself in these terms. He lived a life of despair.

> *He had relationships that were based on despair. He "felt" despair as he drove into work every morning. His effectiveness was a fraction of what it should be. Early in coaching, we challenged him: "Larry, describe despair. Larry, define despair. Let's get it out on the table."*
>
> *Larry was stumped. He had no clue why he related to the word and used it so much. This was a deep revelation for Larry. He began to examine why he always referred to his life in this way. Larry discovered that he was in such a rut that passion and enthusiasm left his life. His energy level was near zero. For no good reason, he had been using despair as a crutch, to get through the tough stuff and everything else. Once his Sherpa took the satisfaction away from Larry's feeling sorry for himself, things changed for the better overnight.*

This can really be difficult for your client. Investigate this topic in depth. Dig deep to get honest answers to these questions:

1. When was the last time you felt a great deal of enthusiasm for your job? (Allow your client to share any work experience in their career, not just their current job.)

2. If an experience or environment that bred enthusiasm was in a different job, what kind of work were you doing at that time? Why aren't you doing that now? What elements of that experience are transferable?

Stimulate your client's imagination. What do they dream about? What's their vision for themselves? How did they answer the first question in the Personal Inventory? Can they recall, without looking back to Journal page 1-3, where they wanted to be in five years? If there were no money considerations or education requirements or expectations, what would your client be doing?

When is the last time someone allowed your client to share the client's dreams? When is the last time your client allowed themselves to think about them?

If your client is stumped, take them back in time. Ask them to do the following:

Create a wish board, a collage of what enthusiasm looks like to you:

- Get a piece of poster board.
- Cut out newspaper articles.
- Cut pictures from magazines.
- Gather snapshots of yourself or others.

You might select a tanned, smiling face, a picture of a peaceful look, a vase of flowers. Find articles or headlines that reflect the things that make you passionate. Paste the articles and pictures on the poster board. Hang it where you can see it every day.

Why might these things matter? Your client may need more direct contact with smiling faces. For example, Jerry, a systems engineer, worked in an isolated environment. He decided he would be better fulfilled with a relational position. So he focused on networking with his colleagues and looked into a job available in his company. Jerry applied for, and got, a position where he could merge his technical background with client and customer service.

Your client tells you that he really wants to be a rapper. After you giggle, appreciate that he is serious. Rapping is an expression of thoughts about a subject or a situation of interest. A rapper is a writer. So tell your client: "Write. Every opportunity you get, write. Then put a beat behind it, a rhythm only you know. It will give you a different approach, an attitude to your work. If you want to share with colleagues, and it seems appropriate, do it. If not, keep the secret for yourself."

Encourage your client to take control, and create pleasant spaces and environments: "You may love fresh-cut flowers. Purchase a bud vase for your desk. Make yourself smile every morning by adding a favorite flower to your vase. Own your environment, and make it work for you."

Keep digging!

Identify whether your client has become so comfortable with their lack of enthusiasm that they no longer can see the value in adjusting. If they once had enthusiasm, then lost it, what is going on? What happened? Make your client be very truthful.

Have them draw it out on paper, using a notes page in their journal: "What did I look like when my enthusiasm was at its peak? By contrast, what do I look like now?"

Revisit Weakness Mountain (Journal page 3-1). Replace your weakness with "Lack of Passion."

Acknowledge that you don't have enthusiasm. You are surviving the day, getting through it.

Observe your behavior. Use your journal to create a record and find patterns. At what point in the day, or in what situations, do you feel you just don't care?

Change. Change your environment, and surround yourself with things that remind you "why it matters."

Evaluate: How well are you doing? Do you see new enthusiasm? If not, try other new ideas.

Can you choose to be more enthusiastic? There is a saying: "As a man thinketh, so shall he be." Teach your client: "Use positive self-talk to feel better. Get in front of a mirror and positively affirm yourself, stating out loud those things that are great about you. Identify maxims that are particularly meaningful to you, and state them out loud every day."

Discovery Shield (Creating Enthusiasm— the first of three tools)

Let's examine your client's gifts. The chara we recommend is an empty box (you pick the size) wrapped beautifully with a gorgeous bow. The box represents the gift you give the world when you are enthusiastic.

Take a look at the Discovery Shield on page 1-4 of your client's journal. It is time to review the "Talent" section of the shield. Have your client list the one gift, the one talent, the one thing they've always been able to do very well. This talent is the foundation of their enthusiasm. This talent drives their primary emotions, because when someone is good at something, they're usually happy doing it. Make sure your client has done a really good job of defining their talent. If not, have them give it some more thought by asking: "What is that one thing you can and will do, no matter where you are? What's your contribution to the world?"

This is a good place to take a client who is searching for enthusiasm, meaning, and excitement. What they love doing will be rooted in their talent. Ask them for examples and anecdotes about when this talent comes out and when it is stagnant: "Record what you feel about that talent. Do you feel passionate about it? If you do, then you are clear about what enthusiasm means."

Discuss people that your client knows who avidly engage in their work. Enthusiasm brings purpose to an activity, task, or job. Work based on a gift becomes the thing we can do well and happily, no matter the circumstances.

As you close this discussion, hand your client the wrapped empty gift and ask them to keep it on their desk as a reminder of their gift/talent. This will be a constant reminder of where they want to go with that talent.

Love Bus
(Creating Enthusiasm—the second of three tools)

The chara is the key to this concept. The chara is a small yellow school bus. It is powerful because it is a visible reminder every day that understanding and welcoming the people in your business life will change the direction of your journey.

How well does your client understand that they are the focus of their organization? Whether your client is a receptionist or the CEO of an organization, their role is vital to the organization's success. As the center of the action, your client needs to attract people to follow, and make those people successful because of their relationship with your client.

We call this concept of bringing people on board the "love bus." The love bus fills up when your client welcomes people into their life: workers, associates, and staff. Before anyone will listen to your expectations, or care about your vision, they have to be on the bus. If you are a manager with an authoritarian approach, you might want to let people on your love bus because they need your support. Accepting them unconditionally on your love bus might be a VERY healthy thing.

Homework on leadership, teamwork, and success might help your client focus on building a following, whatever their job might be. Building it with creativity and enthusiasm will be important.

The Fuzzy Duck Theory
(Creating Enthusiasm—the third of three tools)

People don't care how much you know until they know how much you care. When your client cares about the people around them, amazing things will happen. A stuffed duck is the chara for this concept. Tell the following story as you give your client this chara.

STORIES FROM THE SUMMIT

A first-rate company in Cincinnati commissioned a professional photographer to take pictures of all their staff. Not just people at work, in business attire, but each employee with their favorite hobbies, lifestyles, and with their families. There is Bobbi with her dog, Sam. Dennis is pictured with his fishing gear and his hip waders. The stuffed animals she has been collecting for years surround a smiling Dolores. Her favorite? A fuzzy duck.

The photographs are beautifully framed, hanging throughout the building, throughout the company. Each person knows that their employer cares about them, and that their fellow workers understand them. Everybody has made Dolores feel good by picking out their favorite stuffed animal in the picture. She receives gifts of stuffed animals from her colleagues. These pictures were a simple idea, but they have brought the entire company closer together.

Continue with your client, using these themes to facilitate conversation: We all know that you do not spend all your time being a boss, being a leader. You have to produce, you have to meet deadlines, and you have to work for a living. When you get a chance to lead, to inspire, to teach, to manage, you have to be ready to do it and do it well.

How do you get people to care about working for you? There is only one way. You have to care about them. Be real ... be genuine ... be there for your people. Have fun and be creative. The more fun you have, the more enthusiastic you become. If you enjoy yourself at work, you will blossom, and your enthusiasm for what you do will be apparent.

With the right relationships in place, you can really lead your staff. You can't change the people under you by your own willpower. You *can* change yourself, and change your relationships with the people who work for you. That, in turn, might change the people under you in more ways than you can imagine.

Appreciate that your employee has a life outside this building. Be interested in others, their pursuits, and their work, their homes and families.

So if your client is under-enthusiastic, get them more involved with the people who work for them. Get your client to commit to a relationship based on respect and caring about other people. Your client need not be best friends, or "marry" the people they work with. Your client just needs to connect.

 ## STORIES FROM THE SUMMIT

> *The best manager I have ever met was a man named Francois, a line manager in the world of manufacturing. His people enjoyed their jobs and really respected him.*
>
> *When we asked Francois the secret to his success, he said in a very laid-back way, in his thick French accent: "I walk around the place. I meet the people. I talk to the people. I listen to the people. Don't do much else." Great advice. Give the man a fuzzy duck.*

Be cheerful. Be optimistic. Have FUN! The more fun you have, the more enthusiastic you are and the more people feed their own enthusiasm back to you. Give your client a fuzzy duck and recommend that they connect with their people and learn their passions.

Chapter 8, which follows, covers Phase Four, the organizational route. If you are working with a specific client, you can go to Chapter 9 to get the details on creating the action plan your client needs. The hard work is finished. You are ready to summarize, and to capitalize on the work you have done.

Phase Four: Charting the Course — The Organizational Route

For both routes, the relational and the organizational, and for all ten paths, you'll find training and facilitation we have developed as part of the Sherpa coaching process. All of this is designed to make your client understand their particular issue more clearly, and to take action that produces lasting results. Once you have defined the path your client will travel, you'll use related assessments in their journal and work on the exercises we provide.

Organizational skills are the ways that we get things done, and done correctly, through efficient and perceptive leadership. This is the technical side of your client's job. The organizational route emphasizes the managerial skills of the working person. It's the "business savvy" route. It's a big-picture route, with sweeping views of the client's business life. Paths on the organizational route encompass your client's innate ability to manage.

As you recall, there are five paths on this route, just as there are for the relational route. For each of the paths your client may take, you will offer specific tools and equipment. Some of the things you offer, they will use. Some they will leave by the side of the trail. The Sherpa offers the opportunity to choose. This gives your client the ability to make decisions and create changes they are committed to.

What You'll Find in This Chapter:

- **Leadership Path**
- **Decision-Making Path**
- **Time Management Path**
- **Image and Presence Path**
- **Personal Vision Path**

 THE ORGANIZATIONAL ROUTE

At this point in your coaching, the Sherpa process has led you to a true picture of your client and how they need to improve. For a client taking the organizational route, these are the paths available and the equipment they might find useful:

Leadership Path

- Assessment
- Leadership Analysis
- Recognizing Values

Decision-Making Path

- Assessment
- The Decision-Making Mountain
- Internal Expectations

Time Management Path

- Assessment
- Personal Program
- Prioritization Summary

Image and Presence Path

- Why It Matters
- Client Connection
- Helpful Hints

Personal Vision Path

- PQM—Personal Quarterly Meeting
- The Commercial
- Finding Your Talent

Here's where the organizational route begins. A Sherpa working with a client probably arrived here directly from Chapter 6, where the client chose one of the five paths: Leadership, Decision Making, Time Management, Image and Presence, or Personal Vision.

If that's the case, go straight to the selected path in this chapter and start work. Otherwise, read straight through and gain an overview of the training and development we offer clients on each path along the organizational route.

LEADERSHIP—PATH 1 OF 5, THE ORGANIZATIONAL ROUTE

Some of the questions that may have led you to this path:

- Is your client a good leader?
- Does your client spend time learning and growing as a leader?
- Does your client understand the difference between a manager and a leader?

So much has been said on leadership. You can read a hundred books on the topic and find different interpretations, guidelines, and advice in every one. As a Sherpa, you know the routine: Our goal is not to play on your client's strengths. That's what's gotten them this far, and this is as far as they're going unless they do some things differently. There's a flaw somewhere, a weakness in the way your client uses time, energy, people, or their own resources. As a Sherpa, your mission is to find and fix the weaknesses that hurt your client's ability to lead.

The tools you can offer along the way:

- Assessment
- Leadership Analysis
- Recognizing Values

Assessment (Leadership—the first of three tools)

The leadership assessment is a quick personal inventory. It may serve, as much as anything, to make your client stop talking and start thinking. At some point, clients have to connect with themselves. Perhaps they may realize that they haven't stopped to consider foundational issues in a very long time. That sets the stage for you to do some superior coaching. Your client will turn to Journal page 4-8 and complete the quiz, which includes these five questions:

1. What kind of leader are you? Describe in detail.
2. Give two recent examples of situations in which you were proud of your leadership.
3. Describe a situation where your leadership abilities fell short.
4. Name someone you think is an exceptional leader. Why do you feel that way?
5. List three areas in which you would like to improve your leadership abilities.

Your client should complete this exercise thoughtfully, during a meeting or as homework, and then discuss his answers with you. This will serve as a springboard to identifying good and poor leadership behaviors, and to setting goals and behavior patterns for your client to work on.

A great homework assignment, if your client's a fan of the movies, is to have them watch the movie *Master and Commander: The Far Side of the World* (2002) with Russell Crowe. Ask your client to identify eight leadership traits shown by Captain Jack Aubrey. It's easy to come up with eight items or more. The discussion of your client's answers is always enlightening, and a great opportunity for you to emphasize specific traits of great leadership.

Leadership Analysis (Leadership—the second of three tools)

Our next exercise, on page 4-9 of the client's journal, is thorough and thought provoking. It encompasses every area of leadership imaginable. The best way to use this assessment is to run through it with your client. Do not spend time coaching while you are going through the assessment.

Have your client read each question out loud. Clarify questions, if necessary. Have your client respond quickly to each question with a "first guess" rating of their skills. Don't let them over-think. Get through the assessment; then go back and review.

HOW WELL DO YOU:	CURRENT SCORE 1–10 SCALE AS OF DATE:	WHERE DO I WANT OR NEED TO BE?	SIX MONTHS' REVIEW SCORES
Overall effectiveness			
Recognize your overall strengths			
Recognize your weaknesses			
Select the best course of action			
Evaluate the course of action implemented			
Empowering employees			
Commend individuals for new ideas			
Use suggestions and ideas from project teams			
Allow subordinates to create constructive failure			
Managing employees			
Provide encouraging feedback			
Teach problem solving			
Coach through assignments			
Interacting with peers			
Inspire and guide peers to success			
Establish and build trust and openness			
Understanding accountability			
Set clear assignments and expectations			
Distinguish between urgent, important, and trivial			

continued

HOW WELL DO YOU:	CURRENT SCORE 1–10 SCALE AS OF DATE:	WHERE DO I WANT OR NEED TO BE?	SIX MONTHS' REVIEW SCORES
Follow up on all expectations, yours and others'			
Managing the work			
Set goals that are understood by all			
Praise those who anticipate and avoid problems			
Walk the floor, available to subordinates			
Communicating effectively			
Communicate with clarity to every audience			
Control and use body language			
Present ideas in a logical manner			
Use email effectively and efficiently			
Demonstrating teamwork			
Contribute to discussions, respond positively to requests for information and assistance			
Credit success, avoid blaming others for failure			
Help stop indifference, open and hidden conflicts			
Demonstrating visionary leadership			
Establish and communicate a vision and values			
Gain commitment from your team			

On your second pass, simply highlight your client's lowest scores, values of six or below on the one to ten scale. Then go over those areas of weakness again, without coaching. Have your client read the "trouble spots" out loud. When your client is done, facilitate. Ask them if they see patterns. Do they see a problem in one area that will go away if they solve a tougher, deeper problem somewhere else?

You can see how this can lead to lengthy discussion and introspection. This particular assessment can be a long-term commitment. If you are extending your relationship with your client, this can be a great place to work on multiple issues. If you and your client are on a 12-week schedule, concentrate on only the the most serious shortcomings.

 Recognizing Values (Leadership—the third of three tools)

Leaders give people the benefit of the doubt, and work to bring out their best. Recognizing and supporting people's values, their "why it matters," is the best way to assure them that following you is a good idea.

Put a group of people in a room and ask these questions:

- What was the most important event in your life?
- What would you do if you found a wallet with a hundred dollars in it?
- If you lost your job today, what would you do tomorrow?

Chances are, quite a few people will answer those questions in exactly the same way. These *questions* have something in common, too. They ask about what we place importance on. When you ask these questions, you're finding out a person's values. Values are formed from experience. They are personal, yours and yours alone. Values are fundamentally who you are. They define your direction. Your values are you.

If you take time to understand someone else's values, you will truly begin to understand that person. Understanding how values drive behavior is an important function of being a leader. Using this knowledge could help you figure out, for example, why one of your people might have said or done something inappropriate. If you understand that values are what drive your staff's decisions, you start to look at them quite differently.

It will give you an edge in understanding your staff, and give you the ability to work with them more effectively.

Sheila worked as a waitress in a fast casual restaurant. She showed up every day, always on time. She kept her uniform immaculate and always had her hair neatly tied back. Sheila's supervisor, Ted, was continuously on her back. She kept her customers waiting. He would say to her: "Sheila, you move way too slowly. Didn't your mother ever teach you about speed?" Ted left Sheila feeling degraded, unhappy. She felt like quitting.

Peter, the night manager, noticed all of this, and asked if she wanted to trade shifts. She jumped at the chance. Peter started Sheila off every night by telling her how impressed he was at her promptness and her neatness. He asked her if she could talk to some of the other servers, to help them become more conscious about their breaks and tardiness. Sheila beamed, happy to teach the group the things she understood so well. With that, the group looked up to her. Sheila finally felt great. Her performance improved in other areas, too.

Sheila's values were very clear to her. Because she was conscientious, she was sometimes slow. Reinforcing her values helped her realize her worth and made her a more productive part of the team.

We are not talking about morals or ethics, right or wrong. We are talking about what is important to people. When we refer to values, we refer to what people have made important or critical in their lives.

On one hand we have values, the principles people live by. On the other hand, we have character types, ways of dealing with the world. Let's try to see how values and character types connect.

Let's take a look at some of the character types you work with. As we go along, try to connect some of these character types to different values, to see why people do the things they do:

THE KNOW-IT-ALL.   A show-off, someone who wants to be looked up to . . . so they pretend to know everything.

THE GOSSIP.   You know this one . . . Gossips spend their workday talking and talking and talking about other people. They spend very little time getting their work done.

THE WET BLANKET.   This one has a negative viewpoint on absolutely everything. Complain, complain, complain.

We all run into people who fit these descriptions, all the time. So why do people act like these stereotypes? Let's try to find out.

There are two things everyone wants in life: to be happy and to be successful. To be happy, we want to do the right thing. To be successful, we want to be good at what we do.

Now sometimes, people who act according to these character types are acting out their values, what's important to them. Maybe they are really *trying* to do the right thing. Unfortunately, sometimes they cross the line.

To understand this a little better, we're going to match the characteristic a person takes on with the values they're trying to live by. Here's an example:

Let's take the know-it-alls. Let's say these people value competitiveness. They have always competed. Perhaps the only way they get attention is by winning at what they do. They might be know-it-alls just to make sure that you see them winning. They are doing the right thing in the wrong way, usually at the wrong time.

What if the know-it all places a value on power? The sense of control, authority, and influence is very important. Maybe the know-it-all puts a great deal into being a person of power and influence. After all, how can you be important and influential if you don't know everything about everything? So these types may be trying to do what they think is good and proper. They might be striving to honor one or more of the values we've talked about.

Study the know-it-alls, and discover what makes them act the way they do. Very often, when an employee is wrong, they are trying to be right . . . but are simply going about it in the wrong way. They may be **wrong,** but they're motivated by what is **right.** They're motivated by their values. Keep that in mind the next time someone displays a bad attitude. Try to figure what's important to that person in that situation.

As you can see, values and character traits, figuring out why people act the way they do, is very important. You'll understand your staff a lot better if you walk a mile in their shoes.

You've climbed the Sherpa Leadership path. If you're working through the book with a specific client, skip ahead to Chapter 9, where all the paths rejoin. Otherwise, read on as we discuss decision making.

DECISION-MAKING—PATH 2 OF 5, THE ORGANIZATIONAL ROUTE

Leadership involves making important decisions that affect other people. Problems with decision-making hurt your client's ability to lead, manage and motivate others.

Some of the questions that may have led you to this path:

- Does your client make poor decisions?
- Does your client struggle with every decision?
- Is your client able to stick with a decision once it's made?
- Does your client apologize before announcing a decision?

Decision-making is a complex path. There are many reasons why your client has trouble making decisions. Perhaps the client involves too many people, or too few. Maybe their decision-making involves too much thought, or not enough. We will work through all those possibilities using our "Decision-Making Mountain."

Fighting with alligators can make us forget that our initial objective was to drain the swamp. The demands of the day can make us forget why we do the things we do, why we exist as an organization or as a team. A periodic check on "Why it matters" ensures that the decisions we make are designed to meet the mission.

Decision-making can be hard. Your clients can have it a little easier if they make good decisions about *who should be involved* in their decision making.

Tools you'll use on this path:

- Assessment
- The Decision-Making Mountain
- Internal Expectations

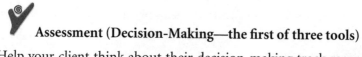

Assessment (Decision-Making—the first of three tools)

Help your client think about their decision-making track record. Examine the quality of the client's decisions, and their timeliness. Talk about times when no decision would have been better than the choice that was made. Talk about some bad decisions and the thought process that led to them. Encourage your client to look for patterns and themes.

There is logic and there is a human factor in how your client makes decisions, and why they sometimes prefer not to make them at all. People handle decisions differently. Some tend to think the environment controls them (high "S" and "C" DiSC scores). Others take control and decide based on logic: "Prove your point" (high D's). Still others will factor relationships into leadership (high I's). All these views will create varied decision-making styles and abilities.

Often, a person is deemed a leader because they will make a decision and stand by it. Stepping up has its rewards. It can be risky, too. Perhaps your client's problem with setting a direction is deciding when to do it and when not to.

Will there be ramifications for making a decision? Always. Some will be positive, some negative. Some outcomes will be easy to predict, others will be totally unexpected. Regardless, your client can learn valuable lessons by consistently thinking back through a decision, good or bad, and looking hard at the ramifications, especially the surprises. It's one of the habits of a great leader.

Our next exercise is one to assess your client's decision-making ability. It's simple: Twelve true or false questions. You can have your client turn to page 4–10 in their journal and work it on paper, or read the questions aloud and have them answer verbally. Reading aloud lets you observe body language as your client responds.

Decisions, Decisions
Answer true or false to each question:

1. I am comfortable with the decisions I make.

2. Reversing one of my decisions is easy for me to live with.

3. I am good at setting priorities.

4. I am an exceptional listener and hear all sides.

5. Building a consensus is easy for me.

6. I am flexible and accepting of feedback.

7. No matter what people say about my decision, I am okay with it.

8. I am willing to break traditions and defy past practice.

9. I completely examine costs and benefits when making a decision.

10. I use my intuition when I make a decision.

11. I am not afraid to make decisions.

12. I don't care how much time it takes to make a good decision.

An answer of "false" indicates an area where improvement can be made. If your client answers all the questions as "true," you should either go back and pick another path if they're telling you the truth, or get to the bottom of it if they're not.

If your client is not a good decision maker, they can improve by surrounding themselves with the proper support system to practice making decisions:

- A good flow of information.
- Advance warning of when a decision is due.
- Good advisers with the time and energy to come up with good counsel.
- A place where the team can gather and brainstorm comfortably.
- Literature and training on decision-making itself.

We look at this assessment as a foundation, a basis for discussion. Center in on the weaknesses relative to your client's decision making. Facilitate. Let them discover answers by forcing them to think it through.

The Decision-Making Mountain (Decision-Making— the second of three tools)

So how will you teach your client to make a decision? We'll be using an expanded tool for decision-making that emulates the four steps in the Weakness Mountain: acknowledge, observe, change, and evaluate. We call this the Decision-Making Mountain. You can refer your client to page 4-11 in their journal for discussion and notes.

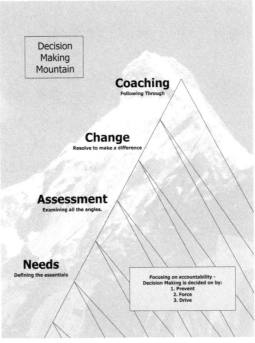

(© Sasha Corporation)

A decision usually involves four phases that you will want to examine. We represent those as four phases in climbing a mountain:

1. NEED: DEFINING THE ESSENTIALS. Your client has to know something is amiss, and acknowledge that it's their responsibility to fix it. This is where your client must gather facts—research the need to make a decision and the urgency of the matter. In this phase of the mountain, your client must manage the normal urge to make a snap decision. That means self-control: managing their own reaction to the information.

2. ASSESSMENT. This step is where you examine "why it matters" and the ramifications of making a decision, good or bad, or leaving things alone. These first two phases present a great opportunity for your client to involve others and share their thinking, invite input, and then evaluate results.

Assessment includes addressing weaknesses and accountability issues. The assessment phase examines how the decision you will be making is related to the accountability you have for the issue. Your accountability will drive the decision, forcing the decision or preventing it.

3. CHANGE. A decision to change means something is going to be different, for better or worse. Prepare people for change. Try to anticipate the unexpected. Broadcast your successes and learn from your failures. There's a big difference between failure that comes from doing nothing and failure that comes when you're trying to do something right.

4. COACHING AND FOLLOW-THROUGH. The most important step: a conscious dedication to the resolution of the issue in every facet. This means creating the desired effect, adding to the knowledge base, building loyalty, efficiency, and team cohesiveness. No one is inherently good at consolidating all these different types of gains. That's why a Sherpa will advise clients to exercise due diligence in follow-through, paying attention to every possible benefit the decision might create.

STORIES FROM THE SUMMIT

Alan is a brilliant executive director in the world of health care. Patients, families, and his staff love him. Alan has a very difficult time making decisions and following through. Because of this difficulty, he can't get his staff to do the work they need to do for him. Why? Because they all know that he will not make a decision quickly and will not (when he does finally make the decision) follow up to see what's been done.

Alan went through the decision-making path. It was helpful to him to revisit expectations. He found the Decision-Making Mountain a helpful reminder on the process he needs to go through to make a decision. He kept the picture of the mountain right on his desk and referred to it every time he had to make a decision. After a month, he was doing much better with telling people what had to happen, and making sure his recommendations were carried out.

Internal Expectations (Decision Making—the third of three tools)

Fear is a powerful motivator, and it can play out in many different ways. A client who's afraid of failure can simply avoid making decisions.

Betty's a veteran manager, well respected in her community. She is called on to make decisions every day, but for two years, she has failed to make some very necessary decisions about reorganizing her company. When she uses the Decision-Making Mountain, she finds that the third phase, change, stumps her every time. Betty will tell you: "I don't know what is wrong with me. Why can't I do this?"

There are two sides to expectations. Clearly, Betty is in a leadership position, delivering expectations to her staff and colleagues all the time. What about the expectations she places on herself? Could the process that we use externally work for internal expectations?

If your client fails to make decisions due to fear, revisit the Expectations Mountain in Chapter 6. Your client has a diagram of the mountain in their Journal on page 3-2, along with their notes from your initial discussions on the topic. Talk them through the "internal dialogue," the way they apply their personal expectations for their own behavior.

This can be a good way to get them past the fear and spurred to action.

That's the end of the Decision-Making path. If you're working with a client, turn to Chapter 9. Otherwise, read on as we discuss time management.

TIME MANAGEMENT—PATH 3 OF 5, THE ORGANIZATIONAL ROUTE

Getting it done: companies have been doing more with less for a long time. We consulted with a global paper company and saw an office stretched thinner and thinner as the company cut costs by not replacing people who left. They were big on cross-training, spreading the work around, piling it higher and higher with each new defection. Time management becomes a very important skill when a leader and their staff are stretched thin.

Some of the questions that may have led you to this path:

- How are your client's organizational skills?
- Does your client say: "There's never enough time"?

- Does your client lack the ability to get everything done during a day?
- Does your client accept more work than can be accomplished?

There are environments where people have too much to do. You didn't arrive here with your client because of that. They have significant room for improvement in the way they manage their time.

Tools you can use on this path:

- Assessment
- Personal Program
- Prioritization Summary

 Assessment (Time Management—the first of three tools)

First order of business: Have your client work through the Time Management Assessment on page 4-12 of their journal and discuss their answers.

1. Can you tell whether the matter you are dealing with is urgent?
2. Do you spend at least one hour each day of uninterrupted time thinking, reading, planning, or doing creative work?
3. How much time per week do you spend developing business relationships?
4. How many times a day do you say "I don't have time"?
5. Can you evaluate your use of time? If yes, describe a day in the life.
6. Is it hard for you to avoid distractions?
7. What is a distraction to you?
8. What do you do to avoid distractions?
9. When a distraction comes along, how do you handle it?
10. What's the most productive time of day for you? _____
11. Prioritize your work projects.
12. Prioritize your life.
13. Do you eat properly? Describe your diet.
14. Do you sleep well most nights? If not, what are your sleeping habits?

Time management is simply organizing your life, prioritizing, and then staying on track. This assessment is designed to find out if your client sets priorities easily.

Go through each question and talk about the answers.

1. Why did you say that?
2. What was the hardest question for you to answer? Why?
3. What question do you think you need to revisit/re-examine?
4. What revelations did you get from this discussion?

Your clients will reveal a lot of themselves in this conversation. Are they in a rut, and totally oblivious? Are they aware of time management issues but still unable to solve them?

One of the keys to time management is teaching your client to be aware of time. What is wasted time? What is useful time? Use the time log to get a handle on this, or to confirm your client's instincts and assumptions about the way they use time.

What does your client use for an appointment book? A handheld device, a paper-and-pencil planner? Learn what your client uses, how they use it, and make it work for them. Do not convert them to a new method. Teach them to use what they already have more effectively. There are numerous time management books out there that will make good reading for your client.

Teach your clients this:

The secret to great time management: Get into good routines and follow them until they become habits. It takes 21 days to form a habit. In your journal, write a couple of new habits related to time management and observe them for 21 days. Use the journal to record how well the habit is developing.

Example:

Review your calendar every morning or evening. Make sure all the "to-do" items are either taken care of or moved to the next day. You will get into the habit of checking this every day, and the way you look at and plan your time will change.

The Personal Program (Time Management— the second of three tools)

Your client will be asked to watch their time and how they spend it. Page 4-13 in the journal shows a basic time log your client can use. Examine whether or not time management is truly the issue. If you have asked enough questions to know your client does not manage their time properly, you can continue down this path.

STORIES FROM THE SUMMIT

> Rob is a plant manager and has a million things to do every day. He cannot get them all done. He strongly believes that time management is his biggest problem. We use the Personal Program to examine his issues further. With the personal program we find out that Rob is WAY more comfortable in meetings and answering emails than he is on the plant floor. The way he chooses to use his time is a symptom of something else, so we decided not to take this path; returned to Phase Three, Destination; and worked on what was really holding him back.

We are going to create a personal program based on examining how your client uses and abuses time. The first step will be the keeping of a time log that you and your client will review together. Your job here is to research, analyze, and change the way your client uses time. Nobody is perfect in their use of time, so there will always be room for improvement.

Write a Time Log (Journal 4-13)

This is straightforward time log—the legend should be created together. In the journal, your legend is blank, so together make sure you create a legend that reflects your client's day-to-day activities and makes it easy for them to keep track.

Ask your client to complete the time log for five working days. This helps the Sherpa examine what really goes on during the client's day.

Example of a legend you can create with your client:

LEGEND:

A administrative

C correspondence (email or phone calls)

D driving

I interruptions

M meetings

Q quality control and inspections

S sales and promotion

Put your client's raw data into a spreadsheet and create subtotals that will categorize and examine their week in detail. If you're working on paper, just make a compilation based on the legend and review it with your client.

Questions to ask when the time log is complete:

- How many casual, drop-in office visitors?
- Is your workspace organized?
- How many of these meetings were timed and had an agenda?
- Did your phone calls last longer or exactly how long you wanted them to?
- Did you need to plan for the unexpected? (See the prioritization summary, next section.)
- Could you have delegated any of these things?
- How much time did you invest in yourself, doing healthy things such as eating well, exercising?
- Can you identify wasted time?
- How early do you wake up and go to bed?
- Did you spend too much time on any one area?

Have your client color code the areas they need to examine further. This makes it easy for them to identify what they're doing during the day. You can use this time log as often as you need to. Examining this time log should be the coach's homework.

You now have everything you need to help your client organize and manage their time. Together, you'll develop strategies that will make their life more manageable.

A time management plan for your client need not be detailed, and it's certainly not something you, the coach, can create for them. Work with the client to see what can and cannot be cut out of their calendar. What does the client's time log look like? Where in their time log can they see room for improvement? Ask questions and try different ways to re-examine the client's day-to-day life.

Don't think you must have every answer to every issue. Work with your client, ask questions, and direct them to making their own decisions on better use of time.

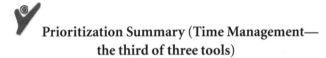

Prioritization Summary (Time Management— the third of three tools)

Your client will find some tools for prioritization on page 4–14 of their journal.

When they have completed this exercise, ask:

- Did you set up priorities for your staff?
- Are they broken down to a fine enough level of detail that things happen the way you want them to?
- How does it feel when you get things done?

The Sherpa Time Management path makes a lot of difference for a lot of people. We've reached the end of this path, so you can turn to Chapter 9 to continue with a client. Otherwise, read on as we discuss image and presence, and a little something called charisma.

IMAGE AND PRESENCE—PATH 4 OF 5, ORGANIZATIONAL ROUTE

"Don't judge a book by its cover." "Clothes don't make the man." In a perfect world, these things would be absolutely true. However in the real world, you never get a second chance to make a first impression. Image is very important.

It was not our original intent to discuss image in a book on business coaching. It's hard to believe that poor image and presence could be a common weakness that derails executive careers. However, more employers than we expected have told us their senior managers are unkempt.

Questions that may have led you to this path:

- Is your client poised, interesting, good at networking?
- When your client walks into a room, do people notice?
- Does your client have trouble believing in their own ability?
- Does your client look good every time they walk into the office?
- Does your client understand that perception is reality?

This path is dedicated to the individual who could use help with walking into a room and making an impression. Image is directly related to who your client is. That is why we give them a pocket mirror as their chara in this path. The mirror will remind clients to do a mirror check before they step out of the house, and help them remember what you'll teach them on this topic.

How can successful men and women be unaware of how they look? Research tells us they simply don't know it's important. Dress codes and the blue-suit, white-shirt corporate uniform have been replaced by "business casual." It's created a lot of confusion. Even Fortune 500 companies allow employees to dress down substantially on days they are not seeing customers.

That has ramifications, all the way around. We are sending each other signals with how we choose to dress. The message might be: It's getting the work done that's important. It might just as easily be: Forget standards; just do what you feel like doing. Because of this, policies are being reversed, but the damage has been done.

As an introductory tool, you might have your client turn to page 4-15 in their journal and do the assessment, in conversation or as homework. This can be a difficult assignment, for both you and your client. It is difficult for people to realize that other people really pay that much attention to them. In some cases, your client may know that people notice appearances, but won't acknowledge that what others think really matters. In real life, no matter what your client would like to believe, they can't move upward based on the quality of their work unless they look the part.

This path can be hard for the Sherpa, too. How do you tell your client that their look doesn't match their goals? How do you say that when they speak, their audience shuts down? The exercise on page 4-15 in the journal can get you started. Here are the questions, with some additional comments for the Sherpa coach:

- Are you aware of others' first impressions of you?

You might ask: "How could I know what others think?" Become an observer at your next couple of business gatherings. Be one of the first to arrive. Watch others enter the room. Pay attention to your impressions. What impressed you most? What impressed you least? What kind of impression do you want to make? How do you do the things that impress you, and avoid doing the things yourself that turn you off?

- What's the value of a first impression?

Your image and presence tell people whether you are credible and trustworthy. They'll judge whether to even entertain a discussion with you. They are evaluating how much time they are going to give you, all in a matter of seconds.

- What do people say when they first meet you? Do people engage with you easily? Are you approachable?

Being able to strike up a relaxed and sincere conversation is another huge part of good first impressions.

- Do you consider business clothing an investment?

Quality is more important than quantity. It is perfectly fine to wear the same clothes every day if they are clean and pressed. When a garment is made well and taken care of, it will last longer.

- Have you been evaluated by a barber or beautician in the last six months?

People often take care of personal grooming at home. Some are better at it than others. To look professional, consult with a barber or beautician at least twice a year, asking for advice on how to maintain your look.

- Can you identify five positive points about your image?
- Are you happy with what you see when you look in the mirror?

No matter what you see, it is where you are right now. Everyone has room for improvement, and you will find yours very quickly.

- When you walk into a room, do people notice?
- When you speak, do people listen?

Discuss with your client how they use words and when. Your client must determine how they affect their listeners. Do they talk so much that it all runs together? Do their words have impact because they come sparingly, at exactly the right time?

Tools you can use on this path:

- Why It Matters
- Client Interactions and Connection
- Helpful Hints

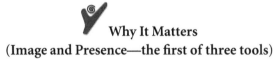

Why It Matters
(Image and Presence—the first of three tools)

Here's a story that demonstrates how attitude is reflected in appearance:

After Ronald Reagan left office as governor of California, he was an unemployed private citizen. He had the freedom to show up at the mall in a T-shirt and tennis shoes if he wanted to. But that's not what he did. He had a larger goal in mind.

As a private citizen, every time he made a public appearance, he acted presidential. He always traveled in a limousine. He wore a business suit every time he was out in public. He carried an entourage, including bodyguards, photographers, and a press agent. He acted like he was very important. The people around him, the people who saw him, believed that he was important. The image he presented reflected a sincere desire to be President of the United States. People believed in his goal, and he achieved it.

 STORIES FROM THE SUMMIT

> Sam is a senior manager who is on the path to becoming a COO of the company. He is a good manager and very skilled at the technical aspects of his position. He is an asset to his company. There is just one little challenge. Sam does not look like an executive, nor does he appear, at first glance, to belong on that track.

The first step is awareness. As a coach leading a client on this path, you'll find it helpful to have someone in authority in your client's life to express that there is, in fact, a problem with the client's image and presence. Often your client will think they look just fine. They won't know what you are talking about. They've dressed, talked, and walked like this for years. You might have to ask pointed questions and issue challenges in some personal areas. Is your client open to being challenged? Can they handle some tough questions?

Review the Perceptions exercise, page 2-2 in your client's journal. If your client did not fill this out in Phase Two, Global View, you'll find notes on this assessment in Chapter 5. The object here: compare your client's self-image with the perceptions of their boss and peers. You can look at previous answers, and see how appearance and image might be related to issues the client brought up, first time around. A person whose boss thinks they're disorganized can be very much in control but give that impression because their appearance is sloppy, for instance.

You can also add new information on this assessment, having your client ask people to rate their appearance and charisma on a scale of one to ten. Using this format gives your client's peers permission to tell the truth. Ask these questions:

- How does my boss expect me to look?
- What image do I need to portray to my customers?

Turn to page 4-16, titled "Image Art," in your client journal. Have your client draw a self-portrait when they feel most empowered, confident, successful, and talented.

The second step is assessment. If possible, put your client in front of a mirror, perhaps even a three-panel mirror, so they can see their own appearance from every angle. Ask the client to do a self-examination from head to toe, and tell you what they see.

What about the garments your client is wearing? What about their attire makes your client feel at their best? List the characteristics of their garments. Does color affect the client's mood? Do they dress the way they feel? Do they look successful? Is everything age appropriate?

Have your client write in their journal about personal grooming and hygiene:

- My hair—is it groomed (cut, colored, styled) by a professional?
- My facial hair—is it always neat? Anything unusual about it?
- Are my nails clean and groomed?
- Eyebrows, nose, and ear hair tamed?
- Am I aware of body odors?
- Teeth clean? Straight?

Your client needs to come up with room for improvement, on their own, and make a commitment with you, the Sherpa, to make positive changes in a fixed time frame.

Then your client must keep learning. Television shows on the subject of makeovers teach what looks good on your body type, how to choose colors, and how to be current without being trendy. These networks are likely to have programs on fashion:

The Learning Channel

BBC

Style Channel

MTV

E (Entertainment television)

HBO

Ask your client to view one of the style shows on these channels once a week, even after your coaching is complete. These shows not only teach you about clothing; they teach you about perception, what friends, family, and coworkers are likely to be saying about you.

The third step is action. It may come down to a wardrobe change. As a coach, you'll need to lead this process. If you are not familiar with business fashion, start reading and researching. Locate a convenient mid-priced clothing store appropriate to your client's gender. They have a tendency to be more private, so you can really teach without being disturbed. Establish a relationship with a salesperson, explaining your role as a coach, and how this person can help you. Know that salesperson's schedule, and only shop when they will be there. You, as a coach, now have ownership over the location for your next meeting with your client, and the confidence that lets you be an expert, in control.

Make sure your client is eased into "shopping mode." Your executive contact may even provide a clothing allowance for your first pass at a better wardrobe. Finance is one part of creating a comfort level. Attitude is another. Tell your client: "This is not about becoming a slave to fashion. We are simply packaging your product." Make sure the client knows that their agenda is your agenda. No particular look will be shoved down their throat. You and a clothing consultant will help them express their personality, and match the demands of their role in business. Assure your clients that they will be bettering themselves, not trying to create someone new. Then, take them to the store you have chosen. Turn them over to the salesperson you've chosen. Let them shop and learn. Don't leave until you've purchased a couple of outfits, or exhausted your client's budget.

Client Connection
(Image and Presence—the second of three tools)

Have you ever known a person who can walk in and light up a room, draw everyone's attention? That person has something we refer to as presence, charisma, charm. It can be defined as a quality of poise and effectiveness that enables a person, especially a performer, to establish a close relationship with their audience. It's a spirit people feel. Maybe it's a gift. Perhaps we all have it in varying degrees. The question is: how does your client get more of it?

Sometimes we can learn most by knowing the desired result and working back to the beginning. Have your client turn to a notes page in their journal and write about these two questions:

1. What comments would you like people to make when you have left the room? List several of them, in detail.

2. What do you want people to think when you walk into a room? Write those out. List several of them.

Go through each comment with your client and discuss what they need to do in order to achieve that response. How do other people create those reactions? The Sherpa is in facilitation mode here, presenting questions, and allowing the client to do all the work.

Now let's lead your client through a scenario, an ordered way of thinking about how they create those desired reactions. We'll examine a situation before, during, and after.

Before

BE PREPARED. Your client must be knowledgeable about subject matter. Don't enter any situation uninformed. Should research not be possible, your client should immediately convert to the role of an enthusiastic student, encouraging others to share their knowledge and experiences.

KNOW THE OBSTACLES OR OBJECTIONS THAT MIGHT INHIBIT REACHING A GOAL. Your client must know their crowd, their customer, whoever they are dealing with. Whether it's an after-hours or a formal presentation, clients must be aware that they are selling, if only selling themselves. Teach them to be energized by the obstacles and look for the objection. Only then can they know when to "close the sale." When your client is prepared, they'll have confidence that they can overcome most any objection or obstacle between them and their goal.

KNOW YOUR LOCATION. Know the place you are going to work. If it's a hotel-based conference, look for room and facility layouts on the Internet. Especially if your client is presenting, they should be comfortable with the space.

- Where are the electrical outlets?
- Where are the housekeeping necessities?
- Will you need a key?
- Is there a gatekeeper, a receptionist, a person who is instrumental to achieving your goal?

During

CREATE VALUABLE INPUT. Your client must not talk simply to fill up space or announce their presence in a conversation. Teach them to find opportunities to provide valuable information or offer constructive opinions when asked. When your client is uncertain about what will be considered valuable, they should make short statements and observe spoken and nonverbal responses, which will cue them about whether to be quiet or continue.

MAKE YOUR PRESENCE KNOWN. Let's return to the definition of presence: "a quality of poise and effectiveness that enables your client to achieve a relationship with their audience." Presence is centered on the impression we make, and goes beyond what we say.

If you wear a color in a conservative environment, make sure it is simple and structured. Posture is important. Clients can develop these characteristics, things that get them noticed in a positive way:

- Stature
- A well-spoken demeanor
- Kindness
- Purpose
- Being visible

Assignment—Pay attention to the individuals you feel have presence. What is it about them that creates that opinion? Pay close attention. Take notes afterward for discussion at a future coaching meeting.

ORGANIZE YOUR SPACE. When making a presentation, arrange your materials for ease of use. Put the things that you will need where you can easily lay your hands on them. Neatly stack things. Minimize your opportunity for error or delay. That creates confidence and avoids negative impressions.

After

EVALUATE. At the end of every day, take five minutes to evaluate. Have your client examine what they'll need to do to follow up and then be prepared for the next day, next meeting, next level of performance.

SET UP A PLAN TO IMPROVE. Work on improvement every day. Set up personal goals such as these:

- Iron the shirt you once wore straight from the dryer.
- Put your materials in a folder instead of carrying loose papers.
- Prepare to make small talk in chance encounters and meetings.
- Look in the business section of the newspaper and update yourself on current events.

Practice. Return to the Weakness Mountain.

Acknowledge
Observe
Change
Evaluate

Helpful Hints (Image and Presence— the third of three tools)

Take your image seriously.

Here are some tips and tricks to improve appearance and presence:

QUALITY IS MORE IMPORTANT THAN QUANTITY. Business clothing is an investment. It is not about how much money you spend. It's about recognizing quality, whether you're at Wal-Mart or Saks Fifth Avenue.

LEARN ABOUT FABRICS. There are fabric blends to accommodate every lifestyle. There are shirts and blouses that are wrinkle free. Wool blends are always the best choice year round. They maintain their color and shape. Cotton and linens breathe well, for comfort in warmer seasons and climates.

CONSULT AN EXPERT. Department and specialty store employees are very knowledgeable. Build a relationship with a salesperson. Each time you shop, check the schedule of that employee and work with them each time. Let them get to know you, your taste and needs. They'll keep you abreast of special promotions you'll be interested in.

PURCHASE THE RIGHT SIZE, NOT THE SIZE YOU WANT TO BE. Have your clothes altered. This creates a neat, put-together appearance. You will feel great in your clothes, even if you don't feel so good about your size and shape at the moment.

YOU MUST BE WELL PRESSED. Do you like to iron? Will your budget allow a monthly dry-cleaning bill? Make a decision to invest time or money in your appearance.

PAY ATTENTION TO YOUR SHOES. Some people claim that you can learn a great deal from the style and condition of a person's shoes. It is impossible to look polished without maintaining your shoes. Wing-tipped lace-up shoes are the preferred men's business shoe because of their classic look.

TAKE CARE OF YOURSELF. You'll come off better when you eat well, drink water, get plenty of rest.

Shopping for clothing:

Become a "regular":
There are benefits to visiting a store often. Your client should learn the cycle of sales and know when they're getting a good deal. They will recognize labels that offer them a well-fitting garment.

Sales, seasons, coupons
The lowest prices come at the end of a season. Buy your clothes for next year at the end of the season. Department store coupons can lower your costs.

Outlets
Outlet stores don't guarantee the best prices. Often, a department store sale will beat an outlet or discount store price. Never pay regular price for a garment unless you really need it, or you feel so good in it that all bets are off.

Labels
Your client may disagree with you that labels are important. We are not talking about labels as a status symbol. We are talking about labels that fit your body, a cut of clothing that works for you. You'll look and feel good in it.

We are always being sized up, evaluated by people who can be important to personal success. Give yourself the best opportunity to make an impression. There are very few things you have absolute control over. Your image is one of them, so work on it.

The Sherpa Image and Presence path ends here. Turn to Chapter 9 to continue with a client project. Otherwise, read on as we talk about career paths, succession planning, and personal vision.

PERSONAL VISION—PATH 5 OF 5, ORGANIZATIONAL ROUTE

As a coach you have a tremendous opportunity to help your client by delivering and drawing out truth.

Delivering Truth

Clients are often lost in the whirlwind of their own mind, life at work, and life at home.

They continue a routine, telling themselves, "This is just the way it is" and "Deal with it." A Sherpa gives a client a rare gift: permission to STOP and give some consideration to who they are and what they really want.

To deliver truth, a coach must force truth by asking questions only the client can answer, and doing it in such a way that the client, at least for a moment, breaks out of the fog and has a truly lucid moment. The coach must ask:

- Who are you?
- No, Who are you really?
- Is that really the true you?
- How do you know?
- Prove it to me.
- Now that you've told me that, what does that mean?

Drawing Out Truth

Once stopped, your client's mind has an opportunity to vacation, purge itself, make room for new thoughts, ideas, and a dream or two. This sets the stage for defining and going after your client's personal vision.

Some of the questions that may have led you to this path:

- Is your client motivated to stay with his job?—private clients
- Does your client need to figure out what to do next?—private clients
- Does your client understand how to start a new job?—private clients
- Is your client stuck in a rut?
- Does your client think their talents are no longer of value?

Clarifying their own personal vision gives your clients a chance to see how well they use their talents and strengths. How do they maximize those strengths in their current position or when seeking a new one? How do they use the job they have to develop skills that contribute to what they want to become?

This path will be the one you travel when a client asks for career coaching. For a private pay client, there may be discussion about leaving their current job. If you've arrived here with a client whose employer is paying the bill, avoid that kind of dialogue altogether.

For any client, you can force answers to the questions we all ask ourselves. What did you want to be and do, growing up? What do you now? What's the difference? How do you find mission and purpose in what you do?

Tools you will use on this path:

- Personal Quarterly Meeting (PQM)
- The Commercial
- Finding Your Talent

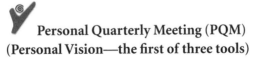

Personal Quarterly Meeting (PQM)
(Personal Vision—the first of three tools)

Personal Quarterly Meeting—This is a one-person "meeting" that you might recommend to a client who needs time away from their office. You can suggest a day trip, a picnic, or a visit to the library. No phones, no communication with the office.

The PQM is your clients' introspective look at themselves for the quarter. Please review Journal page 4-17 with your client and explain the questions individually. It's a personal journey you can assign as homework. Recommend they take the day off and just go to a favorite place and sit there and complete the PQM.

When your client has finished the PQM, the answers to the assessment will provide tremendous opportunities for discussion.

The Commercial
(Personal Vision—the second of three tools)

This exercise can be done in a meeting, with the client writing on a notes page in their journal. The assignment: Have them write one or both of the following commercials and present it to you on the spot.

1. *INTRODUCE YOURSELF TO THE WORLD.*   Write a script to describe the most important features that you want your employer and peers to know about you. Include your skills, strengths, and talents. Time yourself. Thirty seconds is all the time you'll have.

2 *LET YOUR MIND SOAR.*   If there were no requirements, restrictions, or expectations on you, what would you be doing for a living? What elements can you accomplish right now in your current occupation? Give a quick pitch that sells your idea.

Finding Your Talent
(Personal Vision—the third of three tools)

What if it is a struggle to identify your talent?

We are a very busy society. Take ten minutes to take a walk. Check out a sunset. Unwind, and imagine what life would be like if you were always this calm and centered. How do you bring that feeling into your daily routines?

No one's looking. You are all alone. Look in the mirror and tell yourself, in strictly positive terms, all the things you are. When you mention a characteristic, such as easy-going, explore what talents you have that relate to that characteristic.

Still having trouble?

Track your day in your journal. When did you feel like you had all systems rolling? When did you feel excited, productive, knowing you were at your best? Therein lies your talent. Examine those situations, and duplicate the factors that make you great.

Follow a model that mirrors the Sherpa Coaching process:

EXPLORATION.   Draw a picture; take a photograph. What does your client look like when everything is going just right? What's the dream?

> *Example: Gloria's personal vision is to encourage others to reach their goals. She can see herself in front of auditoriums full of people, motivating them to reach as far as they can, exhorting them to believe that nothing is impossible. She pictures herself on stage, under the lights, leaning toward the audience, right arm extended, pointing her finger. Can you see it? Can you feel Gloria? Her vision of herself is so specific, she can go to that place in her mind whenever she needs to encourage herself.*

PERSONAL ASSESSMENT.   So how far is your client today from the vision that they have of themselves? Often, on examination, they will find themselves very close. Others may find that they have a lot of work to do. Then what?

ANALYSIS.   Have your client examine what would it really take to get on the right track. Help them map it out. Include the five W's (who, what, when, where, why). Think about the ramifications of getting there and what will happen once they have arrived. Where will the client's support come from?

DECISION MAKING.   Move forward. Grab it . . . or go. Decide to chip away at it every day, or decide to create a new vision.

PLANNING. Create a checklist, a strategic path. Give yourself time frames for each task. Get others involved. Determine at what stages you will reward yourself.

IMPLEMENTATION. Go for it!

You have reviewed all the paths in both the relational and the organizational routes. You have the hard work behind you. In the next chapter, all the paths come together, and we'll begin work in the next phase.

CHAPTER 9

Goal Setting

A Continuation of Phase Four:
Charting the Course

F ROM HERE ON OUT, it's common ground. You chose a route with your client: organizational or relational. Within the chosen route, you identified a path, a specific topic where you spent significant time and effort changing professional behavior. No matter which path you chose, you're continuing here with the Sherpa process. Here's where all the paths join up again, and we make the final push to the summit.

Now that we have finished the training and analysis that's specific to your chosen path, we'll define further improvements your client can make in their business behavior. Then we'll develop a detailed action plan that goes beyond the coaching engagement.

What You'll Find in This Chapter:

You can organize your conversations in three steps, all aiming toward supporting and sustaining your client's new and improved behavior. The three steps:

- **Defining Needs**
- **Identifying Barriers**
- **QUESTION**

DEFINING NEEDS

Following a path, you've offered tools and training. Your client's goal is the ideal behavior they are working toward. Your client should be able to state one to three specific goals right now, such as:

1. I will use the three-sentence rule in every telephone conference call I participate in.

2. I will not take my staff's poor performance or bad attitude personally.

3. I will solve problems systematically, using the techniques I've learned from my Sherpa.

If your client can't state one or more goals specifically, you should work out a list. The goal or goals answer the question, "What are we going to do?"

Work with your client, and have them complete page 4-18 in his journal with you to help arrive at a specific goal or goals. You can even use these questions to refine and better state a goal they've already arrived at. Answer these eight questions to determine specific actions that support the goal(s).

1. What would make me more productive?

2. What would make my staff (or me) happiest?

3. What would improve my professional relationships?

4. What would make my staff more efficient?

5. What would help me stay focused on my priorities?

6. What changes in behavior will allow me to show my true self?

7. What would revitalize my sense of mission?

8. What could I do to really make my boss proud? myself proud?

We answer these questions to arrive at ideal goals and the best methods for pursuing them. You won't find answers to these questions in this book. Your client will create them. Ask questions. Then ask more questions. Facilitate. Help your client identify meaningful ways to accomplish the change they're committed to working on.

To work out a list, write down every desired behavior that comes to mind. As we explore potential goals, we'll look at the benefits that can come from each one, and at your client's level of enthusiasm about tackling each goal. If your client can't prioritize and come up with top-level goals on their own, bring in the IP factor. This technique helps narrow down your choices. Your client will list all their potential goals in their journal, on page 4-19. The chart there looks like this:

ACTION PLAN	IMPORTANCE 1 (NOT VERY) TO 5 (EXTREMELY IMPORTANT)	MULTIPLIER	PASSION 1 (LOW) TO 5 (VERY HIGH)	FACTOR: MULTIPLY THE TWO VALUES
Arrange regular meetings with top management.	3	X	3	9
Revamp employee orientation.	4	X	2	8
Improve personal rapport with direct report.	4	X	4	16

In the first column, the potential goal is written.

In the second column, the client rates the importance or benefits of achieving the goal (1 is low, 5 is high).

The third column, with the X, indicates we'll multiply two numbers.

In the fourth column, clients rate their personal enthusiasm for achieving the goal, on the same 1 to 5 scale.

In the final column, we multiply the Importance rating by the Passion rating, to produce what we call the IP factor.

This exercise will force your client to calculate the relative importance of each goal they're reviewing. The IP factor produces a value that reflects both the benefits of each goal and the chance your client will be able to work it through to completion. This exercise adds clarity to your client's thought process.

The next step is to answer the "How?" question by creating an action plan. It's important that your client has full ownership of their action plan when all is said and done. They have to be willing to work on it every day, every minute, without prompting from a Sherpa. That means the action plan must be your client's idea.

IDENTIFYING BARRIERS

Spend time in honest discussion of the barriers that inhibit goal setting, action planning, and successful follow-through.

Potential barrier # 1: A negative reaction to the word "goal."

We have all set goals that did not mean very much to us. When that happens, we will not work on them seriously. Allow your client to do a little venting on how well they have set and reached goals in the past. Then lighten it up. Teach your client to embrace the positive aspects of goal setting and prioritization. This is not something to be afraid of. The Sherpa should make it simple and fun.

Potential barrier # 2: The attitude barrier.

Clients sometimes consider goal setting, planning, and follow-through to be exercises in futility. A client who feels relatively powerless might think it's of no use. Remind them: they must *choose* to succeed. Accomplishment of these goals will not happen outside of their efforts. A positive attitude helps organize their thoughts and behaviors. It helps the client move forward positively. We all set goals many times in the course of a day. Let's pay attention to the really important ones.

Potential barrier # 3: Fear of failure.

Often, we fail to set goals because we are simply afraid we might not meet them. Open this up as a topic of conversation with your client. Are they afraid they simply can't do it? Is that fear realistic? Perhaps the fear is related to what others will think of them if they should fail. All these thoughts should be written in your client's journal. More discussion on fear can take place with the Accountability discussion, detailed in chapter ten.

Potential barrier # 4: Fear of success.

Clients might just as easily fear success as they fear failure. Why? It involves a trip into the unknown. What are the ramifications of reaching their goal? They'll have more work to do, perhaps, or more challenges. They'll be more visible, more subject to criticism.

Or maybe your client isn't ready for some other reason, as this story shares:

STORIES FROM THE SUMMIT

We worked with a client who said: "I need a successful company, one that runs itself." Easier said than done. William had quite a few barriers to break through to reach this goal. He was always in crisis mode, and had anger issues on a daily basis. He wasn't sure who he had to replace and who should stay in his office. He needed strategies for dealing with crisis. He had work to do related to anger management. So, needless to say, he was not ready to write his "sit back and relax" goal. The journey of a thousand miles begins with a single step. Our client needed the steps to be clearly defined, in small increments.

Is your client ready to succeed? Any doubts in this area? Have your client draw a picture, using a notes page in their journal, to show you what success looks like, smells like. Have them use all their senses to describe it.

QUESTION

The question has become: What is your client's action plan? This exercise details how your client is going to succeed with each of their specific goals.

You, as a coach, will now walk your client through a series of steps to make sure the goal or goals they commit to will be perfect for them. They'll be adding information and notes on page 4-20 of their journal as you walk through the QUESTION process for each one.

You'll have to know these steps well, so you can facilitate a conversation that refines the client's chosen goal or goals. Have them write their first goal from page 4-19 into the top row of the form on page 4-20.

For each question, you'll walk your client through the rest of the columns, using the steps detailed below. The columns are headed with the letters of the word "QUESTION." Your client will be making brief notes in each column: yes or no, a check mark, a key word or date. Have your client work in pencil in their journal as you lead them through the process. We may be restating his goal or goals as we go along.

Here's how you facilitate that process, one column at a time, on your client's form:

Q: Ask QUESTIONS.   What exactly are we setting out to achieve? What questions can you ask about this goal that you have not asked yet? Encourage your clients to find out whether their goal is stated correctly. Examine the wording of this goal. Talk through the benefits of obtaining the goal, as stated, to make sure it really articulates what they want to accomplish. They can rewrite the goal, if needed, and place a check mark in this column when you see they're ready to move to the next column. The real purpose is to make sure the goal is identified and written exactly as your client wants it to be. The questions help to establish that "perfect" goal.

U: UNDERSTANDABLE.   Make sure your client's intentions are clear and understandable, even to an objective viewer. Do you as a coach completely understand what your client is trying to achieve? Can they explain the goal in a few sentences, in a way that will make sense to their boss and subordinates? Does your client understand the commitment required to succeed?

E: EVALUATE it constantly.   Help your clients set up checks and balances. Together, you need to establish a near-term date to make sure this goal is being worked on, and a regular interval at which they remind themselves to continue work. The Sherpa may want to note the first few dates, and check in with the client to see that work is in progress. If this is not possible, ask your client to identify someone within their company who will commit to helping them stay on track. They may be able to use those individuals that were identified on their Support Mountain (Journal page 2-1).

S: Is it *SPECIFIC* enough?   Create goals that are specific, measurable, and challenging. How do you know when you are succeeding? If the goal is too ambiguous, too lofty, or the action plan too complex, your client will not be able to stay on course.

T: *TRICKS*.   Memory tricks can help your clients remember the tools you've given them. They might note QTIP (quit taking it personally) if that will help them be successful. Facilitate, and compel them to come up with ways they will remember their goal, how to make it happen, and the rewards that await them.

I: Is it *IMPORTANT* enough?   We are looking for goals that are comprehensive and positive. Is the goal under discussion one of the most important your client can achieve? Does it really make a difference? When this goal is accomplished, how will it affect others? Will your client's boss know the difference?

O: *OWN* it.   Can your client say they own this goal? How do they demonstrate ownership? That will involve asking questions such as:

- Do I want the new behavior as part of my life? How badly do I want it?
- Do I truly believe this is a problem? In what way is it a problem?
- Will I be sure to work on this every day?
- How can I prove that I care about this enough to work on it?

As a coach, be careful not to impose your goals for your clients on them. Each goal must be important to them. It must parallel their "Why it matters."

N: *NAME* someone your clients can share this with.   Who can double-check that they are working on this? How can they show this person that they are working on this goal? How can your clients see that they are following this action plan and getting the results they want? External reinforcement is one of your client's keys to success.

STORIES FROM THE SUMMIT

> *Gary was a Vice President of operations. He was straightforward and somewhat intimidating. We spent 12 weeks working on listening. Gary was finally able to put his arms around his weakness and really address it with his staff and peers. His biggest revelation was he was unable to stop talking when he was passionate and excited about something. That led to his people clamming up and not sharing their views and ideas.*
>
> *Gary learned to identify when this happened and constantly worked on this issue. His goal was relatively straightforward but extremely important to his success. His goal was to identify when he needed to stop talking and really listen. Working through QUESTION was perfect, because we covered every conceivable situation and he was prepared to make a positive change.*

The best way to work through this is by an example:

Goal: My body language matches my words and my meaning:

QUESTION: What exactly does that mean? What kind of words might present a problem? Who do you have to watch most carefully when you are around them? When does it happen? Is there a time of day you have to be more careful? Why do your body language and your words not match all the time?

UNDERSTANDABLE: What body language exactly are we looking for?

EVALUATE: How do you know when and if it matches?

SPECIFIC: Who will you be speaking to? When? Where?

TRICKS: How do you remember when you want to be aware of this? What triggers your awareness?

IMPORTANT:	How did you determine that this is important? Can you explain in simple terms why it is important? Why is that?
OWN IT:	Have you delayed pursuing this goal? If so, why?
NAME SOMEONE:	Who will commit to being aware of your body language and words? Consider those people on your Support Mountain.

After you've been through the QUESTION worksheet with your client's goals and action items, it's time to move on. You now have one or more specific, achievable goals to work on. This is the end of the Phase Four, Charting The Course.

We'll continue in Chapter 10 with Phase Five, Setting the Agenda, as we take our client to the summit.

Phase Five: Agenda

So you've finished phase four, Charting the Course. Your client knows what behavioral changes they'll make, and has agreed to the long-term commitment associated with these changes.

If there are paths that still need to be traveled, the Sherpa can go back to travel them along the relational route (Chapter 7) or the organizational route (Chapter 8). As a checkpoint, the Sherpa can turn to the last few pages of Chapter 6 and ask the questions that might show another path that needs to be traveled.

With no more paths to travel, we begin to summarize and have clients evaluate the work they have done. As they approach their personal summit, their dependence on the Sherpa can comfortably come to a close.

The Sherpa now continues up to the summit, pulling together the elements required for sustainability. This is just as important as the work you have already completed. If your progress to date doesn't stick, you haven't achieved your ultimate goal.

Is your client accountable for their behavior? Are they accountable to themselves, or to someone else, to continue working on these issues? To accept the ongoing work associated with the coaching experience, your client needs to develop personal accountability.

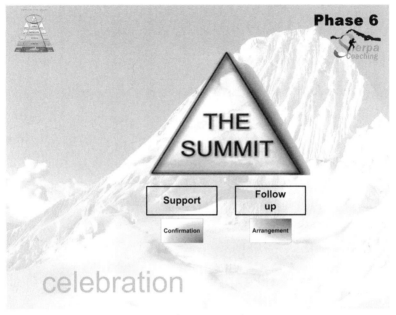

(© Sasha Corporation)

What You'll Find in This Chapter:

- **Commitment**
- **Attitude**
- **Accountability**
- **Journal**
- **Long-Term Outlook**

In Phase Five, the Sherpa ensures that the coaching client gets everything they can from the Sherpa process. Do what you can to make sure the client's commitment to change is sustainable.

 COMMITMENT

Throughout your work, you have been asking your client to determine their level of commitment to the paths you have traveled. This is when the Sherpa calls the client on the carpet. The commitment to positive change in usiness behavior falls into two areas, accountability and attitude. Let's lead our client further into the Sherpa process as they approach their personal summit.

ACCOUNTABILITY

"Unless you hold everyone accountable, you give up the right to hold anyone accountable."

Understanding accountability can be a defining moment for your client. It helps them consolidate their commitment to the changes you have been working on together.

We have developed a model for accountability that addresses its every aspect. You'll review the Accountability House with all your clients, so they'll have a way to better sort through their responsibilities and the responsibilities they assign to others. The Accountability House begins a

(© Sasha Corporation)

four-step process that will be covered in our upcoming book, *The Sherpa Team*. For now, the Accountability House is all your client will need, because it is designed for the individual as a review of personal accountability.

Let's get into the details, starting with Accountability, the portion of Phase Five that every client travels. This is an opportunity to see whether your client has built personal accountability into their life.

What is accountability? Accountability means being totally responsible for actions, events, and behavior, and to furnish a justifying analysis or explanation. Accountability is reflected in the mindset that says: "The buck (the responsibility) stops here." Why should your client truly understand this definition? Accountability is difficult for most people to put their arms around. The Sherpa's Accountability House helps your client figure out their strengths and weaknesses related to the concept of accountability.

THE ACCOUNTABILITY HOUSE

We use the concept of a house, a self-contained unit, and rooms within a house to describe accountability and its components. The Accountability House has four main areas: kitchen, dining room, living room, and foundation. Each area needs to be thought through and discussed with your client. There's a diagram and a place for your client to take notes on page 5-1 in their journal.

Going for a tour around the Accountability House allows your client to understand what it means to be accountable. When they have fully understood each room in the house, they have mastered the meaning of accountability. The house represents accountability because it belongs to you: it's the place you live. Accountability is all about ownership, taking possession. There are ramifications to ownership. This can make accountability a difficult concept to sell and execute well. Sometimes, because it's hard, people ignore it.

Review the house with your client in this manner:

Begin by the definition of accountability. Do you know what it means? You may want to ask your client to create a clear definition, in their own words, as homework for the week. In the interests of time, you may want to offer them this definition.

"Accountability enables activities of a system to be traced to individuals who may then be held responsible for their actions."

Talk about this definition with your client. Break the definition down in small pieces. What are the "activities of a system"? Have them give detailed and precise examples from their organization. What does "held responsible" mean? Get the definition of responsibility before moving on. Your client has to know what accountability means, and create a "buck stops here" mindset for themselves. This means that, no matter what, your client will become the final decision maker, creator, and manager of what needs to be done. They are accountable for moving their company forward, making and acting on decisions day to day, month to month, and year to year.

The Accountability House helps your client see accountability in a way they may never have before. Let's review the four parts of the Accountability House.

The FOUNDATION—Attitude

Chara: It's time to reward your client for the work they have done, and to remind them that this is just the beginning of the work they will be doing long after their Sherpa is gone. Give your clients a colorful, polished stone. This rock represents the foundation they have created for the new behaviors they are striving for. Have them keep their stone on their desk as a reminder to work toward a better understanding of themselves, and to build on their progress and success.

The foundation involves a good attitude. If your client's attitude is good, if you know they will work consistently on their goals and behavior after you're gone, you can skip over the attitude/foundation part of the Accountability House and move ahead to the next room, the Kitchen. Introduce the concept of the Accountability House and say: "You are solid in your foundation. You have nothing to worry about here. Your attitude is positive and it is taking you to the next level, the next room in the house."

A better attitude will fundamentally change your client's life. But let's be realistic. Your client has lived with their attitude for a long time. You know that, and you can tell them so. Move past that and ask: "Do you want anything more? Are you satisfied with the status quo? Are you entirely pleased with where you are?" If you see willingness to work on attitude, spend your last meeting or two in this area, even to the exclusion of working on the summit (Phase Six, Chapter 11).

Here are some indications that you and your client need to continue working here for the rest of the coaching sessions. You know you have attitude issues when:

- Your client tells you they "get it", yet can't produce evidence of any changed behavior.
- Your client falls back into problem behaviors without any remorse, forgetting they've learned another way of handling situations.
- Your client still complains about their boss, staff, and work environment.
- Your client still blames everyone else for their problems.
- Your client is brusque when talking about sensitive topics.

To reach a decision about your next steps, you might want your client to complete the quiz on page 5-3 of their journal, to define a little more clearly what their problem is, and whether you want to tackle it. Your client should answer these true/false questions as false.

1. I was born with the attitude I have today.
2. When my life changes, my attitude stays the same.
3. People should always be able to tell whether I am happy or unhappy.
4. I don't control my attitude. This is who I am.
5. If I don't feel great when I get to work, everyone should know that.
6. It is valuable to vent my feelings.
7. Usually, what's going on at home controls my attitude.
8. Talking about my feelings is the best way to handle an argument.
9. My attitude shows exactly how I am feeling.
10. The people around me affect my mood.

Attitude is all relative. So are your client's answers to these questions. The quiz is designed as a springboard to discussion. Some clients will answer a question as true and have a positive justification for seeing things that way. Don't be arbitrary. Use your facilitation skills to draw out explanations for each answer. Ask questions that might help your client identify negative thinking that's hurting their relationships with others, or their ability to change.

What is your client's attitude like? How committed are they to delving into their QUESTION, as defined in Chapter 9? Does their attitude limit their success in reaching their goal? Perhaps they aren't committed to changing their behavior. Perhaps your client has a negative outlook about their own potential. You know your client well by now. It is time you challenge them to change their attitude.

Discussion around the questions your client has just answered will bring out specific attitude issues. Does your client feel they have no control over outcomes in their life? Does your client allow situations to determine their emotions?

Ask the five W's: Who, What, When, Where, Why?

1. When does the attitude problem appear at its worst?
2. Where does the bad attitude rear its ugly head?
3. Why does the attitude come forward?
4. What happens, or fails to happen, during a bad moment?
5. Who provokes it?

Again you find yourself trying to help your client climb the Weakness Mountain. They have to acknowledge the attitude problem and then observe it. The following exercise will help them do both:

Using page 5-4 in your client journal, score your attitude for the next seven days on a scale of 1 (poor) to 10 (excellent). Either assign an overall score to the day, using the chart at the top of the page, like this:

Day One	6	Day Two	8	Day Three	3	Day Four	4
Day Five	3	Day Six	8	Day Seven	6	average	5.4

or divide your day into parts and assign a score to each one. This can be far more valuable, because it helps the Sherpa note patterns and prompt discussion on specific events. Here's what the bottom of page 5-4 in their journal might look like:

DAY ONE		DAY TWO		DAY THREE		DAY FOUR	
7-12	4	7-12	7	7-12	3	7-12	6
12-5	6	12-5	7	12-5	5	12-5	4
5-12	7	5-12	9	5-12	2	5-12	2
DAY FIVE		DAY SIX		DAY SEVEN			
7-12	3	7-12	7	7-12	7	Average	5.3
12-5	4	12-5	8	12-5	8	Average	6.0
5-12	2	5-12	7	5-12	3	Average	4.5

If they write down the numbers by day part, they can then transfer those values to the chart on page 5-5 in their journal, like this:

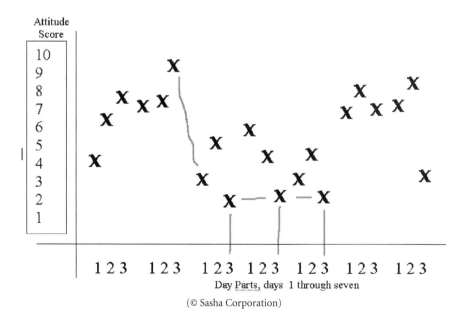

(© Sasha Corporation)

When they show up at your next meeting, you have something you can dig into. Observe the numbers—ask the 5 W's. In this example, the client had a big drop in attitude going from the end of day two to the beginning of day three. Why? What happened? How often does this happen?

The three lowest scores are on days three, four, and five, all in the last day part. Did the client have to work late? start to get run down? Was the evening at home the problem? If so, don't get into personal issues, but point out that a good day at work, like day one, can lead to a good evening. Then direct attention back to attitude at work.

Ask your client: What have you learned from your attitude? Where can you go with this information?

 The KITCHEN

The first room in the Accountability House is the kitchen. Ask your client to think about their kitchen, to describe it to you. Ask your client to draw a picture of it.

A kitchen is very personal. It's all about your client. It is full of the tools, equipment, and techniques that they prefer to use to do the important work of preparing meals for themselves and their families. The kitchen is connected to the lifeline of food. You know where everything is located. That's why we use the kitchen as an analogy for WHAT we are accountable for. The kitchen is the "action item" portion of accountability, your job.

There are three aspects of accountability that should be explored with your client.

1. Does your client understand what they are responsible for doing every day? Are they truly focused on getting their own work done?

2. If your client understands what they have to do every day, do they understand what is not their job? Does your client focus on irrelevant things in their work environment?

3. Does your client "own" their job? When faced with extraneous tasks, can your client say, "It's not my job"? Can your client's manager count on them?

Just as your client's kitchen is theirs in a personal way, so is their job. Does your client stay in their own kitchen? Do they feel free to enter someone else's kitchen and root through it? Ask your client: "Would you ever go to your neighbor's house and open the drawers and cabinets, rearranging things?" Of course not. By the same token, your client must stay in their own "kitchen" at work. Is your client doing that, or do they get involved where they shouldn't? Asking and answering the question "Should I be doing this?" allows your client to be more thoughtful about what they do on a daily basis, their productivity, and why they spend their time the way they do.

Use these two topics for discussion: "What Matters" and "What Doesn't Matter." Don't move on until you are sure your client understands the difference between petty things and things of consequence. Make sure they understand their job, they are committed to it, and know what is theirs to handle and what is not. This may lead to discussion on trivial tasks, distractions, and gossip. If necessary, spend time on those topics. It will be extremely valuable. In our upcoming book *The Sherpa Team,* we'll share more on gossip, and share startling survey results we have produced for client companies.

Let's move to the next room in the Accountability House.

The DINING ROOM

When you think of your dining room, you think of people enjoying time together. It's where you communicate with your family and friends, a place where you ask others for their input and learn more about them.

Think of the dining room as the "people" part of the Accountability House. Looking in this room will tell you whom you are accountable to and who's accountable to you.

Ask your client to list the people in their lives to whom they are accountable. Focus on the people at work. They can use page 5-2 of their journal to do this. Have them write down names, responsibilities, and the level of accountability they have to that person (scale of 1 to 10).

Then dig deeper, and ask your client what it takes for someone to get on that list.

Next, ask about people at work they spend time with, and effort on, who are not on the list. Help your client determine whether any of these individuals should be added to their list. Allow your client a moment to study this list. Then make a very direct statement to them that when they gravitate toward people who are not on the list, they are diminishing their accountability. Accountability and success are linked to one another. Help your client figure out ways to minimize the time they spend with people they don't need to be involved with.

Work through this discussion, and look for revelations by asking questions and prompting for meaningful answers.

 ## The LIVING ROOM

The final room in the Accountability House is the living room. It's where "matters of the heart" are discussed, and where people become vulnerable. It's where your client comes to terms with accountability as they feel it on a personal level.

There are four themes in the living room:

1. The comfort Zone
2. True Outcomes
3. Fears
4. Blame

These themes isolate several difficult issues surrounding personal accountability. Let's examine each one:

Comfort Zone Accountability issues arise with a client who feels comfortable exactly where they are, and thus resists change. Understanding how close your client stays to their comfort zone is one key to helping them improve.

The comfort zone can mean different things to different people. A client who seems adventurous may not be as brave as they seem.

They may take on new projects, unique challenges, all the time. That's because they are confident in their skill set. Ask them to do something that requires learning new skills, and they might go into panic mode. People don't like taking ownership of things they don't know much about.

The best way to see whether your client is stuck in a comfort zone is to draw this picture for them, talking and asking about the zones from the center going outward toward the top of the diagram:

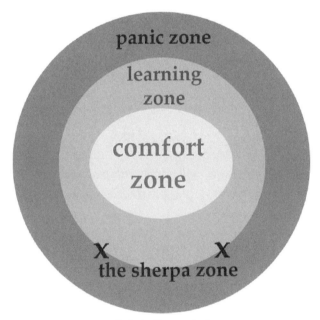

(© Sasha Corporation)

THE COMFORT ZONE	Where we like to stay. We know it. We like it. It's nonthreatening.
THE LEARNING ZONE	A place where you are in control but learning something new. Good examples would be a craft class or a dance class: something new you choose to do, because you are excited about the results.

THE PANIC ZONE   It's a place where you are terrified. You are uncomfortable, because you are not in control. For
some people it's a confrontation, for others it's a
cocktail party. Your panic zone is the place where
fear overcomes your ability to learn.

Then go to the bottom of the picture you are drawing and add the
Sherpa zone. Sherpas want their clients where the X is—right on the edge
of the learning zone, and not quite into the panic zone. The Sherpa's job is
to facilitate change, and to do it quickly. That requires taking the client out
of their comfort zone.

In the Sherpa zone, a client is constantly challenged: not always comfortable, but never in the panic zone. The Sherpa zone is a place where
optimal learning takes place. For our clients, and us, it's a great place to be.

STORIES FROM THE SUMMIT

> *Matt is a plant manager. He is dynamic and spirited. He has moved from
> a big city to a small town. Matt was extremely successful in his job in the
> big city. He now has to connect to his people on the floor and watch them
> do repetitive, boring work. He likes being in meetings, making decisions,
> and answering his emails. His comfort zone is the meeting. He is close to
> his panic zone when he has to spend all day talking with the frontline peo-
> ple. Assuming his responsibility to bring value to that part of his job was a
> fundamental change for Matt. He began to take accountability for his
> people as he got more and more comfortable spending time with them.*

True Outcomes   Sometimes, people will avoid accountability in a
very strange way: They'll go into denial about what's really happening, especially if it involves confrontation or conflict. They constantly look at
their outcomes as positive, even when they know they should be dealing
with an issue more effectively.

The goal, and accountability for reaching it, is so important that they
can't acknowledge defeat. Instead they'll say: "I did the best I could. We

ended up with the best results we could have achieved, under the circumstances." Such clients have to have their feet held to the fire. They must acknowledge that they're not getting the job done. They have to face up to their failures, learn and practice new behaviors, even if it hurts.

In another variation of the "true outcomes" scenario, a client will assume they have more power than they do, or will try to take responsibility for a decision that's not really theirs, because being in control puts them in their comfort zone. In these scenarios you, as the Sherpa, might want to bring up the word "truth": "Do you 'skirt' the truth? Do you always tell the truth? Is this the outcome you want, or the outcome that should be?"

 ## STORIES FROM THE SUMMIT

Bill is a self-motivated plant manager. He has a demanding boss who asked Bill to move one of his supervisors to another department. Bill said: "I don't know about this. Let me get back to you." Bill thought about the pros and cons. He thought about whether the supervisor would benefit, whether the departments involved would benefit. He saw problems and agonized over a decision. Bill took four days of consideration for this question. He went back to his boss and said: "This might work."

The reality was, Bill's boss had clearly made his mind up four days earlier. The true outcome was always going to be: this supervisor is going to move. Bill wanted to be comfortable with the situation, but he made his boss angry because it took him so long to agree to a decision that had already been made.

If Bill had looked at the true outcome involved, he would have realized that his job was to do what his boss told him to. Bill still could have maintained some control when he was told about the move. He should have said, "Yes. Let's do it," right away. Then he could have suggested, for his own peace of mind: "I would like to sit down and evaluate things with you in three weeks."

Fears The next issue we deal with in our living room is fear. What role does fear play in accountability for your client? Fear is a driver that few people spend time dissecting. Fear is a basic emotion that can be hidden yet overwhelming in the work environment. Fear has to be discussed. What makes that discussion valuable is finding the fear that best describes your client's mindset.

Here are some fears:

- Fear of looking foolish or incompetent
- Fear of conflict and confrontation
- Fear of failure
- Fear of the amount of time and effort needed outside the comfort zone

At this point, discuss fear and how it relates to any lack of accountability your client may have. Fear of failure is often a significant problem for individuals who avoid accountability. Successful people don't experience this fear because they have failed before, paid the price, and lived to tell the story. They have confidence that failure will make them better in the long run. *Failing to be accountable* brings deeper pain than simply failing and being accountable for it.

STORIES FROM THE SUMMIT

Working with Valerie is always a pleasure. She is the owner-operator of a small business. She is energetic and task driven. Valerie gets her job done, but she has a fear of losing control. She never wants to be out of the loop. When she is, she feels detached.

What problems can this cause when it comes to accountability? Valerie is unable to delegate, so she does everything herself. She does the most menial tasks because "no one can do them as well as I can." Lost in the details, Valerie can't keep the big picture in mind. She is not moving the company forward as well or as fast as she could.

> *Her fear has driven her to be accountable for someone else's job. She's failing to be accountable for her own. So, delving into her fears, let's her figure out why accountability is so hard for her.*

There are two things human nature tells us to do when faced with conflict: fight or flee. We are wired to respond in one of those two ways if we feel under attack. If your client can admit that this instinct to flee comes into play, help them to develop a personal plan, definite steps they can take to overcome their fear. That means pushing natural reactions to the side, and directing their energy into positive, creative efforts. This process is called sublimation, channeling negative energy into positive pursuits: turning fear into courage, greed into diligence, anger into effort.

Blame   The final issue in the living room of accountability is blame, another big stumbling block for many leaders. Blame is a funny game. Pointing the finger at someone else can come from fear, or from laziness. If you blame, people might go away. If you blame, the problem might go away. If you blame, people might not ask you again. If you blame, you look good and someone else looks bad.

Why is it so easy to blame? Well, it can save someone the effort of being caught up in an issue they never cared about, don't want to be involved in, and don't have the energy for. If your client plays the game of placing blame, the first thing a Sherpa will direct them to do is to fly straight into the face of negative consequences, and get some practice at taking the heat instead of deflecting it.

 ## Stories from the Summit

> *Try taking the blame and see how it feels. I was at a video production with a couple of colleagues. One of my associates was in a rush, and snapped at one of the workers on the set: "Hurry up and get moving. I don't have all day."*

After the shoot was over. The video producer came up to the three of us and pointed right at me. "You were rude to my grip. No one is rude to my people on my set." I said, "Sorry. I didn't mean to upset anyone. Please forgive me."

I hadn't done anything wrong at all, but I took the blame. Why? I didn't think it was worth pointing fingers at someone else. Taking that blame was an experiment on my part. The producer was able to vent and get it over with. The guilty party owed me a big favor. The innocent bystanders marveled at what I had done. It was well worth it, because my stock rose, especially when the producer was told what had really happened.

With a good grasp on accountability, and a way to work through related issues, your client has an advantage over most of their peers.

BROWSING THE JOURNAL

This is one of our favorite parts of the Sherpa process. Sherpa and client go back through the journal, starting from the beginning. Review each page of notes, and each exercise you've used, asking your client: "Was that important to you?"; "Do you remember going through that?"; "What part of this exercise did you like?" When your client recalls an important lesson or a revelation, have your client put a Post-it note or a tab on that page, and have them write something to help them remember why the page has value.

After your coaching has ended, your client will find that their own words are a powerful reminder of the work you've done with them.

THE LONG-TERM OUTLOOK

Every client should work on the QUESTION exercise. Your client has a definite direction: goals, meaning, and measurements. Your client has their QUESTION completed in their journal. Now let's go one step further, and have them open up to the possibility that they can set and achieve goals like this anytime, on their own.

Have your client turn to page 5-6, Outlook, in their journal, to answer these questions:

- What part of the things you have learned will be easy to continue?
- What are some of your other wishes, desires, and needs?
- What else would you like to accomplish on your own?
- What are the benefits of meeting the new goals you have just listed?
- What behavior changes will you be working on in six months? in a year? two years?

Allow time for reasoned, thoughtful answers and encourage discussion. The more ownership your client has of their journal, the more they will use it when you are done.

Now you are ready to move to the final phase, the SUMMIT, with your client.

CHAPTER 11

Phase Six: The Summit

A S YOU ENTER THIS FINAL PHASE, you are finishing up with your client. The Sherpa and the client have both trusted and followed the process. A profound change is already underway in the client's business life. The two of you started as a team, in a relationship built on your meetings, and now you emerge as a better coach and a much-improved client.

Some clients will traverse a path and be through with their Sherpa guide in the usual 12 weeks. Other clients may get stuck early in the process, and need an extension past that period. In other situations, a client may finish one path and need to climb a second or third before the Sherpa's role comes to an end. For each additional path, a six-week extension is probably appropriate. There's always a balance between time, money, energy, and priorities, so your executive contact must approve extensions. Trust their judgment, just as you do your client's. They know things you don't know.

To wrap things up, go back to the first notes page in your client's journal. What were the expectations your client set for you as a Sherpa? Did you reach them? Ask your client to tell you how closely you came to reaching each expectation they had. You'll learn important things from this, and you'll learn different things from each client.

On page 1-2 in your client's journal, we revisit ramifications. Since there's always an equal but opposite reaction to any force in nature, you have warned your client to anticipate the negative consequences of positive changes. Discuss your client's thoughts on ramifications. Ask them

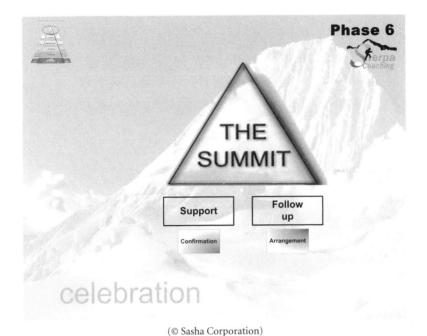

(© Sasha Corporation)

whether they're better at predicting and preparing for unexpected reactions to their changes.

What You'll Find in This Chapter:

- **Support**
- **Follow-up**

You have two very important areas to cover with your client before you end your relationship: support and follow-up. Support means setting up systems that allow other people to reinforce your client's efforts at change. Follow-up means making sure, through personal contact, that your client's new abilities are kept in play.

 **SUPPORT**

The first exercise you will do with your client is the Summit Support Mountain. First, let's look at the support others will provide your client. Take out the Support Mountain and examine it. It's on page 6-1 in your

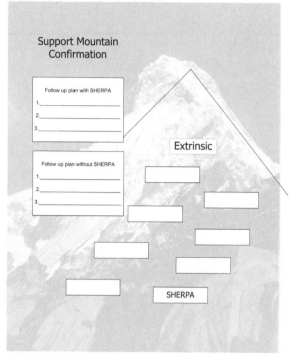

Support Mountain
Confirmation

Follow up plan with SHERPA
1._____
2._____
3._____

Extrinsic

Follow up plan without SHERPA
1._____
2._____
3._____

SHERPA

(© Sasha Corporation)

client's Journal. Your client can copy the names he listed on Journal page 2-1 to this page.

Let's look at the Extrinsic supports, on the face of the Mountain. How complete and accurate is this list of names? Your client should do some reflecting about those who offered support or were selected to participate in their continuous improvement. Discuss each individual on the original Support Mountain. Your client should ask themselves and possibly the people listed:

- Will you be able to continue working with me?
- Be prepared to tell them what you need, and what kind of commitment this might involve: the specifics of their support and the time that may be involved.

If there are people you should remove from your list, include them in your Summit celebration, thanking them for their support. Affirm that they made a difference in your success. Keep them informed as you achieve your future goals.

Are there people who should be added to this group? Give them a job description, including your expectations of them as a member of your Extrinsic Support Team.

Your client is responsible for following up with each person on their list, establishing specific action plans for people on the Extrinsic Supporters list. Those action plans may be simple, short, and sweet:

> Meredith would like her assistant to remind her to stop using the words *want* and *need*.

> David wants his wife to notice when he is calm and cool, when he reacts well to a situation with his son. He needs to hear that she's proud of him. (This is a personal issue, but anger management was this client's chosen path, and that behavior had huge repercussions at home.)

> Rick wants his boss to tell him to stop talking as soon as Rick has made his point.

These are small things, but they create the support and accountability your client needs to make sure the changes stick.

Now let's talk about what your client must do to support others. Use a notes page in your client's journal to write down the names of people who need most from him, going forward.

Answer these questions for each person:

- What do I have to do, specifically, to develop this relationship and make full use of what this person offers me?
- How do I act like a leader with each of these people?
- What does each one need from me?
- How can I make sure to give them what they need?

Example:

Your client writes down "Mary Janet," his personal assistant:

> "She still doesn't grasp the concept of expectations. For the near future, I will help her with this, so she'll develop as a leader and as a team member. MJ needs to connect better with everyone around her, too."

For Leroy, a new subordinate:

"He is new, and he wants to fit in. He needs reassurance that I'll be here until he feels absolutely comfortable with his job. I can learn from his experience working at a competitor, too, if I am open to that."

FOLLOW-UP

You have reviewed the journal, and your client is clear on the direction they will take when you are no longer together. It's time to ensure your work results in a sustainable change. Help your client establish checks and balances. Add these follow-up thoughts to the Support Mountain page in your client's journal.

As you wrap up your relationship, here are some questions you might ask your client:

- How do you know this is going to work for you?
- What conditions have you set up to make sure this works?
- Is there anything else you need to change in your environment?
- Are you happy with your action plans? Will you follow them? How will you notify me when they are accomplished?
- Do you want to follow up with emails on a weekly, monthly, or quarterly basis?
- Do you want to call me (your coach) when you are falling back into old habits?

Here is what we share with all our clients in this last meeting:

- I am your Sherpa.
- We have shared quite a bit in these past few weeks.
- I will be your Sherpa for the rest of your life.
- When there's a genuine need, I will be available for you.
- Keep me posted on your success and the challenges that come at you.

Once a Sherpa, always a Sherpa. Define your expectations for your client and your future connection. You might keep your relationship going with your client for another six months. It might be structured like this:

First two months: phone calls every other week for a half hour.

Next two months: phone call once a month for a half hour.

Final two months: email every other week.

If your client wants this continued contact, it's time to sit down with them and the executive contact (if you have one) to see what's going to be most productive. When you meet, have a fee structure in mind.

Congratulations, you have reached the SUMMIT.

As a Sherpa, you should be very proud of your work with each client. You leave them with an unbelievable array of useful tools and techniques. The journal, your advice, your training, and facilitation will benefit your client forever.

You and your client have reached the top! You're standing on the summit, and it's time to celebrate. Take some time to enjoy the view.

You've learned quite a bit about your client over time. You know the things that encourage them. You know where they need help. You know their outside interests, hobbies, and passions. Offer a gift that reflects those interests, to let your client know that you remembered everything they shared with you. Your gift choices might include bookmarks, trinkets, even children's books designed to encourage your client. Your client will enjoy having a lasting reminder of your time together, and of their goals and dreams.

Talk openly and freely about the successes you've shared during your time together. Have your client acknowledge how hard they worked and how far they have come. CELEBRATE!

CHAPTER 12

The Sherpa Guide

To be a successful Sherpa coach, you'll have to adapt your natural instincts to the Sherpa process. The process is your road map. You only have 12 one-hour meetings. These 12 meetings can make a huge difference in a client's life. The process will drive you. The process will inspire you. The Sherpa process will help you avoid tangents and create a path straight to the summit.

Coaching means creating positive change in business behavior. Both you and your client will experience change. Be aware of what is happening to you personally as all of this is going on. Don't be afraid of your own growth. Change is great for everyone involved, including you.

What You'll Find in This Chapter:

- **Respect the Process**
- **Intuition**
- **Change**

   You've studied the Sherpa coaching process, and along the way, you've learned a few things that are basic to the Sherpa philosophy.

Coaching is a commitment to your client and to yourself. As you take on the awesome task of guiding and encouraging your client to reach for their higher self, you'll be doing the same thing. For a coach, that happens as you spend time preparing for meetings. Because preparation is necessary, you'll devote far more than 12 hours to each client engagement.

Coaching is about facilitation, bringing answers out of people. An athletic coach gets players to develop their strength from within and then apply it. In the same way, a Sherpa coach helps clients do the hard work for themselves. You don't have to always use the perfect words; just bring your client to the perfect place.

How does a Sherpa measure success? By the time you're done, you'll see noticeable improvements in your client's behavior and relationships. A small change can be a profound change. The difference between first place and fifth in an athletic event can be a few hundredths of a second. Often, the Sherpa client will leverage a small change and turn it into a major change in their career, their relationships, and their life.

 ## STORIES FROM THE SUMMIT

Maurie was a hard-working vice president of sales for a restaurant chain. He traveled a lot, and his people were all over the country. His Sherpa coach was brought in because Maurie was in trouble. If he didn't pull his people together and make year-end quotas, he was told, he would be fired.

He needed an overhaul of the way he treated his staff. Maurie and I worked diligently on his management and leadership skills. He was more committed to succeed than any client I ever worked with. I worked with him for two consecutive 12-week sessions. He went from a "below average" boss on his evaluations to an "excellent" boss. He made his quota, and along the way, coaching changed his life. Sherpa coaching created a new manager for his company. This engagement was a huge success.

STORIES FROM THE SUMMIT

> *Van was a "people person," director of a midsized automotive supplier. Although he got along well with his subordinates, Van was largely ineffective as a leader. He challenged coaching, thinking it might teach him to be more manipulative or somehow disrespectful of his staff. He was careful not to do anything that might damage employee relations. He moved slowly, very slowly. One day, Van brought his staff together for a project kick-off, and used the Expectations Mountain. He saw a noticeable improvement in the way people responded. He was thrilled with the results, and began using the process every day. Van continued to be sensitive, but his coaching had made him an effective leader as well as a pleasant one.*

RESPECT THE PROCESS

Teaching at a seminar in South Africa, we were challenged by an audience member who asked: "Why all these steps? This is too confusing. Can't we just choose the steps we need?" Before we could respond, a hospital administrator at the back of the hall stood up and shouted out: "You have to respect the process. Without all the steps, you'll never get any better. You'll just be guessing, like you always have. Respect the process."

Those six words say it all: "You have to respect the process." Without a process, all you can do is guess and react. It is tunnel vision, because your coaching will be driven by whatever is going on that day, with that client. This process draws your client out of their comfort zone and into the Sherpa zone, a place where some people don't want to go but everyone needs to be.

The Sherpa process is designed for the coach, and the included exercise and assessments are designed for the client. Your clients will do what you ask them to do. They won't necessarily know what phase, route, and path they are on, unless you tell them. That doesn't matter because you, the Sherpa, do know where you are and what happens next.

STORIES FROM THE SUMMIT

Cheryl intimidated people. I knew that the first day we met, and I told her so. She wanted to have her problems solved that very day. The Sherpa process allowed us to find out what motivated her to act the way she did. Without certain diagnostic steps in the process, we may have tried to fix an entirely different problem. We focused on creating the correct behavior, and Cheryl became a different person in the way she delivered the demands of the day to her staff.

As you learn the process, you'll eventually master everything in this book. Every trick, tip, and technique should be at your fingertips. Always carry notes about the forms, assessments, and quizzes that appear in your client's journal. You really never know what you are going to need at any time. Be prepared for your client and wherever they may take you.

LEAVING IT ALL BEHIND

Nurses are among our favorite clients. There is a level of caring in their profession that can't be found anywhere else. Day to day, they comfort people and genuinely care about them. Some nurses are capable of "leaving it all behind." Some are not.

Like a health-care professional, you can't survive as a coach if you carry the weight of every case around with you. You might have to follow up or do some research between meetings, but emotionally, you'll need to "let it go."

The Sherpa creates a relationship based on episodes. Each one can be fundamentally life-changing for your client. The successful Sherpa will do the work but not bring it home, emotionally speaking. The Sherpa concentrates completely on the client during every meeting. Your commitment is immediate. You owe your client undivided attention. You owe it to yourself to walk away from your meetings without any undue burdens.

STORIES FROM THE SUMMIT

I love coaching. I look forward to every meeting with every client. Some are less successful than I would like. Some are better than I could imagine. I do the best I possibly can with each client during our time together. I leave them with my help, guidance, concern, and involvement.

I "walk away clean" because I know I can't help my client by being as worried as they are. I don't help my client if I feel the same sorrow they do. I help my client by coming to each meeting with a well-defined process that solves their problems in the workplace. It works for me. I know it can be the same for you.

THE GUMBIE

Ask a new or aspiring coach, "Why did you want to be a coach?" and you'll get a myriad of answers about their background:

- I have worked in HR all my life.
- I counsel people all the time.
- I have trained forever.

And a variety of motivators:

- I need something different after 20 years.
- I want the money.
- I want the status.
- I want to contribute to people's success.

No matter where someone's experience lies, or why he or she wants to be a coach, the Sherpa process has answers. There's nothing more rewarding to us than training a new coach. We call them "gumbies." In the world of mountain climbing, gumbie refers to a novice or inexperienced rock climber. Teaching a gumbie proves the value of the Sherpa process. It validates the development work we have done, because without the process, we would see gumbie coaches tread water and, quite often, drown in the experience.

INTUITION

The Sherpa process helps develop your intuition. Intuition means trusting yourself, following through on your thoughts, beliefs, and insights. Intuition comes from what you see in front of you, the facts of the matter, combined with a mystical knowledge based on instinct.

You can improve your intuition. Like anything else, it takes practice and it takes work. Practice by trusting your coaching decisions, basing them less on fact and more on your personal insight. By responding to your intuition, you'll help your client "read between the lines" in the story of their own life.

Work to develop intuition based on extensive knowledge. Know what resources this book holds for you, so you can apply any resource, any time. Learn all you can about leadership, training, and development. Spend time at the bookstore and the library and use their resources to better yourself.

We have coached many women, and found that female executives value coaching in a very different way than men. Women do not always have the structured environment that men do. Men have their accountants, their lawyers, and their bankers to reinforce their business decisions. Women are often islands. They can feel alone. The coach doesn't have to be brilliant in dealing with legal or financial issues, but they can be a sounding board, a business confidante, and a supporter. Women need women in the business world.

Some of the most successful women struggle with the cost of success. Often, they've compromised their personal happiness for professional accomplishment. In many cases, the expectations women set for themselves are unreasonable. Their support systems don't enable them to reach their goals. Being coached often provides a female executive with the necessary sounding board, a safe place to shed tears of stress without judgment.

"No man is an island" . . . unless, of course, he is a CEO. You've heard it's lonely at the top. Top execs can't fraternize with line-level staff. The question is, with whom do they share the joy and the pain of everyday challenges? One suggestion a Sherpa might offer: Connect with a CEO roundtable at your chamber of commerce, or partner with an executive peer, in or out of your industry. After their Sherpa has moved on, the CEO client will have a group of peers to serve the same purpose their coach once did.

CHANGE—IT CAN HAPPEN TO YOU

We've had tremendous success with the coaches we have developed. They are doing well, and they're very confident. They didn't start out that way, and you won't either. Mastering the Sherpa process involves learning and personal growth.

We'd like to share the stories of three of our newest Sherpa coaches. They are exceptional people with credentials to succeed in this line of work. Becoming a Sherpa has meant learning and growth for each of them.

Maria is a social worker. She has helped people all her life. Her biggest adjustment has been learning to stop *helping* her clients and to start *leading* them to find their own answers. Maria was accustomed to solving every problem people threw at her. She found it difficult to stop. Maria told us this story at the beginning of her coaching career.

Her son is a young father who's had quite a few ups and downs in his life. One day, talking about an issue in his life, he said to Maria, "Mom, I am doing the best I can." She replied: "I know you are, son. I am very proud of you." Her son was shocked: "Mom, that's the first time in my life you didn't try and solve this problem. Are you okay?" Maria said, "Yes. For the first time, I am, and so are you." Maria changed the way she communicated with her son because of what she learned in becoming a Sherpa coach. She stopped solving his and everyone else's problems. She started listening and coaching as needed. She enjoyed her new role as a coach, as a mother, and as a friend.

Rod has had a remarkable life. He has tremendous charisma, what we call presence. It hasn't been easy, especially living life as a devoted single father. Rod will tell you: "Every time I ask a client a question, I ask myself the same question. I really examine how I would answer it and how it looks in my life. This has made me grow and made me realize how much of my life I have taken for granted. I love learning every day."

Rod is so energetic, reporting back to us how the coaching is going. We were on vacation and Rod left this message on voice mail: "I know you are having fun, so I just wanted to tell you 'I am getting it done.'" Rod was getting down and dirty with his client, and he was thrilled about it. Coaching should be an awesome experience.

Angela has been a "ropes course" trainer for a long time, and she's one of the most highly regarded in the country. She knew the ropes, and how to use them in her team-building practice. The world of one-on-one coaching was new to her. She had trained forever, so she felt pretty confident about the whole thing. Angela liked the direction the Sherpa process gave her, but at first she didn't really believe in the process.

Angela's first client was very needy. Angela got caught up with the client, because she liked being needed herself. Angela forgot to follow the Sherpa process. Wherever a meeting went, she would follow. Angela started solving "boyfriend problems." She would even share a drink with her client after a coaching session. This had to stop. After we held a highly charged "respect the process" meeting with Angela, she began to understand that her job was not to be a friend, but to stay completely focused on the process.

What happened to make Angela change? She learned that the process was her salvation. It was the only thing that could keep her focused on her goal. It allowed her to be in charge of her words and the direction of her coaching.

STORIES FROM THE SUMMIT

Staying focused on the process is your "out." If you find yourself getting too close to your client, pull away by saying things like "Back to the process" or "Let's look at our next step." The best example I can think of involves our daughter Dani. When she was a teen, one of our strictest rules was "no more than one friend in the car at a time when you are driving." We were adamant about that rule. She always abided by it.

One recent afternoon, she shared this: "Mom, you know what rule I liked the best when I was driving? The one about 'no more than one person in the car.' I knew I could always use that rule to get out of going to parties I didn't want to go to, or to places I was unsure of. You always gave me an 'out.' " It's the same for coaching, and the Sherpa process. Staying focused on the client, and let the process be your "out," designed to help you stay out of trouble.

THE FUTURE OF COACHING

For 20 years, the computer and software industries struggled with standards. Hundreds of ideas and companies came and went, each trying to gain the market share that would lead to dominance.

Until the Sherpa process set a standard, executive coaching has been in much the same disarray. A *Denver Post* article found chaos and confusion about the definition of coaching, citing "spirituality coaches, relationship coaches, life coaches, business coaches, career coaches, communications coaches, management coaches and leadership coaches," all at the same local convention.

The *Denver Post* was right at that time. Coaching was in chaos. There was no single approach to executive coaching that was considered authoritative. A seminar on coaching sponsored by the Conference Board featured over 30 speakers in a two-day period. Why? No one, at that time, had any answers, so they created panel discussions, trying to figure out what coaching should be. We were invited to speak to an alliance of graduate schools, since they had tried to define coaching with few results.

The Sherpa process and this book create a standard for successful business coaching. It's been designed as an "operating system," an industry standard that coaches and leaders will agree to use and support.

If you're an internal coach for your company, the Sherpa process and practices are all you'll need. For consultants, the adjustment to coaching means selling a new service, and perhaps working with a new type of prospect. Someone starting their own business will need to do much more. When we teach our "Executive Coaching Certification" classes at Cincinnati's Xavier University or other schools, we often have an additional class on how a Sherpa can turn this coaching process into a business. Whatever your role or your plans, devote yourself to learning, and do whatever it takes to make your practice successful.

What's the future of coaching? As we told you when you first opened *The Sherpa Guide,* since there's no significant competition, the Sherpa process will become a solid standard. There are two choices: Operate without a process at all, or with an obscure or discredited process, and you'll have little chance to succeed. Adopt the Sherpa process and become mainstream, instead of being shut out of this lucrative career.

With that in mind, we'd love to hear from the coaches who adopt this process. Tell us what you are doing, how many clients you've coached as a Sherpa, and we'll share information about the total number of Sherpa coaches and clients out there—information that can help you in your marketing efforts.

Email a periodic update to info@sherpacoaching.com, and we'll stay in touch.

One thing that sets the Sherpa process apart is the client journal. The journal has been specially designed as a companion to this book. On the following pages, you'll find a sample of the material in the client journal, the assessments, exercises, and reflective work that each client will do.

.or the professional coach, the journal is a powerful marketing tool that demonstrates added value, proving that you follow an established, well thought-out coaching process. When you prove you know exactly where you are going to lead your clients, you'll get more business.

The journal provides a constant companion, something your client will bring to every meeting as you chart their trip to the summit. When you are done, each client has a permanent record of the work they have done with you, and a constant reminder that there is more work you can do, and more paths you can follow together.

Good luck on your journey.

Brenda Corbett and Judith Colemon, Cincinnati, Ohio, USA

Tools for the Sherpa

THIS CHAPTER CONTAINS TOOLS THAT YOU, as a Sherpa, can use to refine your coaching style and manage your coaching engagements. In the first section, you'll find a number of evaluations and documents that you can use to validate your coaching skills. In the second section, you'll also find a sample of what appears in the client's journal. This material is included for easy reference. However, it is not designed to take the place of the client's journal.

For every client, you should purchase a journal, so they will have an attractive and personal place to record notes and assignments. The client's journal also includes all the exercises and assessments you may use with an individual client.

Let's start with the assessments and documents that will help you become a better coach. Pages numbers for use by the Sherpa coach only include an SC prefix.

SECTION ONE:

SECTION TWO:

Sample Client Journal
Client Journal Order Forms

The Sherpa's Personal
Toolkit − Listening Skills

Use this tool to measure how well you listen. Think carefully about each question. Review the way you "feel" and the way you act, and then write your answers (1-4) on the right-hand column. Your total score provides an important gauge of your listening skills.

When listening, I do the following:	My score:
1 = Almost never 2 = Some of the time	
3 = Most of the time 4 = Almost always	
1. I pay attention, even when I am not interested in the immediate topic.	_____
2. I wait for speakers to finish before evaluating their messages.	_____
3. I listen for feelings as well as subject matter.	_____
4. I stop myself from interrupting the person speaking to me.	_____
5. I listen to people when they speak, even though I have no personal interest in the person.	_____
6. I am aware of my own body language as a listener.	_____
7. I work to make myself really want to listen.	_____
8. I maintain emotional control, no matter what is said.	_____
9. I would rather talk than listen.	_____
10. I am good at summarizing what someone has just told me.	_____
TOTAL SCORE:	_____

What Your Score Means:

34–40   You are an exceptional listener.   Remind yourself to *stay that way*. Can you identify, as a coach, when you lose concentration? Do you recognize and pull back from moments when you are not paying attention? Does your lack of focus have to do with a certain subject or a certain client? You need to know yourself so well that you have "red flags" go up when those situations occur.

26–33 The mark of a good listener. Stand back and watch yourself more carefully. What questions pulled your score down? On which questions did you give yourself 3 or less? Revisit those questions and see if you can figure out what really happens to you in those situations. What is it that distracts you? What is it that you are not interested in?

21–25 You're a fair to poor listener. Allow more listening time in your conversations. You don't want a score in this range if you are considering the world of coaching. You are easily distracted, and just as interested in talking as you are in listening.

20 and Below You have serious listening problems. How do you get along day to day? Develop your skills in this area, think things through, practice new behaviors and retake this test in ten days.

THE SHERPA'S PERSONAL
TOOLKIT – TRUST RATING

SC 1-2

Trust is an important part of coaching.

Let's take a quick snapshot, and see what your "trust rating" is:

Trust factors	My score:
1 = Rarely 2 = Sometimes	
3 = Most of the time 4 = Always	
1. I am on time for appointments and meetings.	_____
2. I make accurate first assessments of people I meet.	_____
3. People believe I have their best interests at heart.	_____
4. I prepare thoroughly for all meetings.	_____
5. People consider me fair, consistent, and even-handed.	_____
6. If something is marked private, I do not touch it.	_____
7. My client would certainly know that I care about them.	_____
8. People can tell me anything, even when they can't tell a partner.	_____
9. I admit it when I don't understand a topic of conversation.	_____
10. People trust my judgment.	_____
TOTAL SCORE:	_____

Your Trust Factor: As you look at your score, keep in mind that trust is a two-way street. That's why some of our questions dealt with your trust for others, and other questions dealt with the trust they place in you.

A score of 34–40: You have a high trust for others. You believe that people, deep down, are mostly good and merit your trust. You have strong relationships because of your trusting nature, however, this can have a negative side—it can leave you vulnerable. You are capable of being trusted. Trust allows you to have a high level of confidence in the people around you, so they'll have a high level of confidence in you.

A score of 26–33:   You are, basically, a believer. You believe in human-kind. But you do not generate trust and confidence easily. You are realistic, not idealistic. Do you think negatively about someone until they persuade you otherwise? Can you persuade someone you have never met that you trust him or her and they should trust you? You'll need to be especially aware of the level of trust your clients give you, and work to improve on it early in your relationship.

A score of 25 or less: You find it hard to trust without proof. Coaching might be tough for you, because you are less than eager to trust. Examine yourself and your trust levels. If you ever have the feeling that there is no one in your life, even the people closest to you, that you can trust com-pletely, you may have a problem to address before you can commit to coaching.

The Sherpa's Personal
Toolkit − Qualities of a Sherpa

In the same way Sherpas are direct and honest with clients, you should be direct and honest about these answers. Coming up with a realistic rating might take some serious thought, or help from people who know you well professionally.

Can I be a good Sherpa coach?:   **My score:**

    1 = Rarely   2 = Sometimes
    3 = Most of the time   4 = Always

1. Listening and paying attention to what people say is easy for me.   _____
2. No one can "put things past me." I am aware of what is really going on.   _____
3. I am spontaneous in my personal life.   _____
4. When I tell a story, people listen with interest.   _____
5. I find it very easy to follow a process.   _____
6. I am comfortable with silence.   _____
7. I can pick out important information when someone is talking.   _____
8. I have strong, positive relationships in my personal life.   _____
9. I ask questions to promote discussion/conversation.   _____
10. People trust me to listen and keep secrets.   _____

                       TOTAL SCORE: _____

Quiz Ratings:

34–40 You're well-suited to the demands of coaching. With the help of the Sherpa process, you can be very successful. You're a natural talent, in need of the structure this book offers.

26–33 You have the potential to be a good coach. Work on those areas where you scored yourself as a 2 or a 3. You will need to know how they affect your clients before beginning coaching. Read on, and you'll learn how to bring these scores up.

20–25 Coaching might work for you, if you bring up your 1's and 2's. Understand that you can't proceed without some introspective work. You can get there. Do not start coaching until you've worked hard in your weaker areas. Much of what you need, you'll find in this book. Guide yourself through the process as you learn about it.

20 and Below You need more development. At this moment, you will find it very hard to be successful as a Sherpa. Continue reading, and take this assessment again, once you have learned more.

The Sherpa's Personal Toolkit – Evaluating a Client Session

This evaluation will help you to become aware of what will eventually be intuitive. You will know what to look for in your next coaching meeting. If your score is low, look back at the coaching qualities in Chapter 1, and see if you can find how to avoid that situation in the future.

Copy this page, because you'll be using it once for each client session as you get started.

Evaluation for Sherpa Coaching sessions:

After your meeting—ask "How well did I do?"

Sherpa's Evaluation	Client Initials: _____ Session #: _____
On a scale of 1 to 5, rate your performance:	Rating / Notes
1. I knew when we needed to stop and work on something specific, before we continued with the agenda I had planned.	
2. Did my client learn today? Was there an "aha" moment?	
3. I was able to keep my client on track.	
4. I was able to help my client produce truths and solutions.	
5. I was at a loss for words.	
6. Did I control the process or did the process control me?	
7. Did I conclude by summarizing the key points of this meeting and setting expectations for the next one?	
8. Did I give the client all I could?	
9. How well did I do? What could I have done differently?	
10. Did I talk too much?	

Sample Client Contract

AGREEMENT for Coaching Services

AGREEMENT, made between Coaching Provider, a (state name) Corporation located in (city name), and _____,
located in _____ (Client):

Coaching Provider (CP) shall provide executive coaching services to Client. CP shall make best effort to provide all services requested in a timely fashion, on a predetermined schedule, which is mutually agreed upon. _____ (usually one hour) of services per week will be provided, over _____ (usually 12) weeks.

Services are to be provided at a location specified by Client within the _____ metro area. Additionally, a DiSC work style assessment and services for interpretation will be provided at a cost of $ _____. (usually included in the base fee).

In consideration of the services rendered by CP to Client, Client agrees to pay a fee of $_____.00. CP will issue billings (when) _____. Client will make payment to CP within _____ days of invoice issuance.

If scheduled coaching sessions are cancelled by Client less than 48 hours prior to the session's date and time, Client agrees to consider the scheduled services as delivered, without rescheduling of the session, and pay invoices related to the cancelled session.

CP warrants that its services will be of professional quality, conforming to generally accepted management consulting practices. The foregoing warranty is in lieu of all other warranties and conditions, express or implied.

All information obtained by CP regarding Client, or the nature and operations of Client's business(es) shall be regarded as confidential and proprietary, and will be safeguarded and kept confidential by CP. Client and will keep confidential all practices and methods of the coaching process used by CP. All licenses and rights to the coaching process are reserved by its author.

CP shall not be responsible for delay or failure to perform which results from circumstances beyond CP's control.

The laws of the State of _____ shall govern this agreement.

ACCEPTED BY:

Coaching Provider   _____ (client)

(signature) _____   _____

(name and title)   _____

date _____   date _____

return signed contract via fax (777) 777-7777, or

to: (_____ address _____)

Report to Executive Contact

Subject: Firstname Lastname
Individual Executive coaching

Dates and number of meetings (list here)

Areas worked on:

- A tendency to be overbearing (intimidation by passion)
- Communication and listening
- Body language

Update: Firstname and I have established an extremely strong relationship. Firstname understands and acknowledges his weakness in communicating with his peers. He came to the realization that if he treats his colleagues in the same way he treats his customers and clients, everyone will benefit.

Firstname is aware that his body language is a powerful communication tool that works in both positive and negative ways for him. He has specific exercises to practice to notice and improve his body language.

Recommendation: Continue to evaluate Firstname's communication at every meeting you attend together. Give him a score from 1-10 if you desire. Make it clear to him that his body language has to match his words and his words should be well thought out.

Continue meeting personally, at least every other week. Make it clear that the conversation is to revolve around his goals and how well he has been communicating.

It was unfortunate that there were several family/personal issues during the time our sessions were scheduled. It definitely made it more difficult to stay "on task" one week at a time. We had to re-schedule on at least four different occasions. That is no one's fault, but needs to be considered when evaluating Firstname's progress.

I would like to have the opportunity to work with Firstname for another 6 weeks at the same hourly rate. We are at the point where profound changes can be made. He is at a turning point in developing his communication. He is focused on what he has to work on. We would analyze, refine, and encourage his new style and success in communicating.

Filed by: _____ Date: _____

SHERPA COACHING CHECKLIST

This checklist will help you make sure you cover every phase and step in the Sherpa process. Copy this checklist to use for every engagement, to validate that you are following the process and making progress.

Sherpa coaching checklist	Completed date	Notes
Phase One: Taking Stock		
1. Your and your client's expectations		
2. Ramifications		
3. Personal Inventory		
4. Discovery Shield		
5. DiSC® Personal Profile		
6. Agreement		
Phase Two: Global View		
7. Support Cell		
8. Who Am I (if needed)		
9. Change		
10. Values Clarification		
11. Benefits Clarification		
Phase Three: Choosing a Destination		
12. Expectations		
13. The Why Questions		
14. Choosing a Route		
6 week intercession—discuss with supervisor/boss/CEO or client progress		

Sherpa coaching checklist	Completed date	Notes
Phase Four: Charting the Course		
15. Training areas		
15. Barriers		
16. Needs		
17. Q.U.E.S.T.I.O.N.		
Phase Five: Agenda		
18. Understanding Accountability		
19. Attitude		
20. Timeline established		
21. Self-evaluation		
22. Journal evaluation		
23. Long-term Goals confirmed		
Phase Six: THE SUMMIT		
24. Support		
25. Follow Up		

EXECUTIVE CONTACT'S EVALUATION

Sherpa Executive Coaching

1. Describe any changes you've seen in your employee's leadership/
   management style as a result of the coaching experience:

   _____

   _____

   _____

2. How have others reacted to the changes?

   _____

   _____

3. Do you think he/she will be able to maintain the changes?

   _____

   _____

4. In your view, where do we still have the most room for improvement?

   _____

   _____

   _____

5. What has our coaching client said about the process?

   _____

   _____

   _____

6. Do have a good general understanding of the coaching process?

   _____

   _____

   _____

7. Your notes and comments:

   _____

   _____

   _____

Midterm: ☐   Final: ☐   Client code: _____   Date : _____

PATH SELECTION

On the Relational Route:

How does the client affect others?	Consider this path
Do they blame others?	**Problem solving**
Do they have trouble dealing with conflict?	*Problem solving*
Do they solve all the problems of their staff, their peers?	*Problem solving*
Do they take things personally?	*Problem solving*
Do they put off solving problems?	*Problem solving*
Do they get their message across?	**Communication**
Do they know how important it is to communicate effectively?	*Communication*
Do they work well with others?	*Communication*
Do they think before they communicate?	*Communication*
Do they understand the difference between talking and communicating?	*Communication*
Can they read body language well?	**Listening**
Are they aware of their own body language?	*Listening*
Do they make a conscious effort to hear their staff, boss, and peers?	*Listening*
Do they know when to stop talking?	*Listening*
Do they feel "surrounded by incompetence"?	**Nonproductive behavior**
Are they too involved in details?	Nonproductive behavior
Do they overuse the words "need" or "want" in their discussions?	Nonproductive behavior
Is anger something they deal with at work?	Nonproductive behavior
Can they identify and deal with nonproductive employees?	Nonproductive behavior
Control issues—Do they have to be in charge of everything?	Nonproductive behavior
Does the word "manipulation" come into conversations? (Either being manipulated or manipulating others?)	Nonproductive behavior

continued

How does the client affect others?	Consider this path
Are they too enthusiastic for their own good?	**Creating Enthusiasm**
Do they spend too much time talking about other people?	*Creating Enthusiasm*
Do they understand that "people don't care how much you know until they know how much you care"?	*Creating Enthusiasm*
Can they identify their talents?	*Creating Enthusiasm*
Are they looking to have a vision for themselves?	*Creating Enthusiasm*
Do they enjoy their job?	*Creating Enthusiasm*

 **On the Organizational Route:**

How does the client affect others?	Consider this path
Are they a good leader?	**Leadership**
Do they spend time growing as a leader?	*Leadership*
Can they describe the difference between a manager and a leader?	*Leadership*
Is anyone following them?	*Leadership*
Do they see importance in developing their people?	*Leadership*
Do they make poor decisions?	**Decision making**
Do they struggle with every decision?	*Decision making*
Are they able to stick with a decision once it's made?	*Decision making*
Do they apologize before announcing a decision?	*Decision making*
Do they allow others to be a part of their decision making?	*Decision making*
Do they make irrational decisions?	*Decision making*
How are their organizational skills?	**Time Management**
Not enough time to get everything done in a day?	*Time Management*
Do they take on more work than they can accomplish?	*Time Management*
Are they happy with their work/life balance?	*Time Management*
Do they understand how to prioritize?	*Time Management*

How does the client affect others?	Consider this path
Are they good at networking, poised, interesting? When they walk into a room, do people notice?	**Image and Presence**
Do they have trouble believing in their ability?	*Image and Presence*
Do they look good every time they walk into the office?	*Image and Presence*
Do they understand that perception is reality?	*Image and Presence*
Are they motivated to stay with their job? - private clients	**Personal Vision**
Do they need to figure out what to do next? - private clients	*Personal Vision*
Do they understand how to start a new job? - private clients	*Personal Vision*
Stuck in a rut?	*Personal Vision*

Section Two

Sample Client Journal

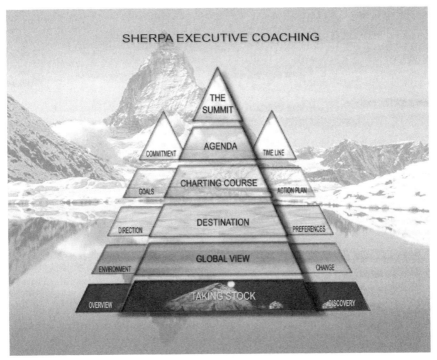

SHERPA EXECUTIVE COACHING

THE SUMMIT

COMMITMENT · AGENDA · TIME LINE

GOALS · CHARTING COURSE · ACTION PLAN

DIRECTION · DESTINATION · PREFERENCES

ENVIRONMENT · GLOBAL VIEW · CHANGE

OVERVIEW · TAKING STOCK · DISCOVERY

(© Sasha Corporation)

Welcome to the Sherpa coaching experience. Your Sherpa coach will guide you through a well-defined process to a personal high point: your summit. This journal is an integral part of the Sherpa experience.

You'll find assessments and exercises designed to accelerate your coaching. Your Sherpa will direct you to the exercises that meet your personal needs. You won't need to complete every exercise. Your coach might either work through an exercise during one of your meetings, or assign one to be completed as homework for your next meeting.

There's also space to take notes and make observations. Many clients use the first notes page to set up a table of contents. This index makes your coaching meetings more efficient. Throughout the rest of this section, you may want to put topic titles on the top of each notes page and use bookmarks to highlight important information.

Table of Contents: Here is a list of the assessments and exercises you'll find in this journal. The pages are numbered with the phase number plus an exercise number. You may want to use some pages more than once. Feel free to copy these pages for your personal use.

PHASE FOUR   Charting the Course Organizational Route

Leadership

    4-8   Assessment

    4-9   Analysis

Decision Making

    4-10 Assessment

    4-11 Decision-Making Mountain

Time Management

    4-12 Evaluation

    4-13 Time Usage Log

    4-14 Prioritization Summary

Image and Presence

    4-15 Assessment

    4-16 Image Art

Personal Vision

    4-17 PQM—Vision

Action Plan

    4-18 Goal-Setting Exercise

    4-19 Filter

    4-20 QUESTION

PHASE FIVE   Agenda

Accountability

    5-1   House

    5-2   List

Attitude

    5-3   Assessment

    5-4   Mapping

    5-5   Graph

Timeline

    5-6   Long-Term Outlook

PHASE SIX   Summit

    6-1   Support Summit

GROUND RULES

_____

_____

_____

_____

_____

_____

_____

_____

_____

_____

MY EXPECTATIONS

_____

_____

_____

_____

_____

_____

_____

_____

_____

RAMIFICATIONS

Keep a log of "perceived changes":

- The change you have made
- An individual's reaction to the change
- Notes

Change	Reaction	Notes

PERSONAL INVENTORY

1. I want to be _____ in five years.

2. My biggest strength in my business is: _____.

3. My manager says _____ about the way I do my job.

4. I am willing to commit _____ hours to my job per week.

5. This really makes me happy: (at work)

_____

_____

_____

6. My biggest stress comes from: _____.

7. My biggest stumbling block is: _____.

8. I come to work because: _____

_____

_____

_____

9. Success looks like this to me:

_____

_____

_____

_____

DISCOVERY SHIELD

3 strengths:

_____
_____
_____

3 weaknesses:

_____
_____
_____

one talent:

_____
_____

why it matters:

_____
_____
_____

(© Sasha Corporation)

WHO AM I?

The top half of the exercise is for your positive traits. What do you do well? In what parts of your personality do you feel accomplished and successful? Fill in each of the 6 circles. On the bottom half of the page, fill in 6 areas of weakness. Your Sherpa will guide you through this exercise.

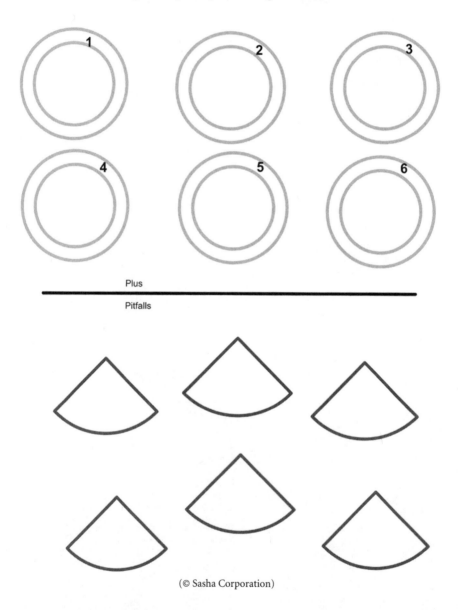

(© Sasha Corporation)

AGREEMENT

Summary of what you have discussed so far and the direction you both want to go.

Discussion Topics   **Next Steps**

_____   _____

_____   _____

_____   _____

_____   _____

_____   _____

_____   _____

_____   _____

_____   _____

_____   _____

_____   _____

SUPPORT MOUNTAIN

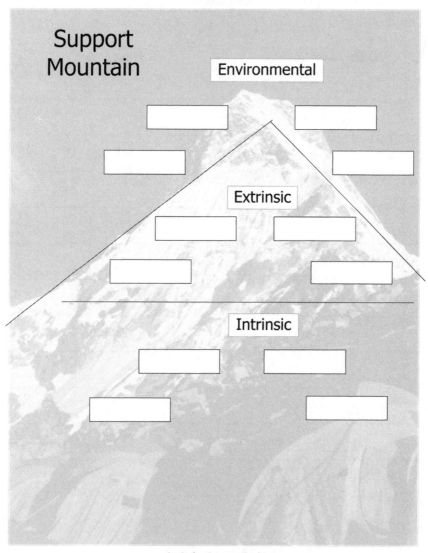

(© Sasha Corporation)

Perception

Use this exercise with your Sherpa's assistance, to define disconnects in your relationships.

1. Name	2. Yrs	3. What do they think I am all about?	4.	5. What do I want them to think about me?	6.	7. Difference between reality and perception	8. What needs to change?
			—		=		
			—		=		
			—		=		
			—		=		

VALUES CLARIFICATION— WHAT IS IMPORTANT?

Values	Prioritize
1. Accomplishment (mastery and achievement)	
2. Advancement (progress up a ladder)	1.
3. Adventure (new and challenging experiences)	
4. Competitiveness (winning, taking risks)	2.
5. Contribution (assisting others, improving society)	3.
6. Cooperation (teamwork, getting along)	
7. Economic security (steady, adequate income)	4.
8. Family Balance (family members are satisfied)	
9. Freedom (independence, autonomy)	5.
10. Friendship (close relationships with others)	
11. Health (physical and mental well-being)	
12. Honesty (truth)	
13. Integrity (sincerity, standing up for beliefs)	
14. Order (tranquility, stability, conformity)	The easiest way to do this is to cross out the values you don't emphasize, then work on the ones you do.
15. Pleasure (fun, laughter, comfort)	
16. Power (control, authority, influence)	
17. Recognition (respect from others, status)	
18. Spirituality (strong religious/spiritual beliefs)	
19. Wealth (making money)	
20. Wisdom (understanding life)	

THE BENEFITS OF YOUR VALUES

Why do you want to get there? If this particular value becomes more important than opposing pressures, what do you gain?

How do you get there? How do you eliminate what's been holding you back? How would you demonstrate that you are living this value more fully?

Benefits	Values
	(transfer from page 2-3)
1. _____	**1.**
Why do you want to get there? Why is it so important? How do you get there?	**2.**
	3.
2. _____	
Why do you want to get there? Why is it so important? How do you get there?	
3. _____	
Why do you want to get there? Why is it so important?	
How do you get there?	

CHANGE BAROMETER

1. Is change easy for you?

_____

_____

2. Have you experienced big changes within the past year? Describe.

_____

_____

3. Did you feel you handled them effectively? properly? on time?

_____

_____

4. Did you feel you handled the change independently? Where did you seek assistance?

_____

_____

5. Did you handle the change with a positive attitude? If not, what were your fears?

_____

_____

6. Could you identify your personal weakness throughout the change?

_____

_____

7. Are you being honest? How do you know?

_____

_____

PERSONAL QUARTERLY MEETING (PQM) CHANGE

Change is the focus of this PQM. Please complete this PQM about change if your Sherpa recommends you explore the changes you are going through. Spend time alone and think about the answers.

For each goal, address three topics:

- **Goal:** The difference between where I am (current status) and where I want to be (vision).
- **Theme:** What am I going to do to get there? What are the obstacles? What are the supports?
- **Idea:** How do I do this? What do I need to do to make this happen?

1. Weekly Goals:

About the change: _____

Theme: _____

Idea: _____

2. Monthly Goals:

About the change: _____

Theme: _____

Idea: _____

3. Quarterly Goals:

About the change: _____

Theme: _____

Idea: _____

4. What am I enjoying most right now?

a. _____

b. _____

Does change affect these things?

_____

_____

5. What am I enjoying the least right now?

a. _____

b. _____

Is change the reason I don't enjoy these things?

_____

_____

6. What part of change really scares me?

_____

_____

7. What part of change am I excited about?

_____

_____

8. Draw a picture of my world right now: 9. A picture of my world after the change:

10. What does change in my company look like, as it relates to me personally?

sample

11. Where do I fit in this change? Where do I want to be in this change?

_____

_____

12. How will I benefit if this works?

_____

_____

13. Ramifications of the change:
Positive:

a. _____
b. _____

Negative:

a. _____
b. _____

WEAKNESS MOUNTAIN

How to tackle weaknesses: Your Sherpa will explain the four steps on this diagram:

Describe a significant weakness:

_____

_____

_____

Work through the mountain:

Acknowledge: _____

_____

_____

_____

_____

_____

Observe: _____

_____

_____

_____

_____

Change: _____

_____

_____

_____

_____

Evaluation: _____

_____

_____

_____

_____

Weaknesses

Evaluate
Meeting Measurements
How well does the new behavior work?

Change
Replacement Behavior
Knowing the RAMIFICATIONS helps you work through the transition.

Observe
Identify when it happens
Keep a log.

Acknowledge
Awareness of weakness
Correctly identify your weakness in a business setting.

(© Sasha Corporation)

EXPECTATION MOUNTAIN

Your Sherpa will lead you through the details of the Expectation process:

Work through the mountain:

Communicate: _____

_____

_____

_____

_____

_____

Commitment: _____

_____

_____

_____

_____

_____

Consequence: _____

_____

_____

_____

_____

Coaching: _____

_____

_____

_____

_____

_____

Expectation Mountain

Coaching
Feedback
Recognition
Re-identification

Consequence
+ and -
Rewards
Accountability

Commitment
Buy-In
Ownership
Repeat

Communicate
Why it Matters
Make Time
5 W's
Details

Identify Expectation
What is an expectation.... Clearly
understanding where and when to use it.
TASKS
Analysis - - think it through!!
Answer the questions - who, what,
when, why, where.
Realistic - ask questions, is it fair?
Consistent? Can they do it?

(© Sasha Corporation)

304

VERIFICATION OF EXPECTATION

Your Sherpa will use this to evaluate your understanding of the Expectation Mountain.

POOR	GOOD	VERY GOOD	EXCELLENT	DID YOUR CLIENT:
				Explain why it matters.
				Give specific details—timeframe, dates, etc.
				Ask for repetition and rephrasing of what was said.
				Create buy-in/ownership.
				Create accountability.
				Clearly explain the consequences.
				Reiterate the consequences/rewards.
				Overall rating.

MIDTERM EVALUATION

1. Describe any changes you've seen in your leadership/management style as a result of your coaching experience:

   _____

   _____

   _____

2. Will you be able to maintain the changes?

   _____

   _____

3. Here is one area I would still like to work on:

   _____

   _____

   _____

4. What has been the most useful aspect of your coaching experience to date?

   _____

   _____

5. What has been the least useful aspect of your coaching experience to date?

   _____

   _____

6. Has this journal helped you sort things out? Have you used it on your own?

   _____

   _____

   _____

7. Other comments:

   _____

   _____

   _____

DIG UP

Your Sherpa will explain this problem-solving technique:

D _____:

_____

_____

_____

I _____:

_____

_____

_____

G _____:

_____

_____

_____

U _____:

_____

_____

_____

P _____:

_____

_____

_____

COMMUNICATION ASSESSMENT

For each of the following, with complete honest reflection, mark the item that best describes your communication style.

1. When conversing with others,
    - ____ a. I usually do most of the talking.
    - ____ b. I usually let the other person do most of the talking.
    - ____ c. I try to equalize my participation in the conversation.

2. While conversing,
    - ____ a. I hold my head still.
    - ____ b. I nod my head at appropriate times.
    - ____ c. I nod my head constantly.

3. When I first meet someone,
    - ____ a. I wait for the other person to make the introduction first.
    - ____ b. I introduce myself with a smile and offer a handshake.
    - ____ c. I usually hug the person.

4. While listening to other people talk,
    - ____ a. I tend to be distracted.
    - ____ b. I listen for meaning and ask questions.
    - ____ c. I watch the person speak, but often don't hear everything.

5. In a brief business conversation,
    - ____ a. I often stand while talking to a person who is sitting.
    - ____ b. I often sit while talking to a person who is standing.
    - ____ c. I follow the lead of the person I am speaking with, and do as they do.

6. As a general rule,
    - ____ a. I tend to be serious and don't smile often while conversing.
    - ____ b. I smile all the time while conversing.
    - ____ c. I smile at appropriate times while conversing.

7. In conversation with someone I don't know well,
    - ____ a. I usually make eye contact.
    - ____ b. I sometimes make eye contact.
    - ____ c. I never make eye contact.

8. When I cross my leg in a seated conversation,

  _____ a.   I cross my leg facing the speaker.

  _____ b.   I cross my leg away from the speaker.

  _____ c.   I bob my foot.

9. In normal conversation, face to face,

  _____ a.   I stand less than two feet away from the person.

  _____ b.   I stand two to three feet away.

  _____ c.   I stand four or more feet away.

10. In business meetings and gatherings,

  _____ a.   I make an effort to remember and use people's names.

  _____ b.   I don't pay attention to names, as I tend to forget them.

  _____ c.   I only learn the names of important people.

11. To end a conversation,

  _____ a.   I often just cut it off, say thanks, and leave.

  _____ b.   I begin to look impatient, hoping the person will get the hint.

  _____ c.   I wrap up with a closing statement.

12. When I'm listening,

  _____ a.   I often cross my arms over my chest.

  _____ b.   I often lean back and relax.

  _____ c.   I often lean slightly forward and face my body toward the speaker.

13. When I have a negative opinion or comment,

  _____ a.   I just come out with it.

  _____ b.   I lead in with a positive comment first.

  _____ c.   I say nothing, to avoid appearing disagreeable.

14. When dealing with team members at work,

  _____ a.   I usually warm up conversations with small talk.

  _____ b.   I usually avoid small talk and get to the point.

  _____ c.   I usually avoid starting conversations.

LISTENING SKILLS ASSESSMENT

Use this tool to measure how well you listen. Think carefully about each question. Review the way you feel and the way you act, and write your answers (1–4) in the right-hand column. Your total score provides an important gauge of your listening skills.

When listening, I do the following:	My score:
1 = Almost never 2 = Some of the time	
3 = Most of the time 4 = Almost always	
1. I pay attention, even when I am not interested in the immediate topic.	_____
2. I wait for speakers to finish before evaluating their messages.	_____
3. I listen for feelings as well as subject matter.	_____
4. I stop myself from interrupting the person speaking to me.	_____
5. I listen to people when they speak, even though I have no personal interest in the person.	_____
6. I am aware of my own body language as a listener.	_____
7. I work to make myself really want to listen.	_____
8. I maintain emotional control, no matter what is said.	_____
9. I would rather talk than listen.	_____
10. I am good at summarizing what someone has just told me.	_____
TOTAL SCORE:	_____

What Your Score Means:

34–40 You are an exceptional listener. Remind yourself to stay that way. Can you identify when you lose concentration? Do you recognize and pull back from moments when you are not paying attention? Does your lack of focus have to do with a certain subject or a certain person? You need to know yourself so well that you have "red flags" go up when those situations occur. Are you there? If not, how do you get yourself to that place?

26–33 The mark of a good listener. Stand back and watch yourself more carefully. What question(s) pulled your score down? On which question(s) did you give yourself a 3 or less? Revisit those questions and see if you can figure out what really happens to you in those situations. What is it that distracts you? What is it that you are not interested in? Can you list the areas of discussion that interest you and those that absolutely do not interest you?

21–25 You're a fair to poor listener. Allow more listening time in your conversations. You don't want a score in this range. You are easily distracted and just as interested in talking as you are in listening.

20 and Below You have serious listening problems. How do you get along day-to-day? Develop your skills in this area, think things through, practice new behaviors, and retake this test in ten days.

Body Language Evaluation

Your Sherpa will lead you through this exercise, designed to analyze and improve body language.

TOPIC #1:   TOPIC #2

RATING, FIRST CONVERSATION 1 - POOR, 5 - EXCELLENT		RATING, SECOND CONVERSATION 1 - POOR, 5 - EXCELLENT
	Eye contact	
	Face-to-Face	
	Distracted/looked around	
	Lean into the speaker	
	Nod head	
	Did not cross arms/legs	
	Didn't send mixed messages	
	Smile	

DAPPER

Your Sherpa will teach you this system for dealing with conflict and confrontation.

D _____:

_____

_____

_____

A _____:

_____

_____

_____

P _____:

_____

_____

_____

P _____:

_____

_____

_____

E _____:

_____

_____

_____

R _____:

_____

_____

_____

ANGER ASSESSMENT

Review your answers with your Sherpa and discuss the areas of concern.

Circle the answer that applies to your personal style:

1. People tell me that I need to calm down.   *T*   *F*

2. I feel tense much of the time at work.   *T*   *F*

3. At work, I find myself not saying what is on my mind.   *T*   *F*

4. When I am upset, I block the world out.
   (watch TV, read, sleep)   *T*   *F*

5. I drink, use drugs, or medication routinely to help
   me calm down.   *T*   *F*

6. I have trouble going to sleep.   *T*   *F*

7. I feel misunderstood much of the time.   *T*   *F*

8. No one listens to me.   *T*   *F*

9. People ask me not to yell or curse so much.   *T*   *F*

10. My loved ones keep saying that I am hurting them.   *T*   *F*

11. Friends and colleagues do not seek me out for my
    opinion and advice.   *T*   *F*

Grading Scale:

Number of "true" responses:

0–2 = MANAGEABLE: You could benefit from relaxation training.
3–5 = MODERATE: You need to learn more about what causes you
        stress and learn stress management techniques.
6 or more = OUT OF CONTROL: You could benefit from learning
        anger management techniques.

EVALUATE YOUR ANGER

Fill out this questionnaire immediately after you have experienced anger.

1. How am I feeling right now?

_____ Anxious   _____ Worthless   _____ Hostile   _____ Depressed

_____ Mean/evil   _____ Revengeful   _____ Bitchy   _____ Bitter

_____ Rebellious   _____ Paranoid   _____ Victimized   _____ Numb

_____ Sarcastic   _____ Resentful   _____ Frustrated   _____ Destructive

Other _____

2. What happened to make me angry?

Anger becomes more understandable and easier to manage if we identify specific events:

_____

_____

_____

_____

3. Who am I angry at?

_____ Myself   _____ My spouse   _____ My partner   _____ My boss

_____ The kids   _____ God   _____ The human race   _____ My life

_____ Men   _____ Women   _____ Other races

_____ Someone specific

_____ A situation (describe):

4. Was it something that happened recently or something brought up from the past?

_____

_____

5. What was the source? Was it something I did or something they did?

_____

_____

6. Why did it happen? Was it an accident? Did somebody push me by doing something deliberate?

_____

_____

7. What is this really about?

_____

_____

8. Why did that "push my buttons"?

_____

_____

9. Is there any truth to it?

_____

_____

10. Other ways I could have handled this experience:

_____

_____

_____

_____

Use these four steps to think things through: (Weakness Mountain)

- **Acknowledge**

- **Observe**

- **Change**

- **Evaluate**

Review your answers—give yourself some time to examine alternate approaches. Discuss with your Sherpa.

LEADERSHIP ASSESSMENT

1. What kind of leader am I? Describe in detail.

_____
_____
_____
_____
_____
_____

2. I was proud of my leadership in this situation. Describe why.
   Within the last week:

_____
_____
_____

   Within the last month:

_____
_____
_____

3. A situation where my leadership abilities fell short. Describe why.

_____
_____
_____

4. Someone I think is an exceptional leader. Describe why.

_____
_____
_____
_____
_____
_____

5. Three areas in which I would like to improve in my leadership abilities:
   a. _____
   b. _____
   c. _____

LEADERSHIP ANALYSIS

Your Sherpa will lead you through this exercise, designed to investigate your leadership abilities.

HOW WELL DO I:	CURRENT SCORE 1–10 SCALE AS OF DATE:	WHERE DO I WANT OR NEED TO BE?	SIX MONTH'S REVIEW SCORES:
Overall effectiveness			
Recognize my overall strengths			
Recognize my weaknesses			
Select the best course of action			
Evaluate a course of action			
Empowering employees			
Commend individuals for new ideas			
Use suggestions and ideas from project teams			
Allow subordinates to create constructive failure			
Managing employees			
Provide encouraging feedback			
Teach problem solving			
Coach through assignments			
Interacting with peers			
Inspire and guide peers to success			
Establish and build trust and openness			
Understanding accountability			
Set clear assignments and expectations			
Clearly understand priorities			
Follow up on all expectations; yours and others'			
Managing the work			
Set goals that are understood by all			
Praise those who anticipate and avoid problems			
Walk the floor, be available to subordinates			
Communicating effectively			
Communicate with clarity to every audience			
Control and use body language			
Listen to staff and respond accordingly			
Use email effectively and efficiently			
Demonstrating teamwork			
Contribute to discussions, respond positively to requests for information and assistance			
Credit success, avoid blaming others for failure			
Help stop indifference, open and hidden conflicts			
Demonstrating visionary leadership			
Establish and communicate a vision and values			
Gain commitment from team			

DECISION-MAKING ASSESSMENT

Review your answers with your Sherpa and discuss the areas of concern.

Circle the answer that applies to your personal style:

1. I am comfortable with the decisions I make.   *T*   *F*

2. Changing one of my decisions is easy for me to live with.   *T*   *F*

3. I am good with setting priorities.   *T*   *F*

4. I am an exceptional listener and hear all sides of an issue.   *T*   *F*

5. Building a consensus is easy for me.   *T*   *F*

6. I am flexible and accepting of feedback.   *T*   *F*

7. No matter what people say about my decision I am okay with it.   *T*   *F*

8. I don't make decisions based on my stereotypes.   *T*   *F*

9. There are no areas (such as costs, benefits) that I ignore when making a decision.   *T*   *F*

10. I use my intuition when I make a decision.   *T*   *F*

11. I am not afraid to make decisions.   *T*   *F*

12. I don't care how much time it takes to make a good decision.   *T*   *F*

DECISION-MAKING MOUNTAIN

Your Sherpa will lead you through this exercise, designed to help with more effective decision-making.

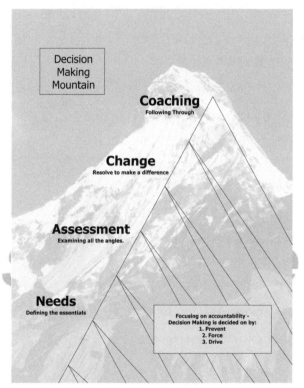

(© Sasha Corporation)

Time Management Assessment

1. Can you tell whether the matter you are dealing with is urgent? Yes ☐ No ☐ If yes, how? _____

2. Do you spend at least one hour each day of uninterrupted time for thinking, reading, planning, or creative work?   Yes ☐ No ☐

3. How much time per week do you spend developing business relationships? _____

4. How many times a day do you say, "I don't have time"? _____

5. How can you evaluate your use of time? Do you need a time log?
   _____

6. Is it hard for you to avoid distractions?   Yes ☐ No ☐

   a. What do you do to avoid distractions?
      _____

   b. When a distraction comes along, how do you handle it?
      _____

7. What's the most productive time of day for you? _____

8. Prioritize your work projects below:
   a. _____
   b. _____
   c. _____
   d. _____

9. Prioritize major elements of your life below:
   a. _____
   b. _____
   c. _____
   d. _____

10. Do you eat properly?   Yes ☐ No ☐

   a.   Describe your diet:

      i. Breakfast   _____

      ii. Lunch   _____

      iii. Dinner   _____

      iv. Snacks   _____

11. Do you sleep well most nights?   Yes ☐ No ☐

sample

TIME USAGE LOG

Copy this for personal use, one page per day.

TIME	EVENT—ENTER A CODE OR DESCRIBE IN DETAIL IF A LETTER CODE DOES NOT APPLY. ADD NOTES TO HELP RECALL SPECIFICS LATER.		
6:30		2:15	
6:45		2:30	
7:00		2:45	
7:15		3:00	
7:30		3:15	
7:45		3:30	
8:00		3:45	
8:15		4:00	
8:30		4:15	
8:45		4:30	
9:00		4:45	
9:15		5:00	
9:30		5:15	
9:45		5:30	
10:00		5:45	
10:15		6:00	
10:30		6:15	
10:45		6:30	
11:00		6:45	
11:15		7:00	
11:30		7:15	
11:45		7:30	
12:00		7:45	
12:15		8:00	
12:30		8:15	
12:45		8:30	
1:00		8:45	
1:15		9:00	
1:30		9:15	
1:45		9:30	
2:00		9:45	

LEGEND:
A - Administrative
C - Communication & Coordination
D - Driving
I - Interruptions, crisis management
M - Meetings
P - Phone Calls
Q - Quality control and inspections
S - Sales and promotion
W - Work at production task

You may use these abbreviations to log basic types of work. Additional notes will be useful for later analysis.

PRIORITIZATION SUMMARY

Copy this for personal use, one page per day.

STEP 1	STEP 2	STEP 3	STEP 4
Things to do today:	How long will each take?	Number in order of importance	Check when completed
Total time: _____			

IDENTIFY INTERRUPTIONS

Who?	What?		How long?	Was it worth it?	Handled properly?
		Total time: _____			

IMAGE AND PRESENCE ASSESSMENT

Your Sherpa will lead you through this exercise, designed to examine your presence.

1. Are you aware of others' first impressions of you?

   _____

2. What's the value of a first impression?

   _____

3. How important are image and presence as part of that first impression?

   _____

4. What do people say when they first meet you?

   _____

5. Do you consider business clothing an investment?

   _____

6. Have you been evaluated by a barber or beautician in the last six months?

   _____

7. Can you identify positive points about your image?

   _____

8. Are you happy with what you see when you look in the mirror?

   _____

9. When you walk into a room, do people notice?

   _____

10. When you speak, do people listen?

    _____

IMAGE ART

What do you look like when you feel most empowered, confident, successful, and talented.

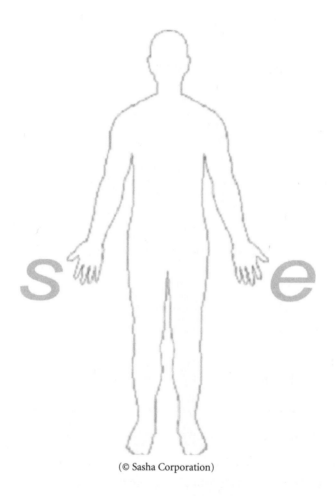

(© Sasha Corporation)

Personal Quarterly Meeting (PQM) Vision

1. What am I enjoying most right now?

a. _____

b. _____

c. _____

What is one thing you can do to make one of these things stand out more in your life? (Refer to PQM- Change for definitions)

Goal: _____

Theme: _____

Idea: _____

2. What am I enjoying the least right now?

a. _____

b. _____

c. _____

How can I get rid of one of these things?

Goal: _____

Theme: _____

Idea: _____

3. What troubles me today? Expand:

_____

4. What is working perfectly right now? Why?

_____

5. This is a picture of my world:

6. **What is one thing I really want?**

_____

_____

7. **Can I initiate it?**   Yes _____ No_____ (if not, go back to #6)

8. **Can I control it?**   Yes _____ No_____ (if not, go back to #6)

9. **Is it achievable?**   Yes _____ No_____ (if not, go back to #6)

10. **What happens if this works? How will I know when I've got it?**

    (Describe evidence in sensory terms of see, hear, feel, smell, taste)

_____

_____

11. **Ramifications**

    Positive:

    a. _____

    b. _____

    Negative: barriers/obstacles

    a. _____

    b. _____

12. **Resources**

    What resources do I need?

    (information, attitude, internal state, training, money, help, or support from others, etc.)

    a. _____

    b. _____

    c. _____

13. **Actions**

    How am I going to do it? What is the time frame is involved?

_____

_____

_____

14. **Assessment**

    How will I know when it is achieved? Measurements:

    _____

15. **If I could do anything and money was no object, what would I do?**

    How would I go about doing it?

    _____

    _____

16. **You have succeeded in achieving what you want.**

    Describe what it looks like:

    _____

    _____

GOAL SETTING

1. What would make me more productive?

_____

2. What would make my staff (me) happiest?

_____

3. What would improve my professional relationships?

_____

4. What would make my staff more efficient?

_____

5. What would help me stay focused on my priorities?

_____

6. What changes in my behavior would show my true self?

_____

7. What would revitalize my sense of mission?

_____

8. What could I do to really make my boss proud?

_____

GOALS FILTER

Your Sherpa will explain the process to filter the goals you will work on after your relationship with your Sherpa is over. This helps you prioritize.

GOAL	IMPORTANCE 1 (NOT VERY) TO 5 (EXTREMELY) IMPORTANT	MULTIPLIER	PASSION 1 (NOT TOO) TO 5 (OVER THE TOP)	EQUALS PRODUCT/ PRIORITY
		X		
		X		
		X		
		X		
		X		
		X		
		X		
		X		
		X		
		X		

QUESTION

Goal Setting and Action Planning

Your Sherpa will lead you through this exercise, designed to clarify your next steps.

Goal Write it out in DETAIL	Q–have you asked enough questions?	U–do you understand it?	E–when to evaluate? Dates	S–is it specific? enough?	T–trick, do you have one?	I–is it important and positive?	O–do you own it?	N–name accountability partner

Personal Accountability

Your Sherpa will explain each room in this house and a process for making accountability a positive factor in your working life.

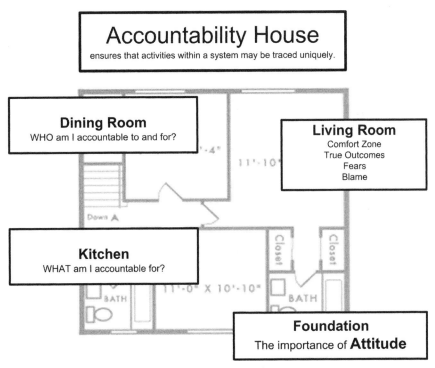

(© Sasha Corporation)

ACCOUNTABILITY LIST

Your Sherpa will lead you through this exercise, asking, "Who are you accountable to?" Discuss.

PERSON	LEVEL OF ACCOUNTABILITY (1–10)	RESPONSIBILITIES INVOLVED
1.		
2.		
3.		
4.		
5.		

ATTITUDE ASSESSMENT

Questions—Circle the answer you think is the correct answer.

1. I was born with the attitude I have today.   F   T

2. When my life changes, my attitude stays the same.   F   T

3. People should always be able to tell whether I am happy
   or unhappy.   F   T

4. I can never change my attitude. This is who I am.   F   T

5. If I don't feel great when I get to work, everyone should
   know that.   F   T

6. It is valuable to vent my feelings.   F   T

7. Usually, what's going on at home controls my attitude.   F   T

8. Talking about my feelings is the best way to handle an
   argument.   F   T

9. My attitude shows exactly how I am feeling.   F   T

10. My mood is affected by the people around me.   F   T

Generally, the best answers are False. It is possible to look at a question
as having a True answer, and have a positive justification for that answer.
Discuss this with your Sherpa. This is intended as a springboard for
conversation and revelation.

ATTITUDE MAPPING

Feel free to copy this page, one for each day as discussed with your Sherpa.

Attitude Graph

Score: 1 is day or day part in which you had a poor attitude, 10 is a perfect attitude.

Day One	___	Day Two	___	Day Three	___	Day Four	___
Day Five	___	Day Six	___	Day Seven	___	Average	___

You can also divide your day into day parts:

Day One		Day Two		Day Three		Day Four	
7–12	__	7–12	__	7–12	__	7–12	__
12–5	__	12–5	__	12–5	__	12–5	__
5–12	__	5–12	__	5–12	__	5–12	__
Day Five		Day Six		Day Seven			
7–12	__	7–12	__	7–12	__		
12–5	__	12–5	__	12–5	__		
5–12	__	5–12	__	5–12	__		

For each score, ask the 5 Ws:

- Who
- What
- When
- Where
- Why

Was this attitude reflected?

ATTITUDE GRAPH

Your Sherpa will explain how to complete this exercise using the information on the previous page.

Attitude Score	1	2	3		1	2	3		1	2	3		1	2	3		1	2	3		1	2	3		1	2	3
10																											
9																											
8																											
7																											
6																											
5																											
4																											
3																											
2																											
1																											
	1	2	3		1	2	3		1	2	3		1	2	3		1	2	3		1	2	3		1	2	3

Day parts for days one through seven: (1-AM, 2-Midday, 3-Afternoon/ Evening)

TIMELINE: OUTLOOK

1. What part of what you have learned will be easy to continue?

_____

_____

_____

_____

2. What are some of your other wishes, desires, and needs?

_____

_____

_____

_____

3. What else would you like to accomplish on your own?

_____

_____

_____

_____

4. What would the benefits be of meeting the new goals you have just listed?

_____

_____

_____

_____

5. What behavior changes will you be working on in six months? in a year? two years?

_____

_____

_____

_____

Support Confirmation

Look up the names that appear on page 2-1 in the extrinsic section of your Support Mountain.

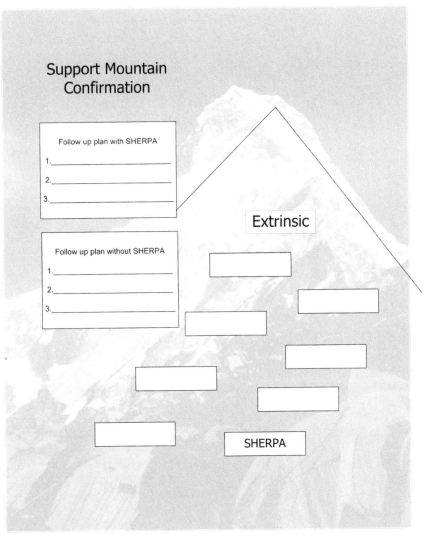

(© Sasha Corporation)

For the Sherpa Coach:

Every client needs a personal journal for the Sherpa Process.
Every Sherpa coach should keep several in stock. Here's how to order:

By mail or fax, provide the information below:

Name: _____

Company name: _____

Shipping address: _____

City, State, ZIP: _____

Phone: _____ E-mail: _____

Please send_____Sherpa client journals at $25.00 U.S. each.
Order amount: $_____.
Shipping and handling: $5.00 U.S. per journal
Maximum shipping charge $25 per order: $_____.

Total Order Amount: $_____.

Payment: Check enclosed_____ MasterCard_____ VISA_____
Other _____

Card number: _____
Expiration date (mm/yy): _____/_____

Cardholder's name (as shown on the card): _____

Authorized signature: _____
(for credit card orders)

Pre-paid or credit card orders, mail to:
Sasha Corporation
P.O. Box 417240
Cincinnati, Ohio 45241
USA

Credit card orders, send a secure fax to: (513) 777-8801 USA

Visit www.sherpacoaching.com to order online.

For the Sherpa Coach:

Every client needs a personal journal for the Sherpa Process.
Every Sherpa coach should keep several in stock. Here's how to order:

By mail or fax, provide the information below:

Name: _____

Company name: _____

Shipping address: _____

City, State, ZIP: _____

Phone: _____ E-mail: _____

Please send_____Sherpa client journals at $25.00 U.S. each.

Order amount: $_____.

Shipping and handling: $5.00 U.S. per journal.

Maximum shipping charge $25 per order: $_____.

Total Order Amount: $_____.

Payment: Check enclosed_____   MasterCard_____   VISA_____

Other _____

Card number: _____

Expiration date (mm/yy): _____/_____

Cardholder's name (as shown on the card): _____

Authorized signature: _____
(for credit card orders)

Pre-paid or credit card orders, mail to:
Sasha Corporation
P.O. Box 417240
Cincinnati, Ohio 45241
USA

Credit card orders, send a secure fax to: (513) 777-8801 USA

Visit www.sherpacoaching.com to order online.

Index